1985

CUBA

WESTVIEW PROFILES • NATIONS OF CONTEMPORARY LATIN AMERICA
Ronald Schneider, Series Editor

†*Mexico: Paradoxes of Stability and Change,*
Daniel Levy and Gabriel Székely

† *Nicaragua: The Land of Sandino,* 2nd edition, Thomas W. Walker

† *The Dominican Republic: A Caribbean Crucible,*
Howard J. Wiarda and Michael J. Kryzanek

Colombia: Portrait of Unity and Diversity, Harvey F. Kline

Honduras: Caudillo Politics and Military Rulers, James A. Morris

† *Cuba: Dilemmas of a Revolution,* Juan M. del Aguila

Also of Interest

Revolutionary Cuba: The Challenge of Economic Growth with Equity,
Claes Brundenius

†*The New Cuban Presence in the Caribbean,* edited by Barry B. Levine

†*Revolution and Counterrevolution in Central America and the Caribbean,*
edited by Donald E. Schulz and Douglas H. Graham

†*Latin American Nations in World Politics,*
edited by Heraldo Muñoz and Joseph S. Tulchin

The Exclusive Economic Zone: A Latin American Perspective,
edited by Francisco Orrego Vicuña

Change in Central America: Internal and External Dimensions,
edited by Wolf Grabendorff, Heinrich-W. Krumwiede, and Jörg Todt

†*Latin America and the U.S. National Interest: A Basis for U.S. Foreign Policy,*
Margaret Daly Hayes

†*Latin America, Its Problems and Its Promise: A Multidisciplinary Introduction,*
edited by Jan Knippers Black

Demographic, Economic, and Resource-Use Trends in Seventeen Caribbean Basin Countries: A Compendium of Statistics and Projections to the Year 2000,
Norman A. Graham and Keith L. Edwards

†*The Caribbean Challenge: U.S. Policy in a Volatile Region,*
edited by H. Michael Erisman

†Available in hardcover and paperback.

CUBA
Dilemmas of a Revolution

Juan M. del Aguila

Westview Press / Boulder and London

Westview Profiles/Nations of Contemporary Latin America

Photo credits: Pages 126 and 160 from the *Miami Herald*; all other photos from AP/World Wide Photos. Reprinted with permission.

Paperback cover photos: (*center*) Fidel Castro, president of Cuba; (*upper left*) shoppers wait in line outside a food market in Havana; (*upper right*) Cubans taken prisoner by U.S. Marines during the invasion of Grenada in October 1983; (*bottom*) Havana. First and fourth photos from AP/World Wide Photos; second and third from the *Miami Herald*. Reprinted with permission.

Copyright © 1984 by Westview Press, Inc.

Published in 1984 in the United States of America by Westview Press, Inc., 5500 Central Avenue, Boulder, Colorado 80301; Frederick A. Praeger, Publisher

Library of Congress Cataloging in Publication Data
Del Aguila, Juan M.
  Cuba, dilemmas of a revolution.
  (Nations of contemporary Latin America)
  Includes index.
  1. Cuba—Politics and government—1959–
I. Title. II. Series.
F1788.D42   1984   972.91'064   84-5178
ISBN 0-86531-563-9
ISBN 0-8133-0032-0 (pbk.)

Printed and bound in the United States of America

10   9   8   7   6   5   4   3   2   1

972.91064
D334

Contents

114,515

Tables and Illustrations

Figures

Photographs

Foreword

A relatively small island just southeast of Florida, Cuba ranks only in the third tier of Latin American nations in population, with 10 million compared to thirteen times that figure for Brazil. But its importance to today's world is certainly far more than its size, population, and limited resources would indicate. Until a generation ago a near protectorate of the United States and a playground for North Americans seeking diversion at a low cost, Cuba has come to represent both the road and the costs of breaking such dependency. U.S. domination is by now history, but the dilemma of marginal viability has been resolved, not by economic diversification but rather by incorporation into the Soviet-led socialist bloc. In return for massive economic subsidization by the USSR, Cuba has assumed a role as the foothold of the Communist world in the Western Hemisphere— sort of a West Berlin in reverse on a much greater scale. As such, its future remains insecure, partially mortgaged to the uncertain tides of the East-West confrontation.

In this context Cuba presents an almost impossible challenge to the scholar who would describe what exists there, explain how this has come about, and analyze why Cuba has turned out to be only the second Latin American nation to experience a complete revolution (after Mexico's 1910 upheaval and subsequent civil war). Indeed, the subject of contemporary Cuba arouses passions in authors and readers alike. Reasoned middle-of-the-road interpretations are not only rare, but usually attacked by both sympathizers and critics of the present regime. Yet a balanced approach, difficult as it is to achieve, is the only valid one. A quarter century of the Castro regime has undoubtedly left Cuba permanently changed in many important ways, but in the process a number of the 1959 revolution's goals have gone unfulfilled or have been pushed aside to make way for new imperatives.

Clearly the coincidence of the 25th anniversary of the Cuban Revolution with a critical election year in the United States underscores the importance at this time of Professor Juan del Aguila's volume in our series *Nations of Contemporary Latin America*. The author, Cuban by birth but with his higher education obtained in this country, is part of a new generation of scholarship on Cuba. Drawing on the vast, albeit often qualitatively deficient, body of literature that has grown up around Castro's Cuba, he cuts through myths and misconceptions to provide a coherent account of the society, the economy, and the political system as it has emerged in the process of the ongoing, if by now largely institutionalized, revolution. Although certainly not underplaying the key role of Fidel Castro—either in the original revolution or in the structured Communist regime that this charismatic leader did so much to bring into existence—the author avoids the common error of equating Castro and the realities of the Cuban nation after a quarter century of his rule.

Del Aguila takes a well-defined position on both the accomplishments and shortcomings of the Cuban Revolution some twenty-five years after it dislodged Batista and his corrupt authoritarian cohorts from power. Moreover, he weaves together the internal and external factors to portray how and why Cuba under Castro has become an important part of the Communist world. The most remarkable facet of the Cuban story in the 1959 to 1965 period is just how Castro managed to attain the position of recognized head of a fully accredited Communist regime in the face of initial and deeply rooted reluctance on the part of the Soviet leadership to accept his almost total conquest of the orthodox Communists of the Popular Socialist Party—long entrenched as Kremlin favorites.

In sum, within the best tradition of this series' scholarship, Dr. del Aguila's book covers a great deal of ground thoughtfully and in an impressively coherent manner. Politics is at the heart of the treatment, but there is also sensitive exploration of the social, economic, and international aspects of Cuban reality. Clarity is achieved without oversimplification, and the final result is a work that not only presents a wealth of information, but even more importantly provides a deep understanding of what has taken place, the dynamic factors in the present situation, and the crucial questions for the years immediately ahead. What more could be asked of an author?

Ronald Schneider

Preface

The Cuban revolutionary process continues to excite intellectual passions twenty-five years after its beginning, due to its profound domestic, regional, and geopolitical consequences. Though in a more restrained fashion than in the 1960s and 1970s, debate on Cuba still rages in the classroom, in the media, in government, and in thousands of households. It is an issue that will not disappear from the public or private agenda, and how one stands on the "Cuban question" is often taken to reflect not only personal beliefs, but ultimately one's own political cosmology. And yet, in the interests of scholarship and simple honesty, the accumulated evidence from a generation of struggle, confrontation, and hope has to be judged in a manner that fathoms the complexity of the revolutionary experience and its documented excesses and abuses. Thus, it is in a framework of critical inquiry that I approached the subject, in an effort to strip away the romanticism and hackneyed commentary that passes as analysis of those dilemmas that Cuba faced and continues to confront.

As I have argued, the need for social and economic development and the desire for cultural emancipation hardly justify the conscious maintenance of totalitarianism, insofar as human freedoms are suppressed by forces that have little to do with the structure of property. In that sense, Cuba ought not to serve as a model for societies struggling to achieve a greater degree of social justice or for those that are committed to a realistic sense of political autonomy. If there is a lesson to be learned, it is that dictatorship is not a solution for the problems of development, because that is self-defeating even for small nations. In short, in order to achieve maturity, a nation, through its leaders, must move beyond railing against the pernicious influences of its neocolonial past.

Several individuals deserve thanks, if not praise, for their disinterested assistance. Enrique Baloyra of the University of North Carolina and Daniel Levy of the State University of New York at Albany—who are friends as well as scholars deeply committed to the study of Cuba and Latin America—made numerous suggestions that invariably improved the work, but they should be (and are) absolved from any of its flaws. Their comments tempered my judgments and assessments. In addition, the corrections made by the editorial staff at Westview Press reinforced my belief that authors should not have fragile egos, and I can now appreciate why that staff has earned a solid professional reputation. In particular, Lynne Rienner deserves to be commended for her encouragement of younger scholars and Jeanne Remington for her commitment to this project. Finally, my colleagues at Emory, especially Eleanor Main and Ken Stein, have been graciously supportive, and our department staff, Linda Boyte and Karen Bussell, have been generous with their time and efforts.

Juan M. del Aguila

Juan M. del Aguila is assistant professor of political science and director of the international studies program at Emory University. Born in Cuba, he came to the United States at the age of twelve and obtained most of his education here, culminating in a Ph.D. at the University of North Carolina. He has published a number of articles on Cuba and Costa Rica, focusing on political change and Latin American relations.

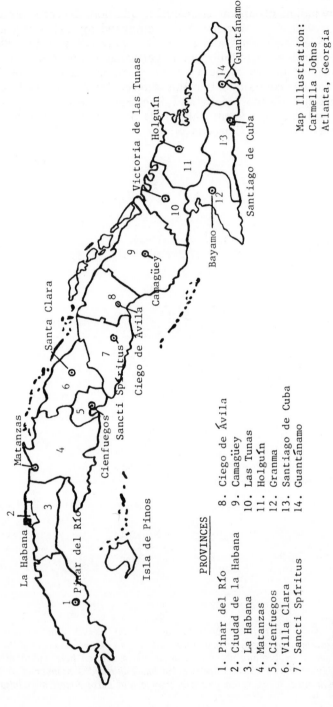

PROVINCES

1. Pinar del Río
2. Ciudad de la Habana
3. La Habana
4. Matanzas
5. Cienfuegos
6. Villa Clara
7. Sancti Spíritus
8. Ciego de Ávila
9. Camagüey
10. Las Tunas
11. Holguín
12. Granma
13. Santiago de Cuba
14. Guantánamo

Map Illustration:
Carmella Johns
Atlanta, Georgia

Map of Cuba

1

Introduction

Cuba's position in the world arena; its standing in regional affairs; the nature of its economic, cultural, social, and political systems; and its unfinished struggle for nationhood are directly affected by the nature of its government, the character of its people, and the will and vision of its current political leadership. A mere twenty-five years after the January 1959 victory of revolutionary forces, the Cuban regime can point with considerable pride to achievements such as a life expectancy of seventy-three years, an infant mortality rate of 17 per 1,000 live births, a literacy rate of 96 percent, per capita income of $1,417, mass education, and the eradication of abject poverty. A well-integrated polity has emerged since the revolutionary period, partly based on militant nationalism, limited political participation, and impressive mobilization capabilities. But, as will be argued here, one cannot estimate either the viability of a society or the success of a revolutionary order exclusively through its material accomplishments. Nation building involves reconciling structural needs with popular aspirations, insofar as these crave for more than minimal material satisfaction.

As will be shown, the Cuban model, featuring economic austerity and political immobility, is beset by dilemmas and contradictions generated by internal pressures, outside forces, and Cuba's unnatural political isolation. In some respects, Cuba suffers from strains typical of developing nations; in other areas, its problems are unique. The outcome of any effort to forge a nation out of disparate elements rests on the availability of resources, the interaction between the few and the many, and the establishment of mechanisms for accountability and the effective expression of the popular will. How historical as well as new dilemmas are confronted and coped with, and what the human and physical costs of transformation add up to, will ultimately decide the outcome of the venture.

This work will focus on the contradictory processes involved in the shaping of Cuba's struggle for nationhood and viability in its postindependence period. Briefly, these are its efforts to create viable political processes in an economically dependent, socially weak society; its efforts to create a national identity in the face of increasing U.S. penetration and

1

involvement; and its commitment to establishing an independent society affirming full human dignity.

This introduction includes a brief review and discussion of Cuba's geographic features and of its population characteristics and demographic profile. Subsequent chapters will cover Cuba's history, society, and culture from colonial times through the 1933 Revolution (Chapter 2); the character and policies of Cuba's prerevolutionary populist/authoritarian order (Chapter 3); the initial policies and structural changes of the post-1959 revolutionary period (Chapter 4); the reasons for the radicalization of the Revolution and the purposes that it served (Chapter 5); the basic features of the Cuban model, including (after 1959) changes in behavioral norms, attitudes, and political culture (Chapter 6); the reorientation of Cuba's foreign policy and its commitment to global revolutionary movements (Chapter 7); Cuba's mass organizations, the vanguard role of the Communist party, and the formalization of leadership and authority (Chapter 8); and finally, the last chapter will offer a critical assessment of the Revolution and Cuban socialism in terms of their ideological congruence, performance, limits, and future prospects.

BASIC GEOGRAPHIC FEATURES

Located at the entrance to the Gulf of Mexico, 112 nautical miles (208 kilometers [km]) from the United States across the Florida Straits, Cuba is the largest island in the Antilles archipelago. With the United States to the north, the Caribbean Sea to the south, Mexico's Yucatan Peninsula to the west, and the Antilles chain to the east and southeast, Cuba is in a central position in the region. Critical points in Central America and the Caribbean such as the Panama Canal, Mexico City, or Caracas are quickly reached by plane. Shipping and trade lanes linking the Atlantic to the American continent pass close to the island.

Cuba's 44,218 square miles (114,525 sq. km) of total surface area lie between 74°08' and 84°57' longitude west and 19°5'–23°15' latitude north, just south of the Tropic of Cancer. The island is some 745 miles (1,199 km) long, its average width is only 60 miles (97 km), and its western region is quite narrow at points due west from the capital city of Havana.

The climate of Cuba is semitropical rather than tropical; the island's location in the path of the trade winds produces pleasant temperatures year-round. The average temperature is 75°F (24°C), dropping to 70°F (21°C) in winter and rising to 81°F (27°C) in summer. Humidity is high, however, with an annual average of 75 percent. Rain falls an average of 80–100 days a year, mostly between May and October; the dry season runs from December to April.

The topography of the island is varied and includes mountain ranges, rolling hills, plains, and numerous rivers and streams. More than 50 percent of the island's total area lies below 3,000 feet (914 meters [m]) and, some 17 percent rises above 3,000 feet in altitude.[1] Fertile valleys, beautiful

Table 1.1.   Cuba's Demographic Growth, 1931-1981

Year of Census	Total Population	Percentage Urban	Percentage Rural
1931	3,962,344	51.4	48.6
1943	4,778,583	54.6	45.4
1953	5,829,029	57.0	43.0
1970	8,569,121	60.5	39.5
1981	9,723,605	69.0	31.0

Source: Adapted from "Censos realizados en Cuba desde 1899 hasta 1981," Granma Resumen Semanal, 8 November 1981, p. 3. Subsequent revisions appeared in Granma Resumen Semanal, 4 September 1983, p. 9, from which the 1981 total was extracted.

beaches, swamps, and tropical lowlands make for a contrasting topography. The principal mountain ranges lie in the eastern, central, and western sections of the island; Pico Turquino, in the Sierra Maestra range, is the highest mountain, at 6,500 feet (1,981 m). Cuba's largest river, the Cauto, runs 160 miles (257 km) from east to west across Santiago de Cuba and Granma provinces in the eastern section.[2]

With 2,187 miles (3,519 km) of indented coastline, Cuba possesses several deep and safe harbors, crucial for domestic and foreign trade and transportation. The harbors of Havana, Santiago de Cuba, Cienfuegos, Nuevitas, and the largest, Nipe, provide a critical maritime infrastructure for a nation dependent on foreign commerce for its prosperity and economic livelihood.

Climatic, geographic, and topographic features clearly affect the economy. Cuba's chief crops are sugar cane, tobacco, coffee, and citrus fruits. Sugar and tobacco are the country's main cash and export commodities, accounting for close to 90 percent of exports in recent years.[3] Minerals such as cobalt, iron, copper, and manganese are also found, as are the world's fourth largest nickel reserves—some 4.2 million tons (3.8 million metric tons) as of the mid-1970s.[4]

POPULATION CHARACTERISTICS

At the time of the 1981 census, Cuba's population totaled 9,723,605 inhabitants, an increase of 1,154,484 persons or 13.4 percent over the 1970 total of 8,569,121. Density stands at 220 inhabitants per square mile (87 per square km), also some 13 percent over 1970. As seen in Table 1.1, 69 percent of the population lives in urban areas, continuing a trend toward urbanization started in the late 1920s. Demographic projections indicate that Cuba will have 10 million inhabitants by 1984 and approximately 12 million by the end of the century.

Table 1.2.   Cuba's Population, 1970 and 1981, by Province

	1970		1981	
Province	Provincial Population	%	Provincial Population	%
Pinar del Río	547,288	6.4	640,740	6.6
La Habana	524,001	6.1	586,029	6.0
Ciudad de La Habana	1,786,522	20.8	1,924,886	19.8
Matanzas	494,486	5.8	557,628	5.7
Villa Clara	700,006	8.2	764,743	7.9
Cienfuegos	296,795	3.5	326,412	3.4
Sancti Spíritus	366,601	4.3	399,700	4.1
Ciego de Ávila	272,731	3.2	320,961	3.3
Camagüey	541,197	6.3	664,566	6.9
Las Tunas	381,831	4.4	436,341	4.5
Holguín	777,262	9.1	911,034	9.4
Granma	641,757	7.5	739,335	7.6
Santiago de Cuba	792,519	9.2	909,506	9.4
Guantánamo	416,115	4.8	466,609	4.8

Source: Adapted from "Población residente y densidad de población por provincias," Granma Resumen Semanal, 8 November 1981,
p. 3.   Column totals for 1981 do not equal total figure cited in
text because revised totals for individual provinces have not
been published in Granma.   Information for 1970 corresponds to
estimates prior to the 1976 provincial realignment.

In terms of distribution by province, a rough index of demographic concentration, the figures in Table 1.2 show that the city of Havana has the largest population, but its percentage of the total had fallen to 19.8 percent in 1981 from 20.8 percent in 1970. No other province has more than 10 percent of the total, but two of the easternmost areas, Holguín and Santiago de Cuba, have 9.4 percent each.

The population of Cuba is young, as is the case in other Latin American and developing countries. Almost 56 percent of the population is under thirty and an additional 35 percent is under sixteen. Although there are no megalopolises in Cuba on the order of Mexico City, São Paulo, or Caracas, the city of Havana, with 1,924,888 inhabitants, accounts for 20 percent of the total population and almost one-third of the urban population and is larger than any other Cuban city on both counts. The second largest city in population is Santiago de Cuba, with 345,289 inhabitants, followed by the provincial capital of Camagüey with 245,235. Cuba has not experienced the high population growth rates that afflict many developing countries; between 1953 and 1970 population increased at a 2.3 percent annual rate and declined to 1.2 percent annually from 1970 to 1981. Cuba's modest population growth contributed to its substantial

Havana, the capital city of Cuba.

level of modernization prior to 1959. In fact, Cuba's demographic regime of the 1950s showed fertility levels and mortality estimates comparable to those found in more advanced countries.[5] In this respect, Cuba is not a typical underdeveloped society in which explosive demographic growth eats up economic resources and creates disturbing social inequalities.[6]

In sum, Cuba's rate of urbanization and population growth have been modest in recent decades, probably due to government efforts to improve the quality of life in the rural areas, large-scale migration out of the country, changes in women's roles, the availability of birth-control devices, and conscious government efforts to "counter the forces that generally contribute to urbanization."[7] Cuba has thus avoided the glaring contrasts found elsewhere in Latin America between urban "ghettoization" and the affluence of certain elites. Conscious government policies since 1959 are largely responsible for eliminating great disparities among social groups.

Ethnically, the population reflects the country's African and Iberian heritages and the nonexistence of Indian subcultures; 22 percent of the population is classified as mulatto, 12 percent black, 66 percent of European ancestry or Caucasian, and 0.1 percent of Asian origin.[8]

Racial cleavages were not deep before 1959 and Cuba was never the racially or ethnically polarized society that can be found in several other

Latin American countries, especially those with substantial Indian populations. Changes in the social system and class structure since the Revolution have further dampened whatever latent class friction existed in the traditional system. Racial and ethnic antagonisms are thus fairly uncommon in contemporary Cuba. Vestiges of the mild institutional discrimination of the past have been outlawed and are gradually disappearing. Nonetheless, there is evidence that, on an individual basis, men and women of different classes and racial backgrounds still hold racist, prejudiced, and stereotyped views.[9]

As the subsequent discussion will make clear, Cuba's political economy was shaped by the dynamics of capitalist development over several centuries, transforming the island into a sugar colony where the existence of slavery perpetuated class and racial divisions. Gradually, the disappearance of slavery and the plantation economy produced new social mores more tolerant of racial differences, partly explaining the absence of enduring racial cleavages.[10]

NOTES

1. Leví Marrero, *Cuba: Economía y Sociedad* (Barcelona: Medinaceli, S.A., 1972), p. 8.

2. Since 1976, Cuba has been divided into fourteen provinces. These are Pinar del Río, La Habana, City of Havana, Matanzas, Villa Clara, Cienfuegos, Sancti Spíritus, Ciego de Ávila, Camagüey, Las Tunas, Holguín, Granma, Santiago de Cuba, and Guantánamo. Except for Granma and Villa Clara provinces, provincial capital and province names are the same.

3. Carmelo Mesa-Lago, *The Economy of Socialist Cuba* (Albuquerque: University of New Mexico Press, 1981), p. 83.

4. Theodore H. Moran, "The International Political Economy of Cuban Nickel Development," in *Cuba in the World*, ed. Cole Blasier and Carmelo Mesa-Lago (Pittsburgh: University of Pittsburgh Press, 1979), p. 261.

5. See Sergio Díaz Briquets and Lisandro Pérez, "Fertility Decline in Cuba: A Socioeconomic Interpretation," *Population and Development Review* 8, 3 (September 1982):515–517.

6. See, among others, Parker Marden, Dennis G. Hodgson, and Terry L. McCoy, *Population in the Global Arena* (New York: Holt, Rinehart and Winston, 1982).

7. Susan Eckstein, "The Debourgeoisement of Cuban Cities," in *Cuban Communism*, 4th ed., ed. Irving L. Horowitz (New Brunswick, N.J.: Transaction Books, 1981), p. 123.

8. "Asciende en Cuba la Población a 9,723,605 Habitantes Según Censo de 1981," *Granma Resumen Semanal*, September 4, 1983, p. 9.

9. The argument here concurs with the view that "the Revolution has not been able to destroy racist, sexist and classist attitudes as rapidly as it did the laws and institutions which gave them sanction." See Oscar Lewis et al., *Neighbors* (Urbana: University of Illinois Press, 1978), p. 527.

10. For an excellent analysis of race relations, marriage patterns, mores, and status during this epoch, see Verena Martínez-Alier, *Marriage, Class and Colour in Nineteenth-Century Cuba* (London: Cambridge University Press, 1974).

Part 1
History, Society, and Political Development

2

Cuba's Struggle for Nationhood

THE EARLY COLONIAL PERIOD

Cuba was discovered on 27 October 1492 during Columbus's first trip, but was settled by Spaniards during the first decades of the sixteenth century. As the island lacked either substantial mineral wealth or a sophisticated Indian civilization, it remained a sparsely populated area of the Viceroyalty of New Spain until well into the eighteenth century.

Cuba's main usefulness to Spain was as a transit point and staging area for expeditions to other Spanish possessions; but its role in the colonial trade system was gradually enhanced as Havana became "a service colony, kept up for the fleets carrying home the main imperial products."[1] In the main, small-scale agriculture and tobacco cultivation provided the economic sustenance for early settlers. By the middle of the sixteenth century, Cuba's white population numbered between six hundred and seven hundred persons, and its Indian population no more than five thousand.

The native Indians, under the *encomienda* system, were employed in searching for and mining gold, clearing forests, and otherwise serving the Spanish settlers.[2] Brutal treatment, disease, poor nutrition, and the insidiousness of servitude quickly reduced the native population, notwithstanding the efforts of friars like Bartolomé de las Casas to improve conditions. As the Indian population declined, black slaves supplied the necessary labor at home and often went along as cooks, cargo bearers, and so forth on Spanish expeditions. Thus, by the early seventeenth century, the twenty thousand or so blacks in Cuba "had become a major factor in the economic and social life of the island," maintaining a subordinate status while their economic potential was recognized by Spain and its colonial officers.[3]

Cuban colonial society was distinguished by the characteristics of colonial societies in general, namely a stratified, inegalitarian class system; a poorly differentiated agricultural economy; a dominant political class made up of colonial officers, the clergy, and the military; an exclusionary and elitist educational system controlled by the clergy; and a pervasive religious system. In addition, the relative isolation of Latin America during the colonial period, due to Spanish imperial dominance, mercantilist practices, and cultural prejudices, produced an inflexible and centralized in-

9

stitutional order ill suited to systemic change. Cuba and much of Latin America were "largely unaffected by those powerful modernizing forces stirring elsewhere in the West," and their political and economic foundations "remained essentially closed, corporate elitist, authoritarian-absolutist, rigidly hierarchical and premodern."[4]

On the other hand, the island's political economy, originally revolving around tobacco and subsequently, coffee cultivation, gradually gave way to a system based on sugar cultivation, production, and export. Slave labor was used extensively in the most arduous aspects of the production of sugar; linkages between Cuba and external forces were subsequently strengthened via the slave trade. Moreover, the English occupation of Havana in 1762–1763 created new opportunities for trade with English possessions in North America and the Caribbean and contributed to the influx of new political ideas, customs, and forms of organization. As new markets were found for Cuba's primary product, mills were built, acreage was put to sugar cultivation, and large numbers of slaves were imported. Following Cuba's return to colonial status under Spain, the latter received increasing revenues from sugar exports.

In sum, growing demand for agricultural products led to Cuba's preeminence as a sugar colony, and the "small scale production of sugar gave way to the dominance of plantation agriculture based on large scale production of sugar and coffee."[5]

The prevailing mercantilist philosophy of the period was grounded in the belief that accumulation of wealth was a necessary ingredient of personal or national power. But it also took into account the social consequences of capitalist production. The unity of capital and ideas gave rise in Cuba to an influential group of thinkers and wealthy oligarchs, men such as Francisco Arango, Ignacio Montalvo, and José Ricardo O'Farrill. These *criollos* (creoles) were learned and widely traveled men committed to the blending of science, technology, capital, and progress so typical of the age; these wealthy *criollos* quickly realized the stifling consequences for Cuba of Spain's restrictive colonial system. They believed that in order for the "sugar revolution" to pay off, new markets had to be found, more slaves had to be imported, and large investments in equipment and machinery had to be made besides the necessary improvements required for efficient production. By the early nineteenth century, creole planters were in a dominant economic position; small farmers tobacco growers and inefficient sugar producers had been driven out by technological, competitive, or financial pressures.[6] The spirit of the age, similar to that in Charleston or New Orleans, has been aptly captured by one scholar:

> From 1792 to 1802 life in Havana took on a new quality; the deep transformation created an exotic world of interrelations and business deals hinging on sugar. It was a world of slave trading, of dried codfish and meat, of rum and molasses, of machines, of cloth for outfitting the toilers, of timber, land, and cattle, of transportation, of financial and trading transactions, of warehouses, road maintenance, merchant fleets and countless other subsidiary

matters. And on top of all this were the non-economic repercussions: a gamut of secret, sordid deals born in the sugar mill and flowering in the University, the Cabildo, the royal medical college, the Audiencia, the Cathedral.[7]

The social contradictions stemming from slavery and colonialism did not impede efforts to improve Cuba's cultural life. Educational opportunities were restricted by birth, wealth, and privilege, but men such as Félix Varela and José de la Luz y Caballero fostered an early sense of nationhood. Luz y Caballero in particular believed in education as a means through which civic virtues are disseminated and present generations are prepared for political action. The creole elite was divided on the issue of independence, but its members could agree on the value of improving Cuba's cultural life. In time the arts began to serve political ends; popular novels like *Cecilia Valdés* pointed to a cultural double standard regarding the social privileges of males in a society in which blacks and women were decidedly subordinate.

On the other hand, there was an absence of genuine liberal thought. Cuba's planters and merchants collaborated with Spanish officials, as yet not considering either political independence or moral retribution. They strongly defended the colonial order; in fact, many had major stakes in it. As a result of official sanctions, technological improvements, and the disastrous effects of revolution in Haiti for that country's sugar exports, "the wealth of Cuba between 1825 and the end of the nineteenth century grew to first class levels,"[8] with sugar earning the bulk of the country's exports.

In conclusion, Cuba's colonial economy responded to external stimuli while retaining its rooted monocultural character. The financial and racial components of plantation agriculture linked to foreign metropolises established Cuba's early dependence and would ultimately lead to tensions, but capitalist expansion and symbolic political gains prevented severe challenges to the colonial political regime. Cultural life flourished among the educated elite, but its social significance was limited by class and racial barriers. Lastly, common interests linked the Cuban economic elite and Spanish officialdom in support of political colonialism. Lacking either clear separatist objectives, a commitment to social revolution, or an effective political/military strategy, Cuba's creole class accepted Spain's periodic concessions, preserved slavery, and accumulated wealth, exchanging political quiescence for economic and social privileges.

POLITICS AND THE TEN YEARS' WAR, 1868–1878

Losing its empire from Mexico to Río de la Plata (Argentina) early in the nineteenth century strengthened Spain's commitment to retain its prized and prosperous Caribbean possessions. Independence-oriented conspiracies involving secret associations and masonic lodges were effectively suppressed by Spain, as were slave rebellions and expeditions of liberation sent from South America to Cuba in the wake of the Latin American wars of independence. Captains General such as Miguel Tacón used repressive policies, censorship, and strict vigilance to combat internal sedition that could challenge Spanish authority. There was interest among annexationist slaveholders in the United States to purchase Cuba to keep Britain from taking advantage of Spain's weakening monarchy, but it did not find much support and gradually dissipated. At midcentury, the absence of a strong commitment to independence among the creoles, the relative economic prosperity of the period, fears of what a free republic would mean for slaveholders, and a repressive Spanish regime conspired to keep Cuba "the ever faithful Isle."

Reformist currents existed, however, and took advantage of brief liberalizations of Spanish rule. The reformers demanded neither abolition nor independence, but sought significant "constitutional reforms" giving creole planters "political control of Cuba, as well as the economic control which they possessed."[9] Their interests were represented by the Reformist party. Founded in 1862, the party worked to bring changes to Cuba's colonial administration and economic system, soliciting as well the ending of the slave trade and Cuban representation in the Spanish Cortes. During 1866–1867, negotiations between the metropolitan government and the reformers' Junta de Información (Junta of Information) on questions of political rights, separation of civil and military powers, and national autonomy for Cuba failed due to the extreme instability and uncertainty in Spanish ruling circles.

Differences among eastern and western planters on the slavery issue (the latter, usually wealthier, were more fearful of social consequences of ending slavery), coupled with the prospect of insurrections causing devastating losses to the wealthier planters, convinced a group of less prosperous white patriots in Oriente led by Carlos Manuel de Céspedes to pronounce in favor of independence on 10 October 1868. Among the reasons cited by Céspedes to justify his call for independence were the Cubans' failure to obtain effective political representation, the continuing limitations on associational rights and freedom of speech, an unjust tax and tariff system penalizing Cuban producers, bureaucratic parasitism, and discrimination against criollos in business and public affairs.

Ten years of bitter and destructive conflict ensued, but the goal of independence was not achieved. Political divisions among patriot forces, personal quarrels among rebel military leaders, and the failure of the rebels to gain the backing of the United States, coupled with stiff resistance from Spain and the Cubans' inability to carry the war in earnest to the western provinces, produced a military stalemate in the final stages. The conflict ended in 1878, but some rebel leaders, principally General Antonio Maceo, refused to accept the terms of the armistice and went into exile. Others, notably Máximo Gómez, accepted the terms despite misgivings, on the grounds that the insurgents were militarily exhausted and politically disunited. Indisputably, the struggle proved costly to both sides; its impact on the economic infrastructure was substantial, including the loss of approximately two hundred thousand Spanish and fifty thousand Cuban lives and the expenditure of some $300 million. The war left the country prostrated, and the deaths of men such as Céspedes and Ignacio Agramonte left a vacuum in Cuba's leadership class.

The Cubans' ability to wage a costly, protracted struggle against Spain demonstrated that proindependence sentiment was strong and could be manifested militarily. On the other hand, before any effort to terminate Spanish control could succeed, differences over slavery, political organization, leadership, and military strategy had to be resolved. In short, the very inconclusiveness of the war left a feeling that the Cubans could and would resume their struggle until their legitimate political objectives of independence and sovereignty were attained.

THE U.S. ECONOMIC PRESENCE

Between 1878 and 1895, Spain abolished slavery (antislavery laws were passed in 1880 and 1886) and introduced political reforms designed to take the steam out of the separatist movement. In addition, an Autonomist movement emerged calling for full political rights for Cubans but maintenance of formal ties to Spain under a constitutional system. Nonetheless, efforts on behalf of Cuba's independence continued on the island as well as abroad, especially in the Cuban emigré communities of the United States.

U.S. interests in Cuba expanded dramatically during the last decades of the nineteenth century. Investments in and commerce with Cuba predated the transformations in American society wrought by the rise of industrial capital and monopolistic fortunes of the Gilded Age. New opportunities attracted financial interests seeking a stake in Cuba's rapidly changing sugar complex. Between 1851 and 1855, sugar and its by-products made up 84 percent of Cuba's exports, and U.S.-Cuban trade during the 1850s— a total of some $20 million—amounted to "about one third of the entire foreign trade of the island."[10] By 1884, the United States was buying 85 percent of Cuba's exports, including 94 percent of its sugar and molasses, and U.S. capital was flowing into ownership of the sugar lands and the newly mechanized mills, into the mining and tobacco industries, and into the nascent railroad network. By 1896, the value of U.S. investments in Cuba was $50 million, and U.S. exports to Cuba in 1897 were valued at $27 million, reinforcing what a Cuban consul general in the United States had once candidly stated, namely that "Cuba was an economic colony of the U.S. even though politically it was governed by Spain."[11]

Political involvement in internal Cuban affairs was restricted largely to commercial matters until the conclusion of the Spanish-American War in 1898. The United States and Spain maintained normal though often tense diplomatic relations; U.S. enforcement of neutrality laws had been lax during the Ten Years' War, and some sectors of U.S. public opinion had sympathized with the Cuban insurgents and their struggle for independence. Interestingly enough, U.S. financial and commercial interests in Cuba expanded—over Spanish objections and despite Cuba's political instability. In other words, Cuba felt the economic influence of the United States on the eve of the War of Independence, exercised directly through U.S. business associations established in Cuba and more intricately through the outward push of U.S. industrial and finance capital.

Cuba's evolving sugar complex was particularly vulnerable to U.S. economic penetration. The capital and technological demands of a recently mechanized and internationally competitive sugar industry led to foreign ownership of Cuba's *centrales* (large mills), with the result that the nation's basic resource was controlled by outsiders. In turn, foreign ownership contributed much to the parcelization of the Cuban economy and the concentration of wealth and little to diversification. And so, according to Fernando Ortiz:

> The great wealth of capital needed for these supercentrals could not be raised in Cuba, and the tendency toward productive capitalism could not be held in check from within. And so the sugar industry became increasingly denaturalized and passed into anonymous, corporative, distant, dehumanized, all-powerful hands, with little or no sense of responsibility.[12]

The United States intervened directly in Cuba in 1898. This action was dictated by the expansionistic and hegemonic impulses of Manifest Destiny, growing imperialistic interests in the Caribbean region, a belief in U.S. naval and military superiority, and domestic pressures in the United States designed to justify intervention on behalf of Cuban insurgents who had been fighting Spain since 1895. U.S. motivations were not the same as those of the Cuban insurgents. From the U.S. standpoint, this would be a war fought in order to deepen U.S. involvement in Cuba and, subsequently, in the Caribbean region itself, while to the insurgents it was a struggle for political autonomy and sovereignty.

WAR, INDEPENDENCE, AND U.S. OCCUPATION

Cuba's War of Independence (1895–1898), and in its wake the Spanish-American War, ended Spanish sovereignty over Cuba and led to three years of U.S. occupation of the island. Cuba formally gained independence without acquiring effective sovereignty for itself, becoming instead a U.S. protectorate under the terms of the Treaty of Paris (1899), the Platt amendment (1901), and the Reciprocity Treaty of 1903.

The war—launched in 1895 as a result of the political, organizational, intellectual, and moral efforts of José Martí (1853–1895) and led by experienced, able generals like Gómez and Maceo—renewed the struggle for independence and forced Spain to pour massive resources into Cuba in order to preserve its cherished colony. By 1897, Spain had some two hundred thousand soldiers in Cuba, at a cost of close to $6 million per month. Obstinately determined to hold on at all costs, Spanish authorities sent General Valeriano Weyler to Cuba, who quickly embarked on a policy of "reconcentration" of the peasant population in the cities, a move designed to isolate the rebels from their potential supporters and to permit the Spaniards to concentrate on the military aspects of war.

The political objectives guiding the Cubans' efforts were framed by Martí, the chief delegate of the Cuban Revolutionary Party, and Gómez, the supreme military commander, in the *Manifiesto de Montecristi*, issued in March of 1895 in the Dominican Republic. In that document, the joint civilian-military leadership established the need to go to war against Spanish obduracy and oppression, mentioning prior efforts to establish a free and democratic republic and calling on the people for moral support of the revolutionary movement. Holding that Cuba's independence could not be viewed as an isolated regional event, as it involved "the uncertain equilibrium of the world," the manifesto forcefully defended Cuba's just cause in favor of "a rigid concept of the rights of man."[13]

The war, essentially a guerrilla struggle, raged back and forth for three years. Rebel columns invaded the western provinces, burning and sacking properties as part of a scorched-earth policy that adversely affected sugar production, domestic commerce, and rural-urban interaction. Spanish attempts to grant autonomy to Cuba in order to retain ultimate control went unheeded by Gómez and other rebel leaders, who, despite recurring political and tactical differences, were irrevocably committed to absolute independence.

"The Cuban question" became part of U.S. domestic politics again in the 1890s. The bloody fighting in Cuba was an issue in the 1896 presidential campaign, turning into a major foreign policy crisis during McKinley's Republican administration. U.S. intervention in June 1898 was strongly supported by both congressional action and public opinion, which had been enraged since the explosion of the USS *Maine* in Havana harbor. Daily press reports commented on the destruction taking place in Cuba, as well as on the cruelty of the "reconstruction" policy and the ineptness of the Spanish administration. In April 1898, reflecting popular sentiment and responding to President McKinley's request for authority "to end the hostilities between the government of Spain and the people of Cuba," Congress passed a joint resolution granting McKinley's petition, but disavowing through the Teller amendment "any disposition or interest to exercise sovereignty, jurisdiction or control" over Cuba once pacification was achieved.

Intervention by U.S. land and naval forces hastened Spain's military defeat. On the other hand, Cuban military commanders, soldiers, and political leaders regarded the U.S. actions negatively, insofar as final victory by the Cubans was foreclosed by U.S. interposition. Cuban sensibilities were further irritated by the United States' establishment of a military government charged with maintaining order as well as with reshaping the island's financial system and its administrative, economic, and political infrastructure. Most Cubans did not view U.S. occupation kindly; they felt

16   CUBA'S STRUGGLE FOR NATIONHOOD

deprived of the opportunity to reconstruct their society—a society paralyzed by years of fighting in a war that had claimed three hundred thousand lives, including those of Martí and Maceo. In effect, once the Treaty of Paris was signed between Spain and the United States, Cuba went from colony to protectorate. The historical objective of a free, independent, and fully sovereign democratic republic was unrealized, and 1.5 million Cubans were still subject to the authority of a foreign power. Despite major improvements in health, education, sanitation, public administration, economics, and finance achieved under U.S. tutelage, the failure to consolidate legitimate political gains out of the sacrifice of two generations created lingering tensions and resentments in U.S.-Cuban relations.

Initially, "Cuban attitudes ranged from moral approval of intervention to violent, outraged rejection of the American role in 1898."[14] The Cubans remained disorganized and politically castrated, unable to reap the fruits of their labor. This had a ruinous effect on the development of genuine national consciousness, as the political system itself was designed and imposed by a foreign power. A dangerous tendency to call on the United States for resolution of internal conflicts developed once the spirit of the Teller amendment gave way to clearly imperialistic designs, creating a pernicious form of dependence and calling into question the nation's ability to govern itself.

THE FIRST REPUBLIC

Cuban independence came in 1902. The politics of the period following independence were characterized by a lack of experience in self-government, uncertain legitimacy, cults of personality, superficial governing doctrines, administrative corruption, and recurring U.S. involvement.[15]

The Cuban Constitution, which went into effect in May 1902, established the framework of a presidential system with the conventional separation of powers. In addition, the constitution included the Platt amendment, granting the United States access to bases and coaling stations; constraining Cuba's sovereignty in financial and territorial matters; and permitting the United States "to intervene for the preservation of Cuban independence and for the maintenance of a government adequate for the protection of life, property, and individual liberty."[16]

Political competition during the first Republican period revolved around loosely organized and personalistic Liberal and Conservative parties; minor parties, some with distinctive regional or ethnic characteristics, also participated in electoral contests. Electoral fraud and administrative corruption were common, and the outcomes of the elections were often considered illegitimate. The government's ability to make binding decisions was poor. Political institutions did not flourish amid clientelistic arrangements revolving around strong local or national personalities.

In turn, politics was viewed as a means of enrichment, and public offices were sought for economic motives. U.S. interventions in 1906–1909,

1912, and 1917 to protect economic interests or to restore political stability underscored the institutional weaknesses of the system and reinforced perceptions that the island was a U.S. colony, that its government lacked legitimate authority, and that its leaders were venal and inept. The practice of looking to the United States for solutions to Cuba's internal problems became common political behavior; factions, leaders, and even presidents sought U.S. assistance on behalf of partisan or personal ends, welcoming intervention. By failing to routinize sound political processes, or to make public policies serve national rather than parochial ends, the system exhibited colonial features and fell prey to manipulation and, ultimately, ridicule. In short, transfers of power were uncertain, and elections "were not perceived as necessarily determining the country's next President, but rather as regularly scheduled opportunities for a show of political strength, and for bargaining among government and opposition forces, political organizations and the United States."[17]

Students, honest labor leaders, and respected intellectuals like Enrique José Varona and Fernando Ortiz—alienated from the political elite—formed part of a rising nationalist intelligentsia committed to reviving Martí's ideals and cleansing the political culture through a national regeneration program. Framing their charges in nationalist slogans and anti-imperialist doctrines, critics spoke of the commercialization of politics and warned of the rising levels and destructive effects of U.S. assets in Cuba. Organizations such as the Cuban Committee of National and Civil Renovation, the University Students Federation (FEU), leftist factions, and the Communist party took up the cause of revolutionary politics and popular agitation. During the 1920s radical university students, an incipient labor movement, and leading thinkers and writers articulated public challenges to the ineptitude of the political regime and the economic dominance of the United States.

The interplay of various antiregime forces, grounded in nationalism but lacking a coherent political strategy or distinct social class base, reflected a deepening cleavage between moderate elements and forces demanding action. For instance, "moderate nationalism" often focused on redressing specific grievances such as the return to Cuba of the Isle of Pines; the other tendency, much more ambitious in its desire for total regeneration, "demanded the abrogation of the [Platt] Amendment, and a total renovation of the political and social structure of the nation."[18]

Numerous challenges to the political leadership of the generation of 1895 stemmed from partially mobilized sectors demanding effective government, economic sovereignty, and social recognition. A precipitous decline in world sugar prices in 1920 from $.225 per pound to less than $.04 per pound set a trend for that decade that contributed to economic insolvency, labor unrest, major banking and financial crises, and deepening foreign penetration, especially into the sugar industry. By 1929, U.S. capital investments in Cuba were valued at $1.5 billion, a more than 700 percent increase over 1909.[19] In addition, the expansion of the sugar industry had driven small and independent farmers into sugar cultivation, creating a dependent relationship between the latter and the mills, with harmful socioeconomic consequences. Cuba's sugar-dominated agricultural system produced spasmodic economic growth and prosperity prior to the Great Depression, increasing the island's economic vulnerability and "sensitizing Cuba to the outside world via foreign trade and commerce."[20] As future reformers and revolutionaries would learn, monoculture retarded diversification, creating a structure of dependence not conducive to the establishment of an adequate industrial or manufacturing infrastructure. As Ramiro Guerra wrote in his classic study *Sugar and Society in the Caribbean*:

> The more Cuba comes to depend on sugar cane, the less possibility there is that it will ever be able to diversify its agriculture and supply its population with consumer goods. Cuba's economic dependence will increase, and we shall be completely and hopelessly at the mercy of the sugar buyers and of foreign governments. The day that Cuba finally becomes one huge cane plantation, the republic and its sovereignty will vanish.

MACHADO AND THE 1933 REVOLUTION

Promised Liberal party reforms following Gerardo Machado's presidential victory in 1924 led to rising expectations and surging nationalism. Machado's approach centered on an impressive public works program and attempts at economic diversification. Hopes were dashed, however, when Machado violated constitutional norms and had himself reelected for a six-year term in 1928 by a controlled congress, arbitrarily ending elections and "instituting a stern and bloody dictatorship with army support."[21] From that point on, Cuban politics took on a violent character. Opposition forces employed terrorism, shootings, and political assassinations, as well as street protests, mass rallies, and strikes, as a means of expressing widespread discontent. The government responded with repression and counterviolence, deepening the rift between popular forces and established—though illegitimate—authority. As a result, a classic prerevolutionary situation emerged "as social forces nakedly confronted one another." Finally, the adverse effect of the Great Depression on public finances, employment levels, national income and labor demands compounded Machado's political difficulties and threatened Cuba's social peace.

The forces arrayed against Machado's repressive dictatorship were heterogeneous in nature, daring in tactics, and often ideologically and programmatically opposed to each other. Among the principal ones the ABC, founded in 1931 and essentially a "new middle-class opposition force grouped as a secret society,"[22] advocated the ending of large land-holdings (*latifundia*), the nationalization of public services, the regulation of foreign investment, social protections for workers, and women's suffrage, among other demands. The Communist party, which had gained adherents from the working classes as a result of poor economic conditions and Machado's antilabor policies, also participated in anti-Machado struggles.

Orthodox in doctrine, subservient to Moscow, and loyal to the Comintern, the Party attacked Machado as well as "petit bourgeois and naively nationalistic" sectors. Tactically, the Party "expanded its anti-imperialist propaganda and its penetration of worker organizations,"[23] rejecting terrorism in favor of street action, strikes, and political agitation. Students, organized in antagonistic factions—the Student Directorate and the Student Left Wing—and divided ideologically and tactically, constituted a third force. The Directorate concentrated on fighting Machado, arguing that transformations should come after the dictatorship ended. The more radical element perceived the regime as an illegitimate representative of a politically corrupt and economically bankrupt system, held together by a cruel tyrant beholden to foreign interests.

The army proved to be a critical contender as well; its support would be essential for either keeping the government in power or improving the prospects of the opposition. Thinking of itself as a guarantor of order and stability, the army had long been politicized. It was structured largely on parochial loyalties rather than merit, and its competence was questionable. It had often been the target of critics who perceived it as an agent of repression; but on the other hand, in seeking to preserve its corporate integrity and viability amidst a violently deteriorating national situation, the army's commitment to the *machadista* regime was not absolute. Simply put, by 1933 "the body military perforce opposed any political movement potentially harmful to the corporate integrity of the armed forces, a requirement transcending in many ways any commitment to the incumbent political authority."[24] Finally, as had been the case since 1898, the United States played the ultimate power broker. The U.S. presence was personified in Ambassador Sumner Welles, President Franklin Roosevelt's personal emissary, who had been charged with ending the crisis in Cuba, restoring political stability, and limiting the damage to U.S. business interests. Ordered to Havana by Roosevelt, Welles arrived in May 1933 and proceeded to start a "mediation" effort designed to return the country to normalcy. Welles did not face a simple task. In fact, Cuba lived in a state of perpeutal agitation, fueled by political intrigues and violence. The fact that the political leadership of organizations like the ABC engaged in violence but spoke the language of reformism further confused the situation.

Welles's negotiations involving the major actors succeeded in getting Machado out. An effective general strike, widespread mobilization, and ultimately the army's withdrawal of support for the regime led to Machado's acceptance of the U.S. plan and his decision to take "a leave of absence." In a major tactical blunder, the Communist party, frozen out of the mediation, agreed at one point to call off its support of the general strike in exchange for legal recognition. Subsequently, the Party's association with a crumbling dictatorship called into question its revolutionary image. The Communists' credibility would be challenged by "a whole generation of unengaged revolutionaries who never forgave them their mistakes,"[25] repeatedly pointing to the Party's sectarianism and lack of vision.

An inexperienced but well-known figure, Carlos M. de Céspedes, succeeded Machado; his weak government was subsequently overthrown in a coup by noncommissioned officers led by an unknown sergeant, Fulgencio Batista. Batista's movement, springing from grievances among the lower ranks regarding troop reductions, pay cuts, and promotion schedules, deepened the political differences that already existed between the enlisted men and the officers due to the latter's collaboration with Machado. Lacking ideological content or a bona fide program of national regeneration, this "lumpenproletariat in uniform"[26] ushered in the Pentarquía, a five-man executive committee headed by Ramón Grau San Martín. Weak and divided, the Pentarquía gave way to a new revolutionary government, which soon became the symbol of Cuba's unfulfilled social, economic, and nationalistic aspirations; this new government was also headed by Grau.

The revolutionary government initiated radical reforms through executive decrees and direct action by Interior Minister Antonio Guiteras, establishing the eight-hour day, cutting utility rates, requiring a minimum of (50 percent) Cubans in the work force in industry and commerce, granting peasants permanent rights to occupied lands, and placing limits on foreigners' land purchases.[27]

Nevertheless, the revolutionary government ruled amidst great uncertainty. It was not recognized by the Roosevelt administration because of its "inability to maintain law and order," it was opposed vehemently by Welles from the outset, and it was feared by business interests for its policies "against latifundism, against a greedy and absorbing capitalism, against wealth, fabulous profits yielding miserable results for the nation."[28] During its tenure, the government received the support of the Student Directorate, the hostility of the Communist party, the tactical blessing of Batista, the enmity of the traditional politicians and the ABC, and the uncertain backing of the army. But, with powerful domestic opponents and ineffective international support, and having failed to create "any political organization or party to mold the masses into a permanent, effective supporting instrument,"[29] the government could not transform popular approval into institutional authority. Administrative disorganization, suspicions between Grau and Guiteras, opposition from the U.S. embassy, and challenges from the army made the government vulnerable and weakened its authority. By late 1933 conspiratorial efforts involving Batista, the traditional politicians, and the U.S. embassy had reduced the number of options available to the government. In short, it was clear that the government's radical policies had brought a degree of unity to its often divided opponents. Also, as Batista's position "depended on his ability to legitimize the commissions granted in 1933 through a settlement satisfactory to organized political and economic groups and Washington,"[30] he willingly moved against the government.

Incapable of withstanding immense domestic and external pressures, Grau resigned on 15 January 1934 and was eventually replaced by Carlos

Mendieta. In Guiteras's own words, the revolution failed when it could not be carried forward on the shoulders of "ideologically-identified men . . . joined together by the same principles and not by the doctrine of 'everyone for destruction.'"[31]

One cannot overestimate the impact of the truncated 1933 Revolution on the following generation's psychological makeup, social agenda, and political tactics. In Cuba's political development, the unfinished business of the 1933 Revolution (subject to each generation's polemics) became goals for sectors committed to restoring Cuba's economic sovereignty, democratizing its politics, and asserting its national will. Moreover, a legacy of social commitment and political defiance was created. Guiteras's emphasis on discipline and unity among the revolutionaries' ranks would be studied and not forgotten, likewise his prophetic view that the phase ending in January 1934 was a "genesis of a Revolution being prepared" more than a "political movement pierced with cannon shots."[32] Thus, in spite of the "basic ambivalent attitude towards the events of 1933–35"[33] held by future political generations, the revolutionary option remained latent through its immediate successors—authoritarianism and social democracy.

SUMMARY

Cuba's evolution from colonial status to nominal independence was shaped by the economic requirements of an expanding sugar complex, as well as by its relations with a weakening monarchy—Spain—and an expansionistic, imperial power—the United States. For most of the colonial period, political activity remained separate from efforts to secure greater economic gains for an expanding but insecure creole elite. More important, class interests were not defined, and social emancipation was hardly contemplated until well into the nineteenth century. Access to culture and education in turn remained restricted, delaying the formation of authentic feelings of community and, lamentably, nationhood.

Frustration became the national mood during and after the U.S. occupation of Cuba; but, paradoxically, foreign hegemony was often welcome. Attempts at self-government failed during the early Republican period due to the absence of legitimating mechanisms guaranteeing popular accountability in public life, as well as to the persistence of a colonialist mentality in the country's political class. With a government dependent on foreign support and domestic acquiescence while mouthing nationalistic slogans, the performance of the political class disintegrated into sterile electoral contests built around semicorrupt clientelistic arrangements. A boom-and-bust economy subject to the vagaries of commodity prices added economic insecurity and insolvency to the unresolved dilemmas of order and legitimacy. The stage was being set for a revolutionary attempt to define the scope of civil and military relations, challenge foreign domination, and reduce social inequities. The efforts of the revolutionary government were thwarted by conservative interests, the United States, and Batista, who personified the modernizing political strongman (*caudillo*). Subsequently viewed as the man who almost single-handedly suppressed a genuinely popular social revolution in the 1930s, Batista and those whom he represented could not conceive of a total break with the United States. In conclusion, an order dependent on foreign involvement for the settlement of internal disputes, riddled with patronage, and unsure of its own sovereignty proved vulnerable to strongman politics. Since the political process hinged on trading personal favors for political support, many in positions of authority used their offices for recruiting loyal followers.

NOTES

1. Hugh Thomas, *Cuba, The Pursuit of Freedom* (New York: Harper & Row, 1971), p. 27.
2. The system involved the apportionment of a certain number of Indians to the early Spanish settlers, reducing the Indians to slavery or to serfdom. An *encomienda* was usually granted for the lifetime of the grantee, but at times it could be passed on to heirs. See C. H. Haring, *The Spanish Empire in America* (New York: Harcourt, Brace and World, 1963), pp. 20–21.
3. Herbert S. Klein, *Slavery in the Americas* (Chicago: University of Chicago Press, 1967), p. 142.
4. Howard J. Wiarda, "Social Change, Political Development and the Latin American Tradition," in *Politics and Social Change in Latin America*, ed. Howard J. Wiarda (Amherst: University of Massachusetts Press, 1974), p. 11.
5. Thomas, *Cuba*, p. 6.
6. Franklin W. Knight, *Slave Society in the Caribbean* (Madison: University of Wisconsin Press, 1970), pp. 16–21.
7. Manuel Moreno Fraginals, *The Sugarmill*, trans. Cedric Belfrage (New York: Monthly Review Press, 1976), p. 41.
8. Thomas, *Cuba*, p. 109.
9. Ibid., p. 233.
10. Leland Jenks, *Our Cuban Colony* (New York: Vanguard Press, 1928), p. 19.
11. Fernando Ortiz, *Cuban Counterpoint* (New York: Vintage Books, 1970), p. 64. Figures are from Robert F. Smith, *The United States and Cuba, Business and Diplomacy, 1917–1960* (New Haven, Conn.: College and University Press, 1960), p. 24.
12. Ortiz, *Cuban Counterpoint*, p. 64.
13. Raimundo Lazo, *José Martí: Sus Mejores Páginas* (Mexico: Editorial Porrúa, S.A., 1976), pp. 67–72.
14. Ramón E. Ruiz, *Cuba, the Making of a Revolution* (New York: Norton, 1968), p. 28.
15. For an overview, see Jorge Domínguez, *Cuba: Order and Revolution* (Cambridge, Mass.: Belknap Press, 1978), pp. 33–53.
16. Federico G. Gil, *Latin American–United States Relations* (New York: Harcourt Brace Jovanovich, 1971), p. 91.
17. Domínguez, *Cuba*, p. 19.
18. Luis Aguilar, *Cuba 1933: Prologue to Revolution* (New York: Norton, 1972), p. 47.
19. Smith, *The United States and Cuba*, p. 29.

20. Domínguez, *Cuba*, p. 23.
21. Gil, *Latin American–United States Relations*, p. 94.
22. Thomas, *Cuba*, p. 594.
23. Aguilar, *Cuba 1933*, p. 123.
24. Louis A. Pérez, Jr., *Army Politics in Cuba, 1898–1958* (Pittsburgh: University of Pittsburgh Press, 1976), p. 66.
25. K. S. Karol, *Guerrillas in Power* (New York: Hill and Wang, 1970), p. 78.
26. Andrés Suárez's felicitous phrase, found in his *Cuba: Castroism and Communism, 1959–1966* (Cambridge, Mass.: MIT Press, 1967), p. 10.
27. Olga Cabrera, *Antonio Guiteras, Su Pensamiento Revolucionario* (Havana: Editorial de Ciencias Sociales, 1974), pp. 103–133.
28. Ibid., p. 104. Translation from text of a Guiteras interview on September 1933.
29. Aguilar, *Cuba 1933*, p. 221.
30. Pérez, *Army Politics in Cuba*, p. 98.
31. Cabrera, *Antonio Guiteras*, p. 181.
32. Ibid., p. 182.
33. Samuel Farber, *Revolution and Reaction in Cuba, 1933–1960* (Middletown, Conn.: Wesleyan University Press, 1976), p. 77.

3

Politics and Development in Prerevolutionary Cuba

Following the brief revolutionary interlude of 1933, Cuban politics passed through a period of realignment, characterized by conservative domination of weak governments, reentry of the nationalist left into the system, and the blurring of civil-military relations due to Batista's central role. A constitutional period gave way to the authoritarian regime of the 1950s. The failure of authoritarianism to cope with the insurrectional challenge paved the way for Castro's rise to power. In this chapter, I assess Cuba's development from the 1930s through Batista's second dictatorship, arguing that neither populist authoritarianism nor reformist social democracy represented viable models, given the former's inherent illegitimacy and the latter's unwillingness to confront Cuba's structural ills. In turn, the discrediting of democratic reformers and the break in the constitutional system in 1952 made insurrectional efforts legitimate. The forces struggling against the authoritarian regime framed their political objectives in democratic, constitutionalist, and pluralist terms—seeking the establishment of a new order but rejecting Marxist-Leninist solutions. In large measure, the politics of prerevolutionary Cuba revolved around failed attempts by democratic as well as authoritarian administrations to create viable institutions. As a result, insurrectional movements emerged, bent on reshaping the polity's basic nature.

REALIGNMENT AND POPULISM

Conservatives supported by the army and the United States controlled the policy agenda for the balance of the 1930s. Batista, secure in his military position and not challenged by either the traditional politicians or sectarian forces, was inclined to take up some of the ideas articulated by reformers. He appealed to déclassé as well as rural elements, maintained good relations with the United States, and risked a partial opening to the alienated, nationalist left at home and in exile. The left, sobered by the outcome of the "revolution," splintered along ideological and partisan

24

lines, with questionable mass support, and without charismatic leadership, could not mount an effective challenge to Batista as long as the latter retained the army's loyalty and partially satisfied various demands. By taking advantage of improved economic conditions, maximizing his political assets, and forcing a realignment favorable to status quo forces, Batista contained the radical legacy of 1933, bringing stability, but not legitimacy, to the system.

External economic dependence alongside competing social claims defined Cuba's political economy. The government's stake in the preservation of a brokered system grew; legislation was passed to stabilize the sugar industry, to grant welfare and social benefits to labor, and to provide for educational and administrative reforms. On the other hand, electoral irregularities, corruption, repression, and military influence in political affairs, when added to the failure of opposition politicians to frame acceptable political alternatives, perpetuated a legitimacy problem unresolved until the 1940s.

Populist policies such as minimum pensions for veterans of the War of Independence, regulation of women's work hours in shops and factories, and expansion of education were enacted during the period. The establishment of service organizations designed to improve living conditions in the rural areas and the passage of the Sugar Coordination Act in 1937 guaranteeing permanent occupancy to medium-sized farmers (colonos) offered some protection for those sectors whose demands were often neglected.[1] Also the character of relations with the United States changed following the 1934 abrogation of the Platt amendment, the signing of the Reciprocity Trade Agreement, the passage of the Jones-Costigan Act, and the creation of the Second Export-Import Bank. These measures, growing out of the New Deal and the Good Neighbor Policy, mitigated the worst effects of the Great Depression, while linking Cuba more closely to the U.S. market and reinforcing the island's dependent status. Domestically, these measures provided resources to governments, enhancing as well the bargaining power of private sugar interests due to the latter's improved economic position. Taking into account the $666 million value of U.S. direct investment in Cuba in 1936 (a marked decline since 1929), "American business interests were generally satisfied with the New Deal's political and economic solutions of the Cuban problem, and these solutions would provide the substance of Cuban-American relations from 1934 to 1959."[2]

In sum, though Cuba's dependent status was not altered through bilateral concessions or through a vigorous expansion of domestic capitalism, the expanded role of the state made it a natural target for private interests' political activities. Without the industrial base, class foundation, or organized mass movements of more advanced Latin American societies, Cuba's populist game relied on the state for limited economic expansion, "securing short-term prosperity and some redistribution of income" without sustaining either for very long and maintaining the tested "practices of personalism and authoritarianism."[3]

The contrast to Batista's populist authoritarianism was provided by the reentry of reformist elements into the system. Founded in 1934 by democratic, nationalist but nonsectarian forces opposed to Batista's virtual dictatorship, the Partido Revolucionario Cubano-Auténtico (PRC-A) aggregated middle-class, professional, working-class, and rural interests around Ramón Grau, building on the programmatic and ideological legacy of the deposed revolutionary government. In a position paper issued in 1936, the party analyzed Cuba's development level, holding that financial imperialism, traditional politicians subservient to foreign interests, and the army accounted for the country's lack of development.[4] Doctrinally, the PRC-A called for "the intervention and control by the state of the national economy," identifying itself as a nationalist, socialist, and anti-imperialist organization eschewing extremism, violence, and the notion of class struggle.

From that point on, the PRC-A became the dominant party on the left, espousing moderate nationalism and vigorous economic reforms. Like other responsible *aprista* (moderate leftist) parties, its clientele included the urban working class, lower-middle-class elements, the rural proletariat, and nationalist intellectuals.[5] According to one scholar, the Auténticos' appeal to latent democratic sentiments and their rejection of militarist approaches meant that "[t]he contrast between the civilian-democratic and the militarist authoritarian traditions remained for a long time one of the key lines of political cleavage, despite the efforts of groups like the communist party to blur the distinction."[6]

Many in Cuba perceived the PRC-A in the 1930s and the early 1940s as the country's "last and best hope." In fact, the party's moral credibility was high, and it represented sectors that had traditionally been disenfranchised. The PRC-A and others also claimed to stand for the "unfinished business of 1933," articulating a view to which many subscribed. Although not yet a mass party able to aggregate heterogeneous interests, the Auténticos were able to turn grievances into political capital, biding their time and exploiting Batista's mistakes.

CONSTITUTIONALISM AND SOCIAL DEMOCRACY

In 1939 Batista, feeling politically secure and wishing to improve his image in the United States and to align with reformist tendencies emerging in Latin America at the time, allowed elections for a new Constituent Assembly. Facing a politically heterogeneous opposition with varying degrees of internal unity and programmatic coherence, Batista overestimated his own labor and mass strength and could not control the assembly. For example, forty-one of the seventy-six delegates elected came from opposition ranks, including eighteen from the PRC-A, sixteen from the Liberal party, and six Communists.[7]

The assembly produced the 1940 Constitution, drafted in a spirit of national unity and democratic hopes. Drawing on the Mexican Constitution of 1917 as well as other charters, the constitution established universal suffrage and freedom of political organization, recognized conventional legal and civil rights, and abolished the death penalty. Social protections for women, children, and workers were framed; racial and sexual discrimination outlawed; and mandatory public education instituted as well. Private property in turn was legitimated in a broad social context, latifundism outlawed, and limits placed on foreigners' land acquistions. In keeping with the philosophical orientation of most delegates, free market principles were subjected to state regulation. The state in turn was charged with "orienting the national economy," promoting national industry, and pursuing agricultural diversification "as sources of public wealth and collective goods." In short, the 1940 Constitution created the legal and institutional framework of a democratic system, enlarging the state's powers in national development, public administration, fiscal, and monetary matters. Basic human rights were recognized and protected. The document sought to legitimate social and economic aspirations with liberal political principles, protecting individual rights while stressing public and collective responsibilities.

In many ways, the contradictory claims of social goals and private interests proved unworkable. Uneven enforcement of critical constitutional provisions due to official neglect, coupled with the limitations of a dependent economy and a failure to place public interests ahead of private gains, meant that commitments turned into illusory goals. The failure to attain these goals often bred cynicism, increasing disrepute for public institutions and contributing to the pernicious delegitimation of constitutional government, which would inevitably affect the system's overall viability.

Batista's victory in the honest and competitive 1940 elections ushered in a period of constitutional governments that lasted until 1952. Despite his military origins, Batista ably expanded the scope of civil authority. He endowed the presidency with legitimacy by governing in accordance with democratic principles, preserving control over the military while improving relations with the Communists, and expanding Cuba's commercial and trade ties to the United States. Increased demand for sugar due to World War II brought growth and prosperity, with modest gains registered in national and per capita incomes; the latter rose from 100 to 137 pesos between 1940 and 1944, though living conditions in the rural areas lagged behind national trends. Agriculture remained the principal source of income and wealth; but wages, salary, and health benefits granted by the 1940 Constitution and instituted through enabling legislation gradually improved the economic and social position of the middle-class and the urban working sectors. In effect, Batista expanded on the populist legacy of the 1930s and respected the boundaries of the active state (that concerned with social and economic matters), while capitalizing on his military background to keep the army in check and preserve constitutional government.

Despite these achievements, the viability of the democratic system was not fully established during Batista's, or for that matter, subsequent administrations. Too many still viewed the state as a treasure to be raided or as a formidable dispenser of political favors. Genuine attachments to the idea of democracy were uncommon. No civic culture as such existed. The system had yet to prove itself.

Batista left office like a good democrat in 1944, going into exile in the United States. Not surprisingly, the enthusiasm of the Cuban people on Grau's inauguration was boundless, aptly described by a U.S. journalist:

> Dr. Grau returned to the presidential palace amidst a wild celebration which lasted three days. He had been forced out of the Presidency in 1934, defeated in 1940, and his triumph was sweet indeed. . . . the island hailed Grau as a great democrat and 'the savior of the nation. . . .' "It is not I who have taken office today" he said, "but the people."[8]

The Auténtico administrations of Ramón Grau (1944–1948) and Carlos Prío (1948–1952) initiated reforms in agriculture, fiscal matters, education, and labor. Maintaining a healthy respect for civil liberties, often pursuing policies friendly to rural and urban labor, but not challenging the presence of foreign interests in the economy nor implementing radical development plans, these administrations reconciled their nationalist impulses with political pragmatism.

Auténtico governments, though tied into Latin America's democratic left and believers in reformist social democracy, held that national development could be advanced in a dependent context. Public subsidies, bureaucratic employment, public financing of private investment, and creation of new state agencies promoted moderate growth in the nonagricultural sector, leading to gains by expanding middle-class and professional groups. In addition, the economic nationalism espoused by the party led to some economic diversification seeking "to reduce the dangers of a one-crop economy."[9] The pace of industrial development was still hindered by market limitations, overconcentration on sugar production, liberal trade and tariff policies, and "ease of access to the main industrial supply centers of the U.S."[10]

Notwithstanding their past denunciations of corruption in prior administrations, Auténtico governments were plagued by extensive official corruption and embezzlement. Political patronage funded with public monies was widely practiced, as was the use of bureaucratic sinecures to reward supporters and adversaries alike. Fortunes were made by several government ministers, and public office was viewed with disdain, cynicism, and disillusionment. These abuses slowly eroded the legitimacy of an immature, and thus vulnerable, democratic order. One of the most obvious sources of corruption and political patronage during Grau's tenure was the BAGA (Bloque Alemán–Grau-Alsina). Grau's minister of education, José M. Alemán, created the BAGA, turning it into a powerful political machine and unofficial financial network controlled by himself and one of Grau's nephews, Grau-Alsina. That gave Alemán considerable power, as the BAGA "came to control the funds of four major ministries plus a number of special funds such as the Lottery Revenue Fund and the Special Public

Works Fund."[11] Alemán himself arrived in Miami in 1948 after two years as minister of education "with $20 million in notes in his suitcase, not to speak of thousands of *caballerías* [roughly, acres] of land, sugar mills, air lines and a score of houses left behind."[12]

Association of individual or governmental dishonesty with institutional laxity brought claims for order, leading directly to a split in Auténtico ranks and to the formation of the Ortodoxo party in 1947. That party, led by the charismatic though psychologically unstable Eduardo Chibás, coined an effective slogan—*vergüenza contra dinero* (honor against money)—becoming a bona fide force on the left. Appealing to the growing middle class, professionals, and intellectuals, and advocating administrative honesty and "no coalitions" with other parties, the Ortodoxos articulated national frustrations.

The Ortodoxo party now saw itself as the heir to the 1933 Revolution, accusing the incumbents of betraying the people once again. This new split on the left was neither ideological nor, substantively, programmatic, having as much to do with Chibás's personal qualities as with his ideas. But Chibás's merciless charges, dramatic and often virulent, echoed in the body politic. For instance, *Carteles*, a then-reputable magazine, reviewed Grau's tenure in 1948 and concluded that "the poor masses have once again been defrauded," pointing out crucial problem areas where his administration's performance had fallen short.[13]

Lastly, Auténtico administrations failed to end—and in fact often spawned—political violence, gangsterism, and urban terrorism carried out by the assorted revolutionary bands and "action groups." Driven by a rampant disregard for public order, often protected and encouraged by government officials, devoid of ideology, and ridden with personal vendettas and internecine political quarrels, the *pistolerismo* (gang warfare) of the action groups further discredited the democratic regime. Not surprisingly, low levels of public ethics and the breakdown of law and order contributed to the emergence of a new type of "revolutionary." This new breed was willing to exchange loyalty for pay, while carrying out threats and intimidation in the name of lofty principles. According to one scholar, this person "was an expert in the use of automatic weapons, loyal only to his tiny independent group, full of contempt for those he referred to as the 'ideologists' in exile, and thoroughly convinced that violence alone could decide everything."[14]

In conclusion, the political aspirations and economic and social expectations spawned prior to the democratic regime were only partially fulfilled by the Auténtico governments. Modernization through reformism ran up against the power of vested interests, foreign capital, and questionable central authority. Preserving liberties while shamelessly insulting public morals constituted a cynical fraud of formidable corrosive impact. To the unfinished agenda of 1933 were added the unrealized promises of the democratic reformers. Clientelistic politics that revolved around personal attachments rather than doctrinal commitments made the system vulnerable to shifting partisan arrangements and manipulation from above. Without an institutionalized party system, unable to draw upon a prestigious democratic tradition, and vulnerable to demagogic appeals, Cuba's political game drifted along on poorly understood, seldom accepted rules subject to veto by force. In sum, weak democratic structures failed to acquire the capabilities essential for satisfying demands. The state, supported by neither a dominant class nor a traditional oligarchy, was itself unable to convert diffuse support into legitimately accepted rule.

DICTATORSHIP AND THE INSURRECTIONAL CHALLENGE

Public loyalty to the democratic order had been weakened as a result of the poor performance of Auténtico administrations compounded by widespread dissatisfaction with the low quality of public life and the cynical behavior of political leaders. In such an atmosphere calls for "law and order" are appealing. In fact, "law and order" is often used euphemistically, masking a desire to return to nondemocratic politics. This is exactly what occurred in Cuba.

Batista's bloodless but well-organized coup in March 1952 ended the constitutional regime and initiated an era of political authoritarianism, measured economic growth, insurrectional attempts, violence, and repression. Cuba's political development was cut short by the coup. It remained frozen in time for the balance of the decade, despite the efforts of radical, moderate, and traditional forces—employing violent as well as legal and accommodationist strategies—to pursue diverse political objectives.

Batista's coup was not solely the result of widespread public dissatisfaction with the civilian administration; there was a strong element of personal ambition as well. Batista knew that he would be unable to win in the presidential elections scheduled for June, and he felt confident of the support of old army cronies, dissident officers, troops of various garrisons, and elements of the Havana National Police. Proclaiming that "worry about the absence of guarantees for life and property," and concern about existing corruption, led him to "accept the imperious mandate" and become chief of state, Batista proceeded to consolidate his authority despite the profound illegality of his actions.

Prominent national figures, business organizations, corporate interests, working-class leaders, and the leadership of the Partido Socialista Popular (the Popular Socialist party—PSP—which was the Communist party) either directly endorsed the coup and rejoiced at the prospect of returning order and stability, or—as was the case with the PSP—tacitly approved the breakdown of the democratic regime. Diplomatic recognition was duly extended by the United States. Except for scattered protests by students, denunciations by some Catholic lay leaders, and isolated instances of civic resistance, the coup provoked neither massive popular repudiation nor formal institutional opposition. In complex fashion, the phillipics of Chibás against previous administrations, the failure of the middle class to assert democratic leadership, the absence of social militancy in working-class ranks, and the widespread conviction that order was preferable to fractious pluralism led to the breakdown of the democratic system. Once done, the rapidity of the takeover and the apparent effectiveness of the conspiracy "dazed public opinion," inducing "a sensation of temporary paralysis in the entire nation."[15]

Batista was unable to legitimate his regime either through elections in 1954, good relations with the United States, or negotiations with traditional politicians and other opposition groups. These failures reduced the probability of restoring constitutionality by institutional means. Realizing the quixotism of legal or electoral challenges, opposition forces gradually assumed a confrontational posture, adopting other means of resistance, including street protests, confrontations with police, urban violence, sabotage, and armed assaults on selected targets.

FIDEL CASTRO: AN EARLY PROFILE

The government was challenged in July 1953 when some 150 men, led by a twenty-six-year-old Ortodoxo militant, Fidel Castro, and including his brother Raúl, Abel Santamaría, Ramiro Valdés, Juan Almeida, Haydeé Santamaría, and others, attacked the Moncada barracks in Santiago de Cuba. Hoping to gain credibility for his revolutionary organization and to demonstrate a willingness to employ armed violence in order to attain diffuse and largely unknown political goals, Castro viewed the attack "as a gesture which will set an example for the people of Cuba," considering its success a fulfillment "of what Martí aspired to."[16] Defeated by Batista's soldiers, most of the attackers, including the Castro brothers, were captured, tried, and sent to prison. Others were killed during the attack or after being captured. But the publicity surrounding the attack, the reports in the press of the cruelties inflicted on the prisoners by the police, and the daring nature of the act thrust Castro into the national consciousness—turning his organization into a potential contender and damaging Batista's prospects for restoring law and order. A trained lawyer with oratorical skills, Castro used the trial to issue a speech as part of his own defense. That speech, subsequently revised and disseminated, constitutes early evidence of Castro's thinking on Cuba's political and economic problems. Portraying his cause as just and inspired by patriotism, Castro called for a return to constitutional government, agrarian reform, profit-sharing arrangements in industry, confiscation of ill-gotten gains by public officials, and minimum grinding quotas for cane planters—hardly a radical program and certainly not one in line with Marxist-Leninist prescriptions.[17]

Castro was released from prison in 1955, under an amnesty decreed by Batista, and moved to Mexico. While in the Isle of Pines prison, he read extensively in world history, political theory, literature, biographies, classics, and Marxist-Leninist writings, in addition to the works of Martí and other Cuban thinkers. Also, he kept up correspondence with colleagues, supporters, and sympathizers, either Ortodoxo associates or other opponents of Batista's regime. By his own account, he maintained a strict routine of self-discipline, study, teaching, and formulation of political strategy and programs. Treated with some leniency and not abused, though subject to the daily humiliations of prison life, Castro spent his time productively. He sharpened his intellect, kept abreast of political affairs, strengthened loyalty bonds with Moncada comrades, and became roundly convinced of his leadership capabilities. As he himself wrote:

> This prison is a terrific classroom! I can shape my view of the world in here, and figure out the meaning of my life. I do not know if I will have a long or short life, whether it will be productive or wasted. But I feel my belief in sacrifice and struggle getting stronger. I despise the kind of existence that clings to the miserly trifles of comfort and self interest. . . . But there are many men who will rise from the ashes like the phoenix; the strong beat of their wings will ring out in the skies over their homeland again.[18]

Other revolutionary groups besides Castro's organization participated in the struggle against Batista in the 1950s. Among these, the Revolutionary Directorate (DR) stood out for its uncompromising ferocity and its commitment to "striking at the top." Primarily a faction of the University Students Federation (FEU), the DR became one of the leading urban organizations fighting the regime. Led by José Antonio Echeverría, Faure Chomón, Rolando Cubela, and others, the DR saw itself not as a revolutionary force seeking total change but rather as an organization with a major political aim—ending Batista's dictatorship. Its attitude was decidedly anticommunist, its membership drawn from student and middle-class ranks, and its broad inclinations democratic and nationalist.[19]

Several of the DR's leaders, including Echeverría, were killed during an attack on the presidential palace in March 1957; other members were subsequently tracked down by police and shot. Though clandestine cells operated through 1958 the reconstituted DR suffered from internal divisions and did not regain its tactical effectiveness. It never became a major political force, being gradually overshadowed by Castro's underground urban networks.

Well-known civic and professional figures, among them traditional politicians, mounted an effort in the mid-1950s designed to bring about an electoral solution to Cuba's political difficulties. The Sociedad de Amigos de la República (SAR), which included Auténtico personalities, student leaders, and various opposition members, engaged in what they called a "civic dialogue" with Batista. The SAR did not have Castro's endorsement or participation. Feeling politically secure, Batista refused their calls for new elections, alienating those with whom a moderate compromise might have been worked out. Moreover, the opposition itself "was profoundly divided between 'politicians' and 'revolutionaries,'—that is those inclined toward a political understanding with Batista and those who would be satisfied with nothing short of the complete abdication of the dictator and his government."[20] Without the proper electoral guarantees, and unable to settle its differences with Batista, the SAR's effort collapsed. As a result, the insurrectional option became increasingly attractive and legitimate, especially to professional and middle-class sectors and members of the 1952 generation, known for its overthrow of Batista. In short, Batista's intractability fed the growing conviction that armed conflict was necessary and inevitable. As has been the case with other Latin American dictators, the curtailing of effective political dissidence transforms opponents into hardened enemies, reducing the options available to moderates and often driving them into the radical camp.

Amid evidence of order, stability, and even incremental economic gains in the mid-1950s, Batista's dictatorship could not appeal for popular support on the grounds that the nation was threatened. Failing to anticipate growing discontent with his dictatorship, Batista governed isolated from the popular pulse, never recapturing his earlier momentum or his image as a populist and reformist, albeit authoritarian, leader. In addition, the basic characteristics of authoritarianism—cronyism, reliance on police and internal security in order to intimidate opponents, sporadic censorship, the lack of a well-defined mentality and development program, and an intricate system of payoffs, subsidies, and bribes designed to buy loyalties and contain antiregime pressures—turned out to be its very weaknesses. Alienated from the urban intelligentsia, unable to mobilize broad popular support, unwilling to open up the political process, and unsure of the effectiveness of politically conservative sectors due to their apathy, Batista's regime gradually became a sad caricature without either vision or conviction.

THE GUERRILLA PHASE

Following his early release from prison and shortly after his arrival in Mexico, Castro and several comrades officially founded the 26th of July Movement (M-26-7). Tracing its origins to Chibás's Ortodoxo party, and defining the movement as "the revolutionary apparatus of Chibás' organization, a grass roots movement . . . without landlords . . . without sugar plantation owners, without stock market speculators, without industrial and commercial magnates . . . or small-time politicos with no-show jobs,"[21] M-26-7 quickly advocated an end to Batista's dictatorship.

Castro's group, involved surreptitiously in military training, fundraising activities, clandestine politics, and study circles, grew in numbers; for instance, Ernesto Guevara, an obscure Argentine leftist doctor, joined the movement in Mexico. At the same time, contacts were initiated with other revolutionary organizations. Although suspicion and profound political differences would later characterize relations between the DR and the M-26-7, in mid-1956 these organizations jointly issued the Pact of Mexico, denouncing any potential electoral solution and restating their commitment to insurrection. The DR itself continued its campaign of sabotage and urban terrorism against the government, disdaining the guerrilla option and creating an atmosphere of tension, uncertainty, and fear.

Preparation for an expedition to Cuba proceeded, involving not only logistical requirements but also coordination with the urban wing of M-26-7 in Cuba, led by Frank País, René Ramos Latour, Celia Sánchez, and others. País had been the leader of Acción Revolucionaria Oriental (ARO) since the early 1950s. Operating clandestinely, the organization by the mid-1950s had "already compiled an insurrectionary record" of bombings, assault and sabotage, merging with Castro's group in late 1955.[22]

Making good on his promise "that we will be free men or martyrs this year," Castro and eighty-one others sailed from Mexico in the yacht *Granma* in late 1956, landing on Cuba's southwest coast on 2 December 1956. Poor communications between the expeditionaries and the urban underground, faulty logistics, rough weather, and intelligence reports available to the Cuban government complicated matters. Followed by army detachments, engaging in skirmishes, and suffering from low morale, the expeditionaries dispersed and some were caught. Several, including the Castro brothers, Guevara, Almeida, and Valdés eventually reached the Sierra Maestra mountains with the help of friendly peasants.

Government denials about the landing as well as press reports alleging Castro's death were subsequently proven false. In addition, the regime's credibility suffered a tremendous blow when *New York Times* reporter Herbert Matthews interviewed Castro in February 1957. The impact of the interview cannot be exaggerated; it established Castro's veracity, portraying him as a sincere freedom fighter struggling against a corrupt dictatorship. The interview also gained the attention of the U.S. press and probably exaggerated the guerrillas' military capabilities. Coming across as a moderate nationalist with democratic ideas, Castro revealed some hostility to the U.S. government while telling Matthews that "you can be sure that we have no animosity towards the U.S. and the American people."[23] Undoubtedly, the publicity rendered immense psychological and political benefits to Castro and his cause, "reaching the darkness of Batista's political prisons," generating public commentary on the guerrillas, and "sending a message of hope for all the militants and sympathizers" of the movement.[24]

Led by a National Directorate headed by Castro and organized in urban and guerrilla wings, M-26-7 issued its Program-Manifesto *Nuestra Razón* (Our Purpose) in mid-1957. It was written by Mario Llerena, a typical representative of the educated, anticommunist, middle-class liberals committed to democracy but compelled to join revolutionary causes. The document established a continuity between M-26-7, Martí, and "the conscience of the Cuban people ever since the beginning of national sentiment." *Nuestra Razón* identified the Four Riders of the Apocalypse conspiring against Cuba's democratic fulfillment as: (1) the colonial mentality, (2) foreign economic domination, (3) political corruption, and (4) military intemperance. Arguing for a necessary war to be followed by a genuine revolution, the program analyzed past historical errors, the failure of the traditional party system, "the subservience of organized labor," the main features of a dependent economy, and "the romantic immaturity of the 1930 generation." Quoting from Jefferson and Lincoln, *Nuestra Razón* stated that the movement "is guided by political thinking that is characterized by democracy, nationalism and social justice," defining the revolution's goals as a free and sovereign country, a democratic republic, an independent economy, and a distinct national culture. Lastly, pronouncements on political economy, public morality, and individual freedoms were followed by a "doctrine of constructive friendship" between the United States and Cuba, disdaining the use of the term imperialism, but allowing Cuba to be "a faithful ally of the great nation to the north and at the same time preserve its right to control its own destiny."[25]

The manifesto opted for reformist approaches rather than radical solutions. It was devoid of Marxist-Leninist formulations, tracing its intellectual lineage to Martí, and it was strikingly similar to the programmatic themes of the ABC and even the Ortodoxo party. At a minimum *Nuestra Razón* committed the revolutionaries to constitutional government and political pluralism, including the preservation of individual guarantees, freedom of conscience, and high standards of public morality. Notwithstanding many other—often conflicting—declarations, messages, and pronouncements regarding revolutionary principles and goals, the manifesto accurately reflected dominant intellectual tendencies within revolutionary ranks.

Castro's tactical political assets, including his ability to command subordinates' loyalty, his skill in playing off adversaries against one another, and his resourceful uses of propaganda, when combined with the army's inability to stamp out the guerrillas, enhanced his position within opposition ranks. Underestimating the rebels' military capabilities and relying on questionable assessments of the army's own strength and morale, Batista's army could not defeat Castro's guerrillas. Batista, failing to reap political dividends from limited economic improvements and unable to convince most Cubans that his regime was preferable to uncertain revolutionary upheavals, could not find a way out of the crisis.

The regime's international position deteriorated significantly when the United States imposed an arms embargo in March 1958 as a means of pressuring Batista to curtail repression and hold honest elections without his own participation.[26] Misgivings among State Department policymakers and U.S. Ambassador to Cuba Earl Smith's suspicions concerning Castro's true political colors affected U.S. assessments of Cuban developments. Opinion was divided between those who perceived Castro as an acceptable nationalist and those who saw him as a radical hostile to U.S. interests.[27]

Contributing to the confusion in Cuba as well as among U.S. policymakers was the fact that the respectable middle-class background of Castro's spokesmen and M-26-7 adherents obscured unresolved ideological conflicts among guerrilla leaders and the urban underground. Probably unknown to the State Department and certainly unknown to the Cuban masses, disputes simmered back and forth during the insurrection. Letters exchanged between Guevara and Ramos Latour in late 1957 reveal the former's Marxist convictions and the latter's feelings regarding the purposes of the insurrection. Questioning the movement's decision to compromise with "bourgeois" elements, Guevara asserted that

> because of my ideological background, I belong to those who believe that the solution to the world's problems lies behind the so-called iron curtain, and I see this Movement as one of the many inspired by the bourgeoisie's desire to free themselves from the economic chains of imperialism.[28]

Ramos Latour, wishing to end "sterile polemics," nonetheless replied:

> Our fundamental differences are that we are concerned about bringing oppressed peoples of "our America" governments that respond to their longing for Liberty and Progress, governments that will be cohesive units that can guarantee their rights as free nations and make themselves respected by the big powers.
> We want a strong America, master of its own fate, an America that can stand up proudly to the United States, Russia, China, or any other power that tries to undermine its economic and political independence. On the other hand, those with your ideological background think the solution to our evils is to free ourselves from the noxious "Yankee" domination by means of a no less noxious "Soviet" domination.[29]

With calculated ambivalence, Castro refrained from endorsing either side, since he was not overly preoccupied with ideological polemics. M-26-7's political program was sufficiently liberal and therefore attractive to broad sectors of public opinion, and Castro wanted it that way. To support either Guevara or Ramos Latour (behind the scenes) meant that a firm commitment to either's arguments had to be made. At that point, such a commitment would have been a tactical disaster. Over time, uncontrollable revolutionary dynamics, the deaths of democratic leaders like País and Echeverría, deepening contacts between the Communist party and the guerrilla leadership from April 1958 on, and Castro's insistence on absolute loyalty gradually increased the radicals' influence and strengthened Castro's personal control.

THE PARTIDO SOCIALISTA POPULAR

The Communist party in Cuba was orthodox in its ideology, conservative in its political behavior, and heir to a collaborationist and tainted legacy. It neither constituted a revolutionary force nor actively engaged in the insurrectional struggle. The Party had limited working-class support, Stalinist leadership, and a poor national image. It did oppose Batista's coup in 1952, but did not convert its opposition into clandestine antiregime activities. Perceiving Batista as a traditional Latin American strongman beholden to U.S. influence but subject to populist impulses, the PSP denounced the regime's illegality without developing an effective counter-strategy of its own. Committed to "mass struggle," sporadic strikes, and tacit concubinage with Batista, the Party denounced the Moncada attack in 1953 as foolish, "putschist and adventurist." It refused to collaborate with action-oriented opposition elements, including Castro's organization. Stating in 1957 that "sabotage and the burning of cane fields"—favorite tactics of the urban underground and the guerrillas—"principally affect workers and small or medium-sized farmers," the party committed itself to waiting until "objective and subjective" conditions made overt challenges to the regime viable and not suicidal.[30]

The Party sought to improve its revolutionary credentials, which had been tarnished by its history of passive behavior, but it was unwilling to risk repression without overt political gains. The Party atrophied on the sidelines as popular sentiment swung against Batista; membership declined from twenty thousand in 1952 to a few thousand by 1958, and the PSP's ossified slogans failed to elicit commitments from youth, middle-class sectors, or respectable opposition in general. The Party, which had survived other periods of official hostility, public indifference, and international disrepute, could not anticipate until 1958 that the insurrectional effort might succeed. In other words, as "Popular Frontists, advocates of a broad anti-fascist union, built on the model designed by the Seventh Congress of the Comintern," Cuba's Communists followed Soviet intentions detrimental to their domestic effectiveness.[31] Nonetheless, once convinced that Batista was doomed, the party sent an old and tested militant, Carlos Rafael Rodríguez, to the Sierra to talk to Castro and other guerrilla leaders, so that they could feel each other out and presumably reach some understanding. Opportunistically and belatedly, Communist cadres collaborated with rebel forces in various activities during the last months of 1958, but without making a major impact.[32]

It is therefore unequivocally clear that the PSP's ideological, political, military, and financial contributions to the struggle against the dictatorship fell short on all counts. Neither the theory of Marxist revolution nor Leninist precepts on strategy and tactics squared with Cuba's objective situation, or with the party's behavior. Consequently, a posteriori claims exaggerating the Party's role in the struggle without mentioning its tactical blunders, its doctrinal sterility, or its ingrained suspicions of bourgeois M-26-7 militants, only deepened antagonisms between these unlikely bedfellows.

THE COLLAPSE OF THE AUTHORITARIAN ORDER

Domestic isolation, rebel military victories in eastern Cuba, and the loss of support from the traditional hegemonist—the United States—convinced Batista that a final military push against the rebels was needed to restore faith in the army and disprove rebel claims of an inevitable victory. The army, attempting to show that the regime had not lost its fighting capabilities, launched attacks against rebel strongholds in the late spring and summer of 1958. These attacks were designed to prevent the guerrillas from advancing eastward and spilling over into Cuba's central provinces. The army did not prevail, despite committing substantial resources to the offensive. Effective rebel propaganda, low morale, poor leadership by field commanders, "and a simple unwillingness among large numbers of officers to continue supporting Havana in the field" led to the army's organizational paralysis and ultimately, to the failure of the offensive.[33] Finding little resistance, rebel columns under Guevara and Camilo Cienfuegos headed westward, reaching the Escambray mountains in central Cuba. The army's disintegration coupled with multiplying popular uprisings and sabotage efforts by the resistance induced military conspiracies against Batista, but these proved pointless once a rebel victory became certain. Finally, fully aware of the army's inept performance, unable to rally popular support following the electoral fraud of 3 November and bluntly instructed by the U.S. ambassador that "he no longer had the support of the U.S. and that he should leave Cuba,"[34] Batista fled at dawn on 1 January 1959.

The breakdown of the authoritarian regime stemmed from its inherent illegitimacy, its refusal to accommodate the needs and demands of citizens, its failure to capitalize on a legacy of military populism dating back two decades, and its unfounded belief that pressures for change could be contained through sporadic repression and military force. In addition, the progressive alienation from the regime of the Cuban middle class reduced the probability that the latter could become a moderating force. Despite the revolutionaries' ambivalent political messages and their limited support among working-class and rural sectors, the regime could neither expand its social base nor effectively exploit the social contradictions in the revolutionaries' goals. Thus, in a situation in which traditional political forces were discredited and no dependable class base existed, popular support gradually moved toward the forces with the broadest and most attractive political appeal. Failing to transform despotic authoritarianism into effective institutional control, or to convert loyalties into capable political organization, Batista's rule rested on a combination of parasitic satrapies, cliques, and internal army politics. Simply put, the authoritarian order could not cope with either the psychological or political dimensions of the insurrectional challenge without transforming itself into a much more coercive regime. Deeply felt commitments to fundamental change growing out of national frustration against the present order and its predecessors built up into a genuine popular revolution. Paradoxically, the breakdown of the authoritarian regime in Cuba illustrates the fragility of presumably reliable clientelistic arrangements, insofar as these cannot substitute for strong central authority. In fact, it was the clientelistic network and its authoritarian supports that stood in the way of genuine democratization. With little doubt, its collapse opened up truly revolutionary opportunities.

A DEVELOPMENT PROFILE OF
PREREVOLUTIONARY CUBA

Some theories of revolution hold that economic deprivation growing out of the general condition of underdevelopment breeds political discontent, something that ultimately threatens the political stability of democratic and nondemocratic regimes alike. A second view holds that improving economic conditions does not always lead to effective demand satisfaction and that a widening "aspirations gap" during the development process itself is what leads to popular rebellions.

As has been made clear up to this point, neither the insurrection nor the social revolution that followed stemmed from popular dissatisfaction with the development pattern of Cuba's dependent capitalism. Political rather than economic or structural factors account for the emergence of revolutionary politics, in the sense that unfulfilled *political* expectations preceded demands for social transformation. In other words, by the 1950s Cuba's social and economic development had produced material welfare for a good part of its population, but substantial differences in the quality of life between urban and rural areas persisted. Asymmetries in the domestic economy due to the dominant influence of sugar and the absence of a dynamic industrial sector added to such a contrast, but economically, Cuba was slowly moving forward.

High levels of unemployment and underemployment, between 16 and 20 percent, characterized an economy geared to the seasonal sugar production cycle, demanding intensive labor for parts of the year but slacking off once harvesting was completed. Seasonal unemployment also affected the rural areas disproportionately, given the existence of a rural proletariat dependent on the mills for employment. As a result, the lack of permanent employment affected rural wage levels and the standard of living, being "the most important explanation for the economic and social backwardness of the majority of rural Cubans."[35]

On the other hand, the proportion of people living in the rural areas—43 percent in 1953—had been declining since the late 1920s. In addition, despite the influence of agriculture in aggregate output and gross national product (GNP), 59 percent of the economically active population was engaged in nonfarm activities, including 20 percent in services and 17 percent in manufacturing. A measure of agricultural diversification had also occurred, improving production of principal foods such as rice, dairy products, and other basic staples like beef, poultry, and pork.[36] Nonetheless, land concentration prevailed due to the extensive holdings of sugar companies and cattle ranchers. In the late 1940s, "less than 8 percent of the farms accounted for almost 75 percent of the farmland, one half of one percent of the farms controlled more than one third of the land, and 85 percent of the farms . . . [had] only 20 percent of the land."[37]

Foreign investment in the economy was substantial by the late 1950s, with U.S. capital dominant in some sectors. For example, in 1958 U.S.

direct investments totaled $1 billion with over $200 million in additional portfolio holdings. Investments in agriculture reached $265 million; $386 million was invested in services and utilities, and the balance in manufacturing, transportation, mining, and petroleum.[38] On the other hand, 121 out of Cuba's 161 mills were nationally owned in 1958, producing 62 percent of the sugar crop, with "Cubanization proceeding even further because many Cubans owned stock in the American sugar companies."[39] National rates of investment and capital formation were often higher than those measured in more advanced countries, reaching 18 percent of GNP and 15 percent of national income in 1957.[40] In sum, despite "the permanent crisis of Cuba's sugar economy—high level stagnation," owing to the political power of organized foreign and domestic interests, which prevented a more rational utilization of the country's economic assets,[41] Cuba's level of development was comparable to that of the more advanced Latin American nations.

In social terms, the expanding middle class constituted between one-fourth and one-third of the population by the late 1950s. A fairly homogeneous culture attenuated social distances, diffusing the extremes of wealth and poverty typical in underdeveloped societies. Cuba had a fairly advanced socioeconomic profile, as evidenced by a literacy rate of close to 80 percent; a per capita income of some $500; and comparatively high rankings in terms of social service deliveries, per capita use of automobiles, communications media, and energy consumption. Lastly, infant mortality rates of 32 per 1,000 live births in 1955–1959 and life expectancy close to sixty years suggest that although inequalities existed in the social structure and distortions affected the pattern of economic development, neither the dual society nor the classic underdevelopment models applied to Cuban society.[42]

In conclusion, by the late 1950s, "Cuba had its share of social and economic problems, but it was not a fragmented or agglomerate nation," ridden with irreconcilable racial, ethnic, or class cleavages.[43] Though its political autonomy remained subject to foreign pressures, the imperatives of capitalist modernization had not obliterated Cuba's cultural integrity, social structure, or economic system. Coping with external forces through structural transformations in order to acquire political viability and greater economic autonomy would be difficult in a capitalist country with scarce resources, but even more so in a society in which the dominant classes did not exercise political hegemony.

NOTES

1. Mario Riera Hernández, *Cuba Libre, 1895-1958* (Miami: Colonial Press, 1968), pp. 147–168.
2. Robert F. Smith, *The United States and Cuba* (New Haven, Conn.: College and University Press, 1960), p. 164.

3. Gary W. Wynia, *The Politics of Latin American Development* (Cambridge: Cambridge University Press, 1978), pp. 165–166. Wynia is referring to the populist game, not to Cuba itself.

4. Ramón Grau San Martín, "La Definición de la Política Auténtica," in *La Revolución Cubana Ante América* (Mexico: Conferencias, 1936), pp. 101–106.

5. Federico G. Gil, "Responsible Parties in Latin America," in *The Dynamics of Change in Latin American Politics*, ed. John D. Martz (Englewood Cliffs, N.J.: Prentice-Hall, 1965), p. 218.

6. Samuel Farber, *Revolution and Reaction in Cuba, 1933–1960* (Middletown, Conn.: Wesleyan University Press, 1976), p. 89.

7. Riera, *Cuba Libre*, p. 167.

8. Ruby Hart Phillips, *Cuba: Island of Paradox* (New York: McDowell Obolensky, 1959), p. 224.

9. Gil, "Responsible Parties," p. 217.

10. U.S., Department of Commerce, Bureau of Foreign Commerce, *Investment in Cuba* (Washington, D.C.: U.S. Government Printing Office, 1956), p. 7.

11. Enrique A. Baloyra, "Political Leadership in the Cuban Republic: 1944–1958" (Ph.D. diss., University of Florida, 1971), pp. 94–95.

12. Hugh Thomas, *Cuba, The Pursuit of Freedom* (New York: Harper & Row, 1971), p. 758.

13. "Lo Que Prometió y No Cumplió el Dr. Grau," *Carteles* 16 (1948):13.

14. Andrés Suárez, *Cuba: Castroism and Communism, 1959–1966* (Cambridge, Mass.: MIT Press, 1967), p. 11.

15. Federico G. Gil, "Antecedents of the Cuban Revolution," in *Reform and Revolution*, ed. Arpad von Lazar and Robert R. Kaufman (Boston: Allyn and Bacon, 1969), p. 300.

16. Carlos Franqui, *Diary of the Cuban Revolution*, trans. Georgette Felix et al. (New York: Viking Press, 1980), p. 57.

17. Ramón L. Bonachea and Marta San Martín, *The Cuban Insurrection 1952–1959* (New Brunswick, N.J.: Transaction Books, 1974), pp. 27–28.

18. A letter from prison quoted in Franqui, *Diary of the Cuban Revolution*, p. 67.

19. Thomas, *Cuba*, p. 927.

20. Mario Llerena, *The Unsuspected Revolution* (Ithaca, N.Y.: Cornell University Press, 1978), p. 65.

21. Franqui, *Diary of the Cuban Revolution*, p. 100.

22. Bonachea and San Martín, *The Cuban Insurrection*, pp. 39–40.

23. Franqui, *Diary of the Cuban Revolution*, p. 141.

24. Bonachea and San Martín, *The Cuban Insurrection*, p. 92.

25. Llerena, *The Unsuspected Revolution*, pp. 275–304, includes the text from which these items are taken.

26. Thomas, *Cuba*, pp. 483–487.

27. For a broader treatment, see Lester D. Langley, *The Cuban Policy of the United States* (New York: Wiley, 1968); or Earl E. T. Smith, *The Fourth Floor* (New York: Random House, 1962).

28. Franqui, *Diary of the Cuban Revolution*, p. 269.

29. Ibid., pp. 273–274.

30. Jorge García Montes and Antonio Alonso Ávila, *Historia del Partido Comunista de Cuba* (Miami: Ediciones Universal, 1970), p. 501.

31. K. S. Karol, *Guerrillas in Power* (New York: Hill and Wang, 1970), p. 150.

32. Bonachea and San Martín, *The Cuban Insurrection*, p. 279.
33. Louis A. Peréz, Jr., *Army Politics in Cuba, 1898–1958* (Pittsburgh: University of Pittsburgh Press, 1976), pp. 154–155.
34. Mario Lazo, *Dagger in the Heart* (New York: Funk and Wagnalls, 1970), p. 176. See also J. Dorscher and R. Fabricio, *The Winds of December* (New York: Coward, McCann and Geohegan, 1980).
35. James O'Connor, *The Origins of Socialism in Cuba* (Ithaca, N.Y.: Cornell University Press, 1970), p. 58.
36. Lowry Nelson, *Cuba, the Measure of a Revolution* (Minneapolis: University of Minnesota Press, 1972), p. 57.
37. U.S. Department of Commerce, *Investment in Cuba*, p. 32.
38. U.S. Department of Commerce, Bureau of Foreign Commerce, *United States Business Investment in Foreign Countries* (Washington, D.C.: U.S. Government Printing Office, 1960).
39. Nelson, *Cuba, the Measure of a Revolution*, p. 62.
40. José Alvarez Díaz et al., *Cuba, Geopolítica y Pensamiento Económico* (Miami: n.p., 1964), p. 427.
41. O'Connor, *The Origins of Socialism*, pp. 19–25.
42. Carmelo Mesa-Lago, *The Economy of Socialist Cuba* (Albuquerque: University of New Mexico Press, 1981), pp. 7–10; Carlos Alberto Montaner, *Secret Report on the Cuban Revolution*, trans. Eduardo Zayas-Bazán (New Brunswick, N.J.: Transaction Books, 1981), pp. 153–158.
43. Richard R. Fagen, "Revolution: For Internal Consumption Only," in *Cuban Communism*, 4th ed., ed. Irving Louis Horowitz (New Brunswick, N.J.: Transaction Books, 1981), p. 370.

Part 2
Revolution and Transformation

4

Revolution and Confrontation

The collapse of authoritarianism in 1959 left a systemic vacuum in the fluid revolutionary environment. Competition among contenders within the revolutionary movement over authority, socioeconomic reforms, programmatic and development matters, and relations with the United States took up much of the 1959–1961 period. Not surprisingly, powerful currents of national euphoria sustained feelings that at long last accumulated frustrations would be addressed through meaningful reforms. In addition, widespread convictions that major changes were in order compelled the government to initiate basic redistributive policies to satisfy legitimate socioeconomic and cultural demands.

Castro and his close associates acquired control over decision making. Opponents within the new regime found their policy preferences subjected to loyalty tests, political considerations, and Castro's amorphous objectives and personal volatilities. In short, the early phase of the Revolution featured internal power struggles, major redistributive policies, changes in the political culture, ideological ambiguity, and escalating tensions between Cuba and the United States.

INTERNAL CONFLICT AND REDISTRIBUTION

Seizing power on the heels of a national institutional collapse opens opportunities for creating a new order; at the same time competing demands and the need to fulfill explicit promises impose burdens and constraints on those assuming political power. Programmatic, political, and ideological difficulties traceable to the insurrectional period but exacerbated by popular expectations and pressures by the United States affected the policy agenda of the revolutionary regime. The new government's need to move forward in order to establish its credibility, expand its social base, and demonstrate its resolve overcame gradualist approaches mindful of legal or constitutional parameters.

Generally speaking, the developmental views of moderate, liberal, and revolutionary sectors were not in conflict with each other. Land reform, salary and wage benefits for workers, regulation of foreign interests, administrative reform, diversification of production, industrialization, and

45

curtailment of sugar's influence in the economy were all accepted goals on which a near-consensus existed. On the other hand, many expected constitutional government and a restructuring of relations with the United States, the former to come through electoral means and the latter through firm but amicable negotiations. Castro was aware of those expectations. During the Revolution's early months he had been ambivalent on the schedule for national elections but had insisted that they would be held. Responding to criticism in the U.S. media regarding the perceived radicalization of the Revolution, Castro reaffirmed the latter's democratic nature in May 1959.

Early policies redistributed wealth and income, improved the purchasing power of urban workers and the lower middle class—the popular sectors—and expanded services through public and private means. For example, confiscation of properties belonging to Batista or his close associates was followed by reductions in utility rates and urban rents, rationalization of the tax structure, abolition of legal race discrimination, improvements in social and state services, and new infrastructural ventures.[1] Conditions in the rural areas as well as the tenure of land ownership and the availability of credits and technical assistance to peasants were addressed through an Agrarian Reform Law enacted in May 1959 that established the powerful National Institute for Agrarian Reform (INRA) with Castro as its president. The law established a "vital minimum" of 27 hectares (66.7 acres) for homesteads, granting priority to renters, squatters, and sharecroppers, while limiting individuals and corporations to ownership of a maximum of 400 hectares (988 acres). The country was divided into twenty-eight zones; each zone would be administered by an INRA appointee and INRA would be responsible for the provision of basic health and educational services as well as technical and financial assistance.

Collectivization and redistribution of land changed the tenancy structure, bringing the state fully into agricultural affairs as an administrator, monitor, and regulator of production. INRA organized Cooperatives, Farm Units Under Direct Administration, and Sugar Cooperatives from the expropriated holdings. By May 1961, following the expropriation of U.S.- and Cuban-owned sugar mill lands, total surface affected by the land reform measures was 4,438,879 hectares (10,964,031 acres), or 44 percent of total farm lands.[2] By the same date, some 167,000 canefield workers had joined cooperatives, with an additional 50,000 still hiring out for private wages.[3] In addition, since from the Revolution's standpoint organizing workers, small farmers, and the rural proletariat was as significant as changing their economic status, the National Association of Small Farmers (ANAP) was created in 1961, with membership rising close to 150,000.[4]

The Agrarian Reform Law, along with other populist measures undertaken in 1959, enhanced the socioeconomic position of the peasantry, the urban proletariat, and the lower middle class, increasing their purchasing power and contributing to a rise in living standards while preserving the basic capitalist system. Delivering on needed reforms strengthened the regime's support among the popular sectors, but it created opposition among cattle ranchers, big landowners, some businessmen, and foreign property holders. Nonetheless, despite the regime's "statist, populist, anti-market, consumptionist and nationalistic tendencies,"[5] affecting middle- and upper-class interests, individual businessmen and firms cooperated with the regime, advancing tax payments and supporting tributary reforms.[6]

It appeared to many that the revolutionary regime was committed to fulfilling promises made in previous decades by both moderates and radicals. The energy displayed by the regime in confronting what it perceived to be "obstacles to development" added to its popularity, but it also led many to wonder just what was happening. Gradually, supporters as well as opponents of the regime came to the view that this would no longer be "business as usual"—that a profound social project was unfolding, the final outcome of which could not yet be visualized.

The new regime was convinced that sugar monoculture lay at the root of Cuba's structural ills by making the economy vulnerable to harmful price fluctuations and contributing to seasonal unemployment and "rural rootlessness." It chose to de-emphasize sugar production, diversify agri-culture, and encourage industrial development. If successful, industrial development would reduce Cuba's internal dependence on sugar, create additional employment opportunities, reduce the need for many imports, and improve the country's foreign trade position through variations in trade that presumably would bring in greater earnings. This strategy was in line with mainstream Latin American developmental thinking; economists like Raúl Prebisch had proposed import-substitution industrialization as a viable strategy for countries with development levels comparable to Cuba's. Along these lines, modernization depended on the successful establishment of industrial and manufacturing complexes and required substantial in-vestments in industry, capital goods, and industrial technology. That consumption would have to be sacrificed in order to reallocate resources for investment purposes was not appreciated at the time. Optimistic assessments of Cuba's industrial potential prevailed among economic policy-makers, as did the view that "heavy industry would put an end to unemployment and to dependence on imports for basic industrial equip-ment."[7] That a small market flooded with U.S. consumer and durable goods could sustain major efforts at industrial expansion without incurring scarcities, bottlenecks, and persistent shortfalls between demand and supply was not fully considered.

Eradicating economic evils associated with a dependent capitalist system dictated that statist practices and antimarket philosophies govern policymaking. Prior to any formal commitment to a socialist model, the regime instituted reforms reducing the economic and political influence of the private sector, such as the Urban Reform of October 1960 which socialized Cuban-owned businesses and privately owned real estate. Though the passage of that law was due partly to deteriorating relations with the United States, it further undercut the private sector's position and expanded

Table 4.1. Collectivized Sectors in Cuba: 1961

Sector	Percentage of Ownership
Agriculture	37
Industry	85
Construction	80
Transportation	92
Retail trade	52
Wholesale & foreign trade	100
Banking	100
Education	100

Source: Adapted from Carmelo Mesa-Lago, "Economic Policies and Growth," in Revolutionary Change in Cuba, ed. Carmelo Mesa-Lago (Pittsburgh: University of Pittsburgh Press, 1971), p. 283.

the state's role. The state thus demonstrated its use of summary powers and revealed its commitment to nonmarket mechanisms for regulation of economic activity. Also, capitalizing on the unused capacity of the economy during this early period reduced the probability that consumptionist pressures would eat up critical resources. In fact, during a phase in which the economy was still relatively mixed, industrial production rose 17 percent in 1959 and 29 percent in 1960, with improvements in wages, salaries, and employment levels.[8] Lastly, combined efforts to "de-sugarize" the economy, begin industrial projects, create jobs, change the land tenure system, and redistribute wealth through central mechanisms meant changing Cuba's political economy. Large-scale nationalization of U.S. businesses and firms during the second half of 1960 accelerated the pace of socialization by extending state control over the basic means of production. As shown in Table 4.1, critical sectors were totally in state hands by 1961, and although 63 percent of agriculture remained in private hands, INRA's role was self-aggrandizing.

Structural changes combined with populist, redistributive measures signaled the regime's willingness to incur domestic costs and risk internal opposition in order to gain the support of déclasse elements and popular sectors, thereby showing its domestic and foreign adversaries that its commitments were real. Moreover, by sacrificing economic rationality to political considerations and social mobilization, the regime showed an early willingness to trade performance for revolutionary commitments. That tendency clearly produced various imbalances and dislocations. As Mesa-Lago has commented, disappearing market forces

were not substituted by planning and central orders, partly because of a lack of a clear economic program and due to the alienation of former managers and technicians usually replaced by enthusiastic but unskilled revolutionaries. The net result of this situation was widespread economic disorganization.[9]

Postponement of crucial political decisions on economic grounds made little sense to leaders whose basic aim was to advance the power of the state over private interests in order to abolish the system of property, wealth, and class that the Revolution was committed to destroy. Supply and demand did not matter. Who lost what did not matter. What the economic costs might be down the road did not matter. What was crucial was furthering the revolutionary process, doing rather than thinking, moving rather than standing still. Many remembered "the generation of 1930," especially those, in the words of a popular poem, "hunted and shot on the streets, murdered while sleeping, fighting in the trenches of defeated revolutions." This, they vowed, would not happen to them.

The revolutionaries, taking themselves, their view of history, and their immediate political situation seriously hammered away on all fronts against the church, the university, labor, and organized professional interests. They created a "we" versus "they" climate and portrayed all their opponents as enemies of the people and counterrevolutionaries. The newspapers *Avance* and *El Mundo* were seized by the government in January 1960, and in March the country's leading television station, CMQ, was itself seized, continuing a trend designed to stifle criticism and intimidate the press. Unanimity, not dissent, was sought. As long as the leadership retained the support of its natural clienteles and chose to employ coercion in order to force compliance, the strength of its social base and the efficiency of its internal security units overcame elite resistance. By activating class forces and provoking sectoral clashes, "the radicalism of the leadership had in various forms filtered down to the masses," and the masses enthusiastically supported the "various measures Castro periodically and unexpectedly produced after long night sessions of the revolutionary leadership."[10]

Once it became evident that a radical social revolution committed to the destruction of the capitalist order and "bourgeois" society in general was in the making, led by individuals seeking total power, internal though divided opposition emerged in an attempt to reverse authoritarian and dictatorial trends. That opposition, motivated by something other than a desire to restore social privileges or capitalist profiteering, involved Catholic organizations, disaffected M-26-7 cadres, respected democratic figures, and other anticommunist elements.

CASTROITES AND COMMUNISTS (I)

The intensification of the revolutionary process forced nationalist reformers, revolutionaries, and communists either to support further radicalization, acquiesce and disengage, or commit themselves to overt and covert resistance. In addition, the creation of revolutionary organizations like the Committees for the Defense of the Revolution (CDR) in 1960 extended regime controls to the level of the masses. The CDR began as neighborhood committees designed to protect the Revolution from its internal enemies. They constituted the revolutionary organization par excellence, emphasizing vigilance as well as revolutionary militancy and individual sacrifice. According to Richard Fagen, the committees were "expected to integrate, socialize and mobilize the masses, implement revolutionary policies and programs and protect both the material and social resources of the Revolution."[11]

Once Castro discarded the electoral option—on the grounds that such frivolities would divert the masses from greater tasks—the means through which legitimate resistance could be mounted were severely curtailed. Non-identification with the direction of the Revolution carried personal costs; domestic critics of the regime were portrayed as obstructionist lackeys of U.S. imperialism. The consistent attacks on the press, labor, and independent organizations as the "hour of solid and impenetrable unanimity" approached were worse than censorship, "because censorship forces oneself not to speak one's own truth, but unanimity forces one to repeat another's truth without believing it."[12]

Castro's calculated ambivalence regarding the role of communists in the regime and his refusal to break with them deepened the split between moderates and radicals, especially after Major Huber Matos's denunciation of communist activities led to his arrest, trial, and imprisonment.[13] Major Matos was military commander of Camagüey province at the time of his arrest. As a noncommunist nationalist committed to democracy, Matos was torn between his loyalty to Castro and the Revolution and his opposition to dictatorship. In that, he was the prototype of many who also felt uneasy about Castro's personal ambitions and the communists' creeping influence. Matos had denounced the communists in a speech in April 1959, but he hoped that his letter of resignation in October would force Castro to unequivocally state his intentions regarding communism. Castro's reaction was swift and ruthless. Matos was arrested, accused of treachery, tried, and subsequently sentenced to twenty years' imprisonment, along with other officers who were loyal to him.

Opposition to Castro was embodied in groups such as the Movimiento Revolucionario del Pueblo (MRP) and the Movimiento de Rescate Revolucionario (MRR). These groups were made up of former Castro colleagues and anticommunist and nationalist elements. Engaging in clandestine antiregime activities—in some cases supported by the CIA—these opponents sought to prevent the consolidation of a leftist dictatorship led by Castro. In addition, struggles raged within M-26-7 between unconditional followers of Castro and Marxist elements close to Guevara and Raúl Castro on the one hand and nonsectarian forces on the other. Gradually, the moderates lost influence, through disillusionment, personal withdrawal, defections, purges, or arrests and imprisonment. Invariably, Castroite loyalists and communist sympathizers gained greater political, ideological, and administrative control. The Rebel Army remained loyal to Castro's leadership as well. In short, through 1960, hopes for a national, democratic, and social revolution rather than a revolutionary dictatorship quickly faded, amidst a climate of domestic repression, censorship, intense underground activity, growing communist influence and polarized class politics.

Castro relied on his own appeal, charismatic qualities, and unparalleled audacity to transform personal leadership into hegemonic authority. He subordinated ideological dogma to tactical considerations, delaying as long as possible his commitment to either Marxist socialism or authoritarian reformism. Leaving ideological interpretations to Guevara and retaining freedom to manuever vis-à-vis domestic antagonists as well as real or potential foreign adversaries, Castro invoked themes of sacrifice, patriotism, struggle, and *cubanidad* (the essence of being Cuban)—rather than ideological truths—to justify revolutionary measures. Having once condemned capitalism as a "system that would kill men with hunger" and criticized communism for "wiping out man's freedom," Castro insisted on revolutionary solidarity in the face of foreign aggression and domestic class enemies. In time, organizational imperatives and the necessity of finding an international patron willing to partially meet Cuba's economic and defense needs delegitimated criticism of either the communists or of Cuba's emerging ties with the Soviet Union.

In essence, Castro's relationship with the Communist party stemmed from his desire to limit the damage inflicted on the regime by the progressive defection of proven but noncommunist revolutionaries, as well as from the need to enlist Soviet support. It was tactical demands rather than ideological affinity to revolutionary comradeship that led Castro to the PSP. The PSP capitalized on the political opportunity, providing Castro with an organizational network based on discipline, unity, and command. Taking advantage of the fluidity created by Castro's vacillation on final political choices, the Party accepted measures like the expropriation of foreign properties despite ideological reservations. Most important, the Party offered solid contacts with Moscow, a well-elaborated anti-imperialist ideology, access to international propaganda resources, and a remarkable record of political resiliency.[14] Simply put, the union of Castroites and communists was one of strict convenience for both. The Party was willing to accept a subordinate position in exchange for any role at all; it vindicated its strategy of creeping encroachment, capitalizing on the anti-U.S. character of the Revolution without explicitly demanding that Castro at once convert to its official faith.

For Castro, the knowledge that anticommunist feelings ran deep among some revolutionaries—especially those belonging to the DR or the urban underground—was not as critical as his belief that personal animosities must not threaten the regime's survival. Thus, efforts to force Castro to repudiate communism went nowhere,[15] especially after the Soviet foreign minister's visit to Cuba in early 1960 established needed economic ties between Havana and the Kremlin.[16]

To sum up, seeking to exploit unfolding revolutionary dynamics and straining to fit the Cuban case into the framework of orthodox revolutions, the PSP reaped the windfall produced through the fallout among moderates, Castroite loyalists, and known Marxists. Enhancing its standing from that of a discredited fringe group to a revolutionary force due to the radicalization of the Revolution, the Party became an official though subordinate member of the regime well before Castro's conversion to Marxism-Leninism in December 1961.[17]

CULTURE AND THE REVOLUTION

Revolutionary changes in the 1959–1961 period affected popular culture as well as the arts, cinema, literature, and journalism. From the outset, many writers, artists, and intellectuals sympathized with the Revolution, often feeling compelled to participate in a process of social change and cultural emancipation. Established figures like the writer and social critic Jorge Mañach were swept along in the euphoria of the first months; the support of others, such as the novelist Alejo Carpentier, lent intellectual prestige to the revolutionary process. Writers, poets, and literary critics sought to redefine the idea of "culture" itself, infusing their work with zeal, social significance, and political commitment. In a society in which the "man of letters" was not widely admired and in which belonging to a "cultural intelligentsia" raised suspicions, the new climate of freedom was widely hailed.

Magazines like *Lunes de Revolución*, then headed by Guillermo Cabrera Infante, opened its pages to hitherto unknown writers; *Lunes* at times also reproduced works by José Luis Borges, Pablo Neruda, William Faulkner and others in the effort to improve the quality of literary, even ethical debate. In fact, the whole revolutionary experience had a dramatic impact on intellectuals in Europe and Latin America; both Jean-Paul Sartre and Pablo Neruda, among many others, visited Cuba during this period.

The organization of the government press (Imprenta Nacional) in 1959, the Cuban Institute of Arts and Cinematography (ICAIC—Instituto Cubano del Arte e Industria Cinematográficas), and a major publishing house—Casa de las Américas (House of the Americas)—opened up new outlets for creative works. Culture was revolutionary, ideas had value, critical thinking was becoming respectable. The new day had emerged.

Such an explosion could not remain isolated from the struggles being waged inside the Revolution's ranks. By mid-1961, as communist leaders began to assume prominence in politics, their influence over the content of "cultural works" (articles, poems, novels, movies, and so on) began to be felt. For example, Edith García Buchaca, director of the National Council of Culture (CNC), and other PSP members like Alfredo Guevara (head of ICAIC), sought to put an end to what they perceived were "divisive currents" being encouraged by some newspapers and magazines. *Revolución* (M-26-7's organ) and *Lunes* were singled out, as was the film *P.M.* Cultural officials alleged that *P.M.* "created the impression of a people that had not acquired any consciousness of the national problems and preferred to dance, get drunk and forget," since the film showed people enjoying their leisure time.[18]

The situation acquired immense political significance as it dealt with a potentially explosive issue: the role that critics might play in a revolutionary process. Would the Revolution tolerate independent thinking if it came from within the ranks? To what extent must ideological criteria condition works of art and literature? Was the imposition of cultural uniformity an explicit political objective? Such questions did not remain unanswered.

As would happen again and again, Castro himself set the limits on cultural and artistic freedom. In June 1961, in his famous *"Palabras a los Intelectuales"* ("Words to the Intellectuals") Castro allowed that "the whole group of artists and intellectuals who are not genuinely revolutionaries can find within the Revolution a place to work and create," because the Revolution had no intention of suppressing freedom of expression. In fact, writers and poets would help in satisfying the people's cultural needs, because "the artist creates for the people, and so the people in turn raise their cultural level and draw nearer to the artist." Finally, Castro resolved the issue between what would or would not be permissible by laying down the following formula: "Within the Revolution, everything; against it, nothing." Needless to say, the regime reserved for itself the right to judge what was, or was not, acceptable. In the words of one of Castro's former close associates, the resolution of the conflict in such terms meant "the historic death of a new and free project of revolution," an eye-opening manifestation of cultural Stalinism.[19]

RELATIONS WITH THE UNITED STATES

The U.S. stake in Cuba was substantial in 1959, as was discussed in Chapter 3. U.S. investments in Cuba totaled $1 billion and Cuba received 65 percent of its imports from the United States, while sending the United States 75 percent of its exports. U.S. influence was evident in culture, values, and lifestyle, as well as in traditional political and economic matters. Cuba's middle and upper classes were familiar with American ways; they often sent their children to study in the United States and otherwise admired U.S. economic affluence and democratic stability. In short, members of "high society" as well as ordinary Cubans felt a mixture of admiration, respect, and awe for their northern neighbor. They felt quite comfortable with Cuba's dependent position without fully considering how close bilateral ties between an industrial giant and an underdeveloped society affected the latter's struggle for identity. Clearly, there were also those who benefited from the asymmetries in the relationship, either in association with U.S. capital or from numerous business, financial, and commercial interactions between Cuba and the United States.

In a major respect, the Americanization of the middle class was itself a reflection that its cultural values and sense of identity in Cuba were in flux, directly affected by U.S. influences. The Cuban middle class was characterized by political inertia, ideological ambivalence, and "social isolation" and by its lack of a developed sense of national consciousness.[20] Its leaders did not think that they had a "national mission" to carry out, least of all when such a mission might mean challenging the United States. That option, in short, was inconceivable, and that fact helps to explain the sense of puzzlement and betrayal prevailing in the middle class once it became clear that the United States was unwilling to remove Castro no matter what the cost.

So, although Cuban nationalism paled beside the pervasive Yankee-phobia of other Latin American societies, the dominant U.S. economic presence—from glittering neon signs to Campbell's soup to "usted si puede tener un Buick" (you too can have a Buick)—offended defenders of Cuba's economic sovereignty and cultural integrity. Moreover, many on the left focused on the "incestuous" relationship among dictators, domestic and foreign capital, and U.S. imperial ambitions, correctly pointing out that if Cuba was not a colony, it was certainly a subordinate, client state. Specifically, U.S. support for Batista had reinforced the view that U.S. policy invariably supported friendly dictatorial governments (conveniently forgetting the 1940–1952 period) unwilling to alter either Cuba's subordinate political status or move ahead on a path of independent development. Lastly, members of the democratic left in Cuba and Latin America felt that the United States failed to distinguish between nationalist reformers committed to stable social and economic change and Marxist-Leninists, pointing to Jacobo Arbenz in Guatemala in the early 1950s—whose commitment to structural change was perceived as threatening U.S. interests— as a case in point. What all this adds up to is that, as Gonzalez has correctly noted, "by the late 1950s Cuban nationalists had accumulated a backlog of emotion-laden grievances towards the United States,"[21] feeling that U.S. interests had to be challenged if Cuba was ever to realize its potential sovereignty, economic viability, and cultural emancipation.

It is also true that many participants in the insurrection and in the government during 1959–1960 believed that an assertive, self-confident, and economically prosperous Cuba did not threaten vital U.S. interests; they expected cooperation from the United States for a post-Batista government. In other words, they felt that economic nationalism preceded full sovereignty and that restructuring U.S.-Cuban relations was necessary in order to gain national viability. On the other hand, a total break with the United States was almost unimaginable, given Cuba's location, the record of past U.S. interventions, and the psychological hold U.S. society retained on Cuban elites. Thus, how revolutionary Cuba would deal with the United States—and vice versa—became more than an inconsequential foreign policy matter. It turned into a major issue dividing the radicals committed to ending U.S. influence and the moderate reformers believing in necessary adjustments but, ultimately, accommodation.

Perceptions about Castro himself in the U.S. government and to a lesser extent in the media and American public ran along the following lines. There were those, like U.S. Ambassador Earl Smith, who were suspicious of Castro's intentions, certain of his antidemocratic leaning, convinced of his anti-U.S. attitudes, and sure of his procommunist inclinations. At a minimum, Castro represented trouble for U.S. interests; at the very worst, he was a committed revolutionary driven to challenge U.S. hegemony.

A second group, including reporters like Herbert Matthews of the *New York Times*, some intellectuals, and liberal spokesmen, felt that Cuba needed a revolution and that Castro was a welcome change from the corrupt politicians of the past. In fact, they saw him as a dedicated, idealistic, nationalistic leader opposed to dictatorship as well as communism. They believed that the United States could deal with Castro and revolution, that it should support changes in Cuba's political and socioeconomic structures, and that it must not confuse a desire for order and liberty with Marxist inclinations or communist conspiracies.

Finally, there were those who viewed Castro neither as a traditional strongman nor as a doctrinaire, disciplined Marxist. Instead, he was seen as an immature but effective leader, without a well-formed view of how to lead a revolutionary movement and not overly concerned with abstract or philosophical matters. They believed that Castro harbored anti-U.S. feelings and that he realized the obstacles to full development that U.S. hegemony presented, but that he was sufficiently astute to follow a prudent course. In Cuba itself, individuals subscribing to the third view were found in the urban wing of M-26-7, in positions of leadership in some unions, and in sectors of the Catholic church. For them, the Revolution could be nationalist *and* democratic. Restraining Castro's *caudillo* (political strongman) temperament would be a problem, but they firmly believed that Castro would not throw his lot in with the communists. Lastly, through organs such as the newspaper *Revolución*, pro-Castro nationalists hoped to steer the revolutionary process away from dogmatism and sectarianism, giving rein to authentically Cuban aspirations.

As often happens when information and images are filtered through personal prejudices or bureaucratic systems, each characterization of Castro captured part of his personality, missing Castro's megalomaniacal, authoritarian tendencies as well as the depth and scope of nationalist feelings generated by the Revolution itself. In a nutshell, if the assumption that Castro "would come around" proved to be unfounded, so did the expectation that the Revolution would crumble in the face of the right mixture of U.S. diplomatic and political pressures or economic sanctions. In effect, the various forms of external aggression hardened revolutionary resistance without increasing U.S. leverage.

In classic action-response terms, U.S.-Cuban relations went through a period of mutual uncertainty, escalating challenges, and ultimately, rupture and military confrontation. Specifically, actions by the regime—such as the Agrarian Reform Law of 1959—affected relations, since the United States insisted on adequate compensation, though it did not dispute Cuba's right to expropriate properties. Other measures against U.S. interests involved the takeover of the Cuban Telegraph and Telephone Company, and government-ordered rate reductions for the U.S.-owned Cuban Electric Company. Also, prior to the major wave of nationalizations in late 1960, the Cuban government "intervened" in U.S. mining and hotel interests.[22]

Despite provocations, recriminations, and hostile rhetoric, the Eisenhower administration chose a policy of caution and circumspection toward Cuba rather than a decidedly antagonistic one, at least through the spring of 1960. For instance, Castro's visit to the United States in April 1959 reassured those who felt that he was inclined to get along with the United States, though in his meeting with Vice-President Nixon the latter presumably became convinced that Castro was either "extremely naive" or already beholden to communism. U.S. officials suggested that they would look favorably upon a Cuban request for economic aid, but later complained about inadequacies in the compensation for expropriated lands and properties belonging to U.S. nationals.

Cuba's attempt to overthrow the Dominican dictator Trujillo, the summary trials and executions of Batista henchmen, Castro's purposeful snub of U.S. Ambassador Philip Bonsal by failing to receive him for several months, the cancellation of elections, and increasing communist penetration of the army, labor, the media, and bureaucracy contributed to escalating suspicions about Castro's true intentions. Most important, in February 1960 Soviet Foreign Minister Anastas Mikoyan arrived in Havana, where he signed an agreement providing credits of $100 million to Cuba for the purchase of industrial equipment, various other materials, and technical assistance; the USSR also agreed to purchase over 400,000 tons (362,812 metric tons) of sugar in 1960 and an additional 4 million tons (3.63 million metric tons)[23] through 1964. Military and foreign policy matters were also discussed. According to Jorge Domínguez, "this agreement did not necessarily determine the shift to socialism," since full diplomatic relations between Cuba and the USSR were not restored until May 1960, "but it was a major economic and political turning point for the revolution."[24]

With Soviet commitments offsetting potential U.S. economic retribution—the sugar quota being the key matter—relations between the United States and Cuba worsened following the takeover of U.S.-owned oil refineries in June 1960 when these refused to process Soviet crude. The regime viewed this as a major challenge "not only with regard to its foreign and commercial policies but on strategic grounds as well," and it seized the refineries.[25] Moving swiftly, the United States played its major economic card in July, suspending the balance of Cuba's 1960 sugar quota: 700,000 tons (634,921 metric tons). Reasons for doing so involved domestic considerations as well as a desire to increase pressure on Castro; "it was an act of economic warfare aimed at a 'change of government' in Cuba."[26] Though not immediately, Cuba confiscated the remaining U.S. assets in Cuba, including sugar mills, utility companies, banks, and numerous U.S.-owned businesses and firms—raising the total value of expropriated assets to $1.5 billion.[27]

Economic warfare, charges during the 1960 presidential campaign that Eisenhower had "done nothing" about communism so close to the United States, and the never-forgotten Guatemalan episode, during which forces supported by the Central Intelligence Agency (CIA) overthrew a leftist government, made a final confrontation all but inevitable. Unquestionably, "the Guatemalan precedent seem[ed] to be relevant in explaining United States policy," given U.S. military superiority, unclear Soviet signals, and the belief that "economic pressures and external and internal discontent" would overwhelm the regime.[28] In fact, the decision to recruit, equip, and train a Cuban exile force was made in March 1960, as part of a four-point plan involving the creation of a Cuban government in exile, utilization of propaganda assets, contacts with clandestine anti-Castro groups in Cuba, and the invasion force itself.[29] Castro's own intelligence network, public bickering among exiles, and U.S. media reports assured the non-secrecy of the presumably covert operation, adding tension to the already highly charged bilateral context, while allowing Castro to prepare Cuba's defenses and reduce the probability of the invasion's success. In any case, following Castro's demand that the U.S. reduce its embassy staff in Havana, the Eisenhower administration severed diplomatic relations with Cuba in January 1961.

A popular and widely held view contends that U.S. policies in the 1959–1961 period offered Castro poor domestic and foreign policy choices, left him with little room to maneuver and thus encouraged his radical impulses. For example, it is often asserted that insisting on U.S. notions of legality and fairness regarding treatment of regime opponents in Cuba or takeovers of property in a revolutionary environment diverted the focus from larger efforts, namely Cuba's attempt to create a new order and embark on a path of successful development. From that standpoint, the United States could have been more accommodating, asserting its security interests without needlessly antagonizing Castro or constantly referring to the communist menace in Cuba. In short, it is argued that Castro was driven into the Soviet bloc, forced to obtain economic and military protection from an unnatural source during a period of extreme tension with the United States.

Others argue that Castro's decision to seek Soviet assistance stems from his conviction that the regime's survival depended on reducing Cuba's vulnerability to U.S. moves and that in a bipolar world, the only potentially capable source of protection was the Soviet Union. From this perspective Castro's behavior is entirely logical, within normal rules of international politics, typical of the behavior of small states in a system dominated by two antagonistic major powers. Thus, since the enlistment of Soviet support neither reduced Castro's political space nor imposed intolerable costs—at that point—on other internal or foreign policy matters, confrontation with the United States became a manageable policy.

My own appraisal is as follows. The conflict with the United States revolved essentially on security rather than on economic matters. From the U.S. standpoint, Cuba's alignment with the communist bloc threatened the United States' regional position by giving the Soviets a potential strategic forward position during a period of rigid bloc politics. For similar reasons, following the Bay of Pigs fiasco and Castro's ideological conversion to Marxism, the United States moved to isolate Cuba in the hemisphere by imposing an economic embargo and obtaining OAS support for suspending trade and commercial relations with Cuba. In short, U.S. policies toward Cuba can best be explained on national security grounds, namely that the "United States must insure that no unfriendly regimes are established near American borders," often demanding that "American power be used to prevent the possibility of unfriendly regimes in Central America and the Caribbean."[30]

On the other side, reasonably convinced that in order to survive, the Revolution had to become *more* not less radical, Castro escalated his demands, matching U.S. moves with often unanticipated responses. The link between U.S. actions and Cuba's internal dynamics became obvious prior to the Bay of Pigs invasion. Escalating challenges unleashed the forces of nationalism. An effective internal security apparatus, Castro's own dynamism, weak countermobilization, and superior tactical resources increased Cuba's probability of successfully resisting armed invasion. In sum, domestic mobilization sustained by charismatic leadership and impressive demand satisfaction had given the regime substantial staying power by 1961. The tendency of domestic and foreign opponents to underestimate the energies generated through confrontational politics contributed to major planning and tactical blunders by the CIA and the Kennedy administration, dooming the Bay of Pigs expedition before it hit Playa Girón.[31] In fact, the expected strong anti-Castro reaction inside Cuba never materialized. CIA estimates regarding Castro's unpopularity, and hence the degree of assistance the brigade could count on, also fell short. Finally, Kennedy's decision not to deploy U.S. air power from ships patrolling the approaches to the Bay of Pigs meant that Castro's air force had full control of the skies. With a decided advantage in the air and on the ground, and without having to cope with massive internal resistance, government forces overcame the brigade. Militarily, but more important, politically, this was a major victory for the revolutionary regime.

The consequences of the U.S. defeat were felt beyond Cuba itself. By failing to topple the regime, the invasion cemented Castro's domestic standing, demoralized the remnants of internal opposition and substantiated Castro's charges about "imperialist aggression." In terms of its overall impact, it was clear that

> the Bay of Pigs affair added new fuel to the fires of anti–United States critics throughout Latin America. It cast doubts not only on the integrity of the United States, but also on its qualifications for leadership and even its military ability. Castro, on the other hand, stood stronger and more defiant than ever; he was now definitely committed to the Soviet camp and determined to extend his revolution to other Latin American countries.[32]

SUMMARY

Revolutionary changes restructuring class, property, political, and foreign policy relationships eliminated a dependent capitalist order replete with U.S. influence without establishing well-defined institutions, demarcating authority, or identifying enduring sources of legitimacy. The elimination of legal channels for domestic opposition enhanced Castro's leadership role, bringing forth a repressive, authoritarian political regime committed to further political consolidation but with diffuse ideological characteristics.

Governmental takeover of the means of production, changes in Cuba's foreign commercial and trade policies, reliance on Soviet bloc technical and economic assistance, and the introduction of central planning mechanisms had favorable short-term social and political consequences, but in the long run they stifled production in basic commodities and gradually lowered consumption.

In foreign policy terms, movement toward the Soviet bloc entailed neither irrevocable ties nor total subordination to Soviet goals. Not willing to commit itself fully to a revolution without a Communist party in the vanguard, the Soviets waited for an enhancement of the PSP's influence in the regime, as well as for clearer formulations by Castro regarding his own ideological preferences. Though supporting Cuba seemed to make strategic sense, logistics and geography could create problems for the Soviets in the event of a direct confrontation with the United States. Other sources of potential friction involved the Cubans' unabashed revolutionary fervor, the absence of either cultural or historical affinity between Cuba and the Soviet Union, and the fact that the Soviets' "sense of solidarity was in direct proportion to their total ignorance of the situation and problems of that country."[33]

From Cuba's standpoint, the need to obtain long-term economic and technical assistance was as important as obtaining the perceived military and defense protection the Soviets offered. Thus, domestic imperatives, Cold War rivalries, and an untested belief that the Soviets would place revolutionary fraternity ahead of traditional balance of power approaches compelled Cuba to assume the risks of associating with a distant and alien communist state.

Finally, successful confrontation with the United States and the rapidity with which capitalism was abolished created the belief in Cuba that "history could be bypassed" and socialism built through obviating basic economic laws. Developmental dilemmas requiring concentrated attention were inadequately addressed, and inexperience, amateurishness, and poor administration plagued subsequent economic projects. The revolutionaries, committed to the economics of plenty, wanting to preserve distributive gains, and placing unbounded faith in their new mentors, would find that managed, noncapitalist development involved wealth creation and growth as well as revolutionary zeal.

NOTES

1. Archibald M. Ritter, *The Economic Development of Revolutionary Cuba* (New York: Praeger Publishers, 1974), pp. 70–71.

2. Michel Gutelman, "The Socialization of the Means of Production in Cuba," in *Cuba in Revolution*, ed. Rolando E. Bonachea and Nelson P. Valdés (Garden City, N.Y.: Anchor Books 1972), pp. 238–253.

3. James O'Connor, *The Origins of Socialism in Cuba* (Ithaca, N.Y.: Cornell University Press, 1970), p. 108.

4. Ibid., p. 121.

5. Carmelo Mesa-Lago, *Cuba in the 1970s*, rev. ed. (Albuquerque: University of New Mexico Press, 1978), p. 5.

6. Rufo López Fresquet, *My 14 Months with Castro* (Cleveland: World Publishing Co., 1966), pp. 117–121.

7. K. S. Karol, *Guerrillas in Power* (New York: Hill and Wang, 1970), p. 214.

8. O'Connor, *Origins of Socialism*, pp. 268–271.

9. Mesa-Lago, *Cuba in the 1970s*, p. 5.

10. Samuel Farber, *Revolution and Reaction in Cuba, 1933–1960* (Middletown, Conn.: Wesleyan University Press, 1976), p. 219.

11. Richard R. Fagen, *The Transformation of Political Culture in Cuba* (Stanford, Calif.: Stanford University Press, 1969), p. 80.

12. Luis Aguilar León, *Cuba, conciencia y revolución* (Miami: Ediciones Universal, 1972), p. 128.

13. Castro himself spoke at Matos's trial, after accusing his former comrade of treachery. Released in October 1979, after completing his full sentence under abominable conditions, Matos now lives in the United States and is engaged in anti-Castro efforts.

14. For an excellent analysis of the PSP's strategy in the early phases of the Revolution, see Samuel Farber, "The Cuban Communists in the Early Stages of the Cuban Revolution," *Latin American Research Review* 18, 1 (1983):59–83.

15. Hugh Thomas, *Cuba, The Pursuit of Freedom* (New York: Harper and Row, 1971), p. 1281. Thomas speaks of an effort by noncommunist M-26-7 members to "draw up an ultimatum to Castro demanding that he publicly reaffirm his hostility to Communism."

16. The USSR and Cuba signed an economic protocol. Besides purchases of sugar, the Soviets were to lend Cuba $200 million for twelve years at 2.5 percent interest.

17. Controversy still rages regarding Castro's ideological beliefs. Cuban scholars tend to view his "conversion" and subsequent commitment to Marxism-Leninism with some skepticism. Others contend that Castro had to "hide" his true convictions during the insurrection lest he alienate liberals and moderates who opposed Batista. Castro himself has confused matters even more by defining himself as a "humanist," as a "Marxist idealist," and as a "utopian." Speaking in Berlin in 1977, he said:

I myself, was a utopian before becoming a Marxist . . . When I read the *Communist Manifesto* as a student, I began to cease being a utopian socialist to become a Marxist socialist. I still don't know to what extent I'm still a utopian and to what extent I've become a Marxist-Leninist—perhaps I may even be a bit of a dreamer.

Michael Taber, ed., *Fidel Castro Speeches* (New York: Pathfinder Press, 1981), p. 27.

18. Julio Matas, "Theater and Cinematography," in *Revolutionary Change in Cuba*, ed. Carmelo Mesa-Lago (Pittsburgh: University of Pittsburgh Press, 1971), p. 439. For commentary on literature in the early years, see Seymour Menton, "La novela de la revolución en Cuba," *Cuadernos Americanos* 23 (January-February 1964):23–41.

19. See Carlos Franqui's delightful *Retrato de Familia con Fidel* (Barcelona: Editorial Seix Barral, S.A., 1981), esp. pp. 267–273.

20. For discussion, see Gilbert W. Merkx and Nelson P. Valdés, "Revolution, Consciousness and Class: Cuba and Argentina," in *Cuba in Revolution*, ed. Bonachea and Valdés, pp. 82–109.

21. Edward Gonzalez, *Cuba Under Castro: The Limits of Charisma* (Boston: Houghton Mifflin, 1974), p. 65.

22. Cole Blasier, *The Hovering Giant* (Pittsburgh: University of Pittsburgh Press, 1976), pp. 76–78.

23. Ibid., p. 189.

24. Jorge Domínguez, *Cuba, Order and Revolution* (Cambridge, Mass.: Belknap Press, 1978), p. 146.

25. Blasier, *Hovering Giant*, p. 191.

26. Paul E. Sigmund, *Multinationals in Latin America: The Politics of Nationalism* (Madison: University of Wisconsin Press, 1980), p. 108.

27. O'Connor, *Origins of Socialism*, p. 165.

28. Sigmund, *Multinationals in Latin America*, p. 106.

29. Peter Wyden, *Bay of Pigs, The Untold Story* (New York: Simon and Schuster, 1979), pp. 24–25.

30. Edward J. Williams, *The Political Themes of Inter-American Relations* (Belmont, Mass.: Duxbury Press, 1971), pp. 21–22.

31. In addition to Wyden's *Bay of Pigs*, see Tad Szulc and Karl E. Meyer, *The Cuban Invasion* (New York: Ballantine, 1962); Haynes Johnson, *The Bay of Pigs* (New York: Norton, 1964); or the relevant sections in Arthur M. Schlesinger, Jr., *A Thousand Days* (Boston: Houghton Mifflin, 1965) and Theodore Sorensen, *Kennedy* (New York: Harper and Row, 1965).

32. Federico G. Gil, *Latin American–United States Relations* (New York: Harcourt Brace Jovanovich, 1971), p. 233.

33. Karol, *Guerrillas in Power*, p. 209.

5

The Politics of Survival

The government's attention, from the early to middle 1960s, was largely taken up with the consolidation of the regime, the centralization of political power, the restructuring of the various components of the revolutionary coalition (M-26-7, DR, PSP), and the initiation of development strategies emphasizing industry over sugar production and agriculture. During that period, internal opposition slackened, mobilization reached impressive levels, various revolutionary organizations merged in order to enhance internal unity, ideological commitments were clarified, and the Cuban Communist Party (PCC) was unveiled in 1965.

Clashes between communists and other revolutionaries had reduced the communists' political influence. By the same token, Castro's proclamation in December 1961 that "I am a Marxist-Leninist, and I will be one until the last day of my life" induced the erroneous belief that orthodox communist ideology would substantially influence the regime's foreign and domestic policies. Regional isolation, imposition of the U.S. embargo in 1962, and suspension from the OAS in 1964 created real and perceived enemies. The sense that Cuba was externally besieged was particularly acute following Soviet capitulation during the 1962 missile crisis, but Castro's trips to the Soviet Union in 1963 and 1964 reduced some of the political friction between the two nations and elicited further Soviet economic and technical assistance.

In this chapter, I will analyze how the consolidation of a Castroite regime perpetuated rather than solved pressing developmental problems and how organizational decisions shaped the emergence of a mobilizational regime that lacked institutional solidarity and was not dominated by the Communist party. An assessment of regime performance in key areas will also be provided in order to establish the outcome of several policy initiatives.

LEADERSHIP AND CONSOLIDATION

Castro's regime relied less on organization than on his ability to elicit mass support and maintain order through direct popular appeals. It was sustained by its own revolutionary momentum, massive mobilization campaigns such as the 1961 "Campaign Against Illiteracy,"[1] and a widespread feeling that the Revolution faced formidable developmental and external challenges. The fact that distributive policies expanded the regime's support and placed its social adversaries on the defensive in turn enabled the leadership to exercise authority without having to worry about legitimacy. The political currents generated during the period of initial transformations carried over into the phase of consolidation, even though economic difficulties emerged and Cuba felt isolated and threatened. Political resilience in the face of poor economic performance and foreign policy challenges became a dominant trend—almost a hallmark—of the total revolutionary process, reducing the possibility that economic dislocations or external aggression would have unmanageable political repercussions.

Although Castro's personal authority was unchallengeable, persisting struggles over ideological, organizational, and administrative matters retarded the emergence of a solid Castroite regime in which loyalty to the leader determined one's position, influence, and political longevity. Paradoxically, bureaucratic growth went on without parallel efforts at institution building. Organizations such as the Central Planning Board (JUCEPLAN), INRA, numerous other specialized agencies such as the National Institute of Savings and Housing (INAV), the National Institute of Tourism (INIT), and several new ministries increased the state's management capabilities, but were neither connected to nor monitored by formal political structures. Power, in short, flowed from Castro and his close associates. Guevara, for example, became something of an economic czar, heading the national bank and the Ministry of Industries. Thus, the Revolution advanced in an institutional vacuum, with little attention paid to the costs of bureaucratic disorganization.

An extremely diffuse political environment prevailed, with centralizing mechanisms in place but without permanent institutional control. Orders, guidelines, and directives went from top to bottom, leaving the principal mass organizations (CDR, FMC, UJC, ANAP, CTC)[2] entirely out of the decision-making process. Quite clearly the absence of mediating institutions or rules of political behavior reinforced Castro's special relationship with the masses—sharpening his radical impulses, honing his freewheeling style, and absolving him of any responsibility if things went sour. As Edward Gonzalez has stated, the revolutionary dictatorship "based itself on the rapid mobilization of the masses and proceeded to break down the hitherto pluralistic, institutionalized fabric of Cuban society." That very process broke formal ties between leaders and followers, reduced accountability to a minimum, subjected mass behavior to charismatic guidance, and freed Castro from "those organized and institutionalized constraints on his power that he had proposed to observe" once upon a time.[3] Unquestionably, unrestrained personal power could lead to total dictatorship, and the very process of sociocultural transformation strengthened rather than retarded consolidation of such a dictatorship.

In order to enforce a proper code of revolutionary conduct, popular tribunals were established during the 1960s. Staffed by laymen and with

A woman walks down a Havana street past signs proclaiming the twenty-fifth anniversary of the Revolution.

undefined jurisdiction, the tribunals dealt with a variety of mostly non-criminal offenses. Set up in neighborhoods, factories, and in the rural areas, these courts imposed penalties, including incarceration. But the poor skills of the legal and administrative personnel meant that the fairness of "revolutionary justice" was often violated. In time (1973) these tribunals were incorporated into a restructured legal system.

In fact, the regime created new political opportunities as the sources of private power disappeared and as the superior position of the dominant sectors was undercut through statization and social confrontation. That vacuum, which expanded as the process of transformation deepened, was filled with new clienteles. For instance, Maurice Zeitlin has shown that in large numbers, peasants, agricultural laborers, and in particular, the "politicized" sectors of the working class, supported the Revolution.[4] Militant *cederistas* (CDR members), radicalized elements in the urban popular sectors, and many from the lower middle classes were part of the Revolution's social coalition. Altogether such elements formed a large and stable core. A sense of participating in an epic process of change led by an invincible *caudillo* strengthened those sectors' emotional attachments to the revolutionary process. Castro himself remained immensely popular.

In such an environment, in which the distribution of power inside the regime was not as crucial as the purposes to which power was demonstrably put, revolution is conducted in the name of collective leadership principles, but the charismatic element, far from being enveloped by the bureaucratic organization, becomes transformed into a supergovernment. Traditional Latin American personalism resolves itself in private government. From this stems the social origins of terrorism of the socialist type.[5]

CASTROITES AND COMMUNISTS (II)

If the Revolution's social base was to be expanded, some central means had to be found through which popular support could be organized. The mass organizations served mobilizational interests, but the absence of a ruling party suggested that the leadership preferred to exercise direct authority in order to preserve its own autonomy.

What role the PSP would play in the regime once the commitment to socialism was made involved questions of internal unity, the Party's relationship with the Soviet Union, and the extent to which Party militants and leaders would assume key bureaucratic, administrative, and political roles. According to Leninist revolutionary theory, the Communist party must lead the revolutionary process as the sole representative of the peasantry, working class, and progressive intelligentsia, "pulling the masses" along and presumably advancing interests and demands on the latter's behalf. As the revolutionary process deepens, the Party itself consolidates effective control mechanisms, relying on a strategy combining discipline in the ranks with ideological purity in order to firm up its dominant role. Revolutionary doctrine also allows tactical alliances between the Party and "progressive sectors of the bourgeoisie," in the form of the conventional popular front or in other arrangements. In this case, however, the Party's inability to lead owed more to the resistance of the Castroites than to its own weak standing with previous popular movements, and communist efforts to jump on the revolutionary bandwagon were often perceived as opportunistic.

In essence, consolidating the regime meant that the Revolution would either follow a Castroite path, or be directed and controlled by other forces, namely the PSP. Though the PSP was quietly dissolved in 1961 as a party, militants and leaders took advantage of unsettled political conditions to assume positions of importance in the Schools of Revolutionary Instruction and elsewhere in order to guardedly expand their influence. These special schools for the leadership cadres were of critical importance, their principal task being "the ideological formation of revolutionaries, and then, by means of the revolutionaries, the ideological formation of the rest of the people."[6] PSP participation in the training of cadres allowed the Party to impose ideological rigor on individuals presumably groomed for future leadership positions. On the other hand, a self-proclaimed socialist revolution without the established Communist party at the front was ideologically irreconcilable and politically unprecedented. Such an incongruence was particularly sharp in Cuba, where a "Leninist party, properly accredited to the Comintern, had been established on the island for the past 35 years and according to accepted ideas, was the only one entitled to lead the working class and the people forward to socialism."[7]

The need to integrate the surviving elements of M-26-7, the DR, the PSP itself, and "the masses" into a single, more manageable organization capable of responding more effectively to the leadership's demands led to the creation of the Integrated Revolutionary Organizations (ORI) in early 1962.[8] Aníbal Escalante, a former PSP secretary, participated in its creation, along with Castroites and others. Escalante was bent on carving out a considerable role for the Party in leadership and administration; but his efforts were taken by Castro as an attempt to impose communist control over the Revolution at the expense of loyal and tested revolutionaries. Denouncing the ORI as a "sectarian organization" and Escalante as "abusing the faith placed in him" by furthering his own ambitions, Castro moved to oust Escalante from the organization and ensure that it would not turn into a parallel, potentially hostile political bureaucracy. According to Castro, Escalante—in this instance—and historically "the very international communist movement" had made great mistakes; Escalante was directly responsible for "having promoted that sectarian spirit for personal reasons," seeking to create not a vanguard or workers' party but a "straightjacket." Finally, testifying to the personal valor and revolutionary commitment of those unable "to recite from memory a Marxist catechism," Castro stated that the ORI was a "mere shell of an organization," excluding the masses and thus "lacking in Marxist, proletarian sense."[9]

Escalante's ouster was followed by a purge of other communist militants from bureaucratic and political positions, a move that strengthened the hand of Castroite loyalists and indicated that Castro would interpret Marxist-Leninist ideology in line with his own preferences and inclinations and not necessarily those of "recognized authorities." By blaming Escalante and his sectarian followers, Castro stopped short of discrediting the Party as a whole. He in effect gave the Party a second chance while demonstrating a willingness and ability to take on real and potential challenges directly and in devastating fashion. The Party preferred to survive despite the political defeat and humiliation suffered by one of its top figures; the remnants of the "old communist leadership immediately lined up behind him [Castro], accepting his supremacy both ideologically and politically, and in terms that spelled out unconditional surrender."[10]

Castro, successful in this first major clash with the communists, moved to place loyal subordinates in key decision-making positions, and the creation of a formal party was delayed further. In 1963, the United Party of the Socialist Revolution (PURS) appeared; its national directorate included members of various revolutionary organizations, but the power of communist leaders to effect major organizational changes had clearly been curbed. Not yet enshrined as a formal Communist party but recognized by the Soviet Union as a "fraternal party," the PURS directorate acquired new powers over the mass organizations and the bureaucracy. Its members would subsequently be involved in coordinating and supervisory functions, mobilization, political education, and propaganda activities.[11]

The conflict between Castroites and communists flared up again in 1964. In this case, the settling of an old score between communists and former members of the urban underground led to the trial, conviction, and execution of Marcos Rodríguez.[12] Rodríguez had been denounced by members of the former DR for collaborating with Batista's police at the time of the assault on the Presidential Palace in 1957. Rodríguez confessed to having provided the police with information regarding the hiding place of Juan Pedro Carbó, Fructuoso Rodríguez, Joe Westbrook, and José Machado, DR members who had been captured and shot in Havana. Rodríguez at the time had been a member of the *Juventud Socialista* (Socialist Youth) and had subsequently gained the protection of PSP members Joaquín Ordoquí and his wife, Edith García. Major Faure Chomón, the minister of communications and a former DR leader, testified as the principal witness against Rodríguez, condemning the accused for treachery. The court, in turn, sentenced Rodríguez to death. Castro's personal intervention at that point held up the execution. A second trial brought out contacts between Rodríguez and other PSP leaders who had in fact protected Rodríguez from revolutionary justice by facilitating his departure from Cuba to Eastern Europe. Following Rodríguez's own testimony, as well as that of Chomón (again), former high PSP members, officers of state security, and Castro himself, the court upheld the prior sentence and Rodríguez was shot.

Shrewdly approached, full of tension, revealing secret intrigues, and in grand confessional style, Castro's testimony was conciliatory of the Party, though individuals were singled out for past errors and questionable judgments. Castro found disclosures indicating less than total harmony among the various factions in the regime distasteful, and so he sought to minimize harmful divisions by pointing to personal deviations rather than organizational misconduct. According to Suárez, "Castro's posture had been so unequivocally 'unitary' that the whole affair offered an excellent opportunity to end once and for all the 'factional spirit'" feeding rancor among revolutionaries and threatening his leadership.[13] Castro's participation in the trials, as well as his insistence that divisions among revolutionaries were damaging, indicated that he, and he alone, would act as final arbiter of intraregime disputes. Only in a personalist dictatorship can the will of many be surbordinated to the word of one individual. In this case that individual was a leader restrained by neither law nor custom, and who felt compelled to interfere in political, legal, cultural, and economic matters.

Absolution of the Party in 1964, organizational imperatives, probable inducements from the Soviets, and the certainty that the new Cuban Communist party (PCC) would be controlled by Castro himself led to its unveiling in 1965. Castroites filled the Central Committee, Secretariat, and Political Bureau, with the first showing a high proportion of military officers. A breakdown of Central Committee members showed that 58 percent came from military ranks, 17 percent served in various bureaucracies, 10 percent were political figures or leaders, and the rest were drawn from

Table 5.1.   Membership in Top Organs of the Cuban
             Communist Party, 1965

Political Bureau	Secretariat
Fidel Castro	Fidel Castro
Raúl Castro	Raúl Castro
Osvaldo Dorticós	Osvaldo Dorticós
Armando Hart	Blas Roca[a]
Juan Almeida	Faure Chomón[b]
Ramiro Valdés	Carlos R. Rodríguez[a]
Guillermo García	
Sergio del Valle	

[a]former PSP member
[b]former DR member

Source: Cuba Socialista, November 1965, p. 9.

educational, cultural, organizational, and other backgrounds.[14] Communists
held 23 positions in the 100-member Central Committee, 2 in the 6-
member Secretariat and none in the 8-member Political Bureau. Only 5
out of the 100 Central Committee members were women. They were
Haydeé Santamaría (the wife of PCC Secretary for Organization Armando
Hart), Vilma Espín (Raúl Castro's wife and the president of the Federation
of Cuban Women [FMC]), Celia Sánchez (Fidel Castro's personal secretary
and long-time confidante), and two former PSP members. As shown in
Table 5.1, Castro himself became first secretary of the Cuban Communist
party and the top member of the Political Bureau in addition to being
prime minister and commander in chief of the armed forces. Castro held
the top position in the party, the government, and the military, and his
brother Raúl ranked second in all three. The interlocking membership by
the Castro brothers in top party, state, administration, and military roles
emerged as a permanent characteristic of Cuba's structure of political power,
with additional key positions occupied by loyal revolutionaries from the
ranks of M-26-7. That scheme has carried over into the 1980s.
     Unveiling the restructured party did not mean that it would function
as a vigorous Marxist-Leninist organization in terms of national leadership.
Total membership during the mid-1960s was only several thousand, and
even though cadres played a role in instructional and ideological tasks,
their competence as well as the Party's doctrinal standing and institutional
role were questionable. In no way was the PCC a leading ruling institution,
since its doctrine did not legitimate the Revolution's program and its leaders
failed to influence Castro's behavior. Altogether,

     the ideological state of the party corresponds to its desolate organizational
     condition. It is the question of the two sides of one and the same coin. The

PCC has no program. Anyone inquiring of its ideology is invariably referred to Fidel's speeches whose contradictions are notorious; anyone who actually refers to them does well to take recourse to the most recent of them; for, to repeat what Fidel said a few years ago can have the most unpleasant consequences.[15]

ORDER AND CHANGE: AN ASIDE

In the final analysis, the consolidation of the regime involved more than centralizing political power in the hands of a revolutionary elite, effectively suppressing internal challenge, or sanctioning opposition and dissent. Above all else, consolidation meant demonstrating staying power—political endurance—and coping with adverse economic conditions without surrendering political initiative or losing essential popular support.[16] If difficulties, scarcities, hardships, and contradictions were not resolved, these did not, in large measure, lead to major legitimacy problems or, more critically, to widespread and pernicious questioning of the Revolution itself. For instance, it was precisely in the 1964–1965 period that the regime suppressed armed "counterrevolutionary" activities in the Escambray mountains and elsewhere. Though the regime deployed superior military force against what were by then semi-isolated groups, the counterrevolutionaries' failure to generate widespread resistance was partly attributable to the regime's popularity.

Governing through exhortation limited the leadership's ability to transform popular aspirations into minimal satisfaction of social and economic demands. At the same time, in a situation in which economic deterioration means that promises will not be fulfilled, mobilization often compensates for effective demand making and even participation. Appealing to nationalism, calling for sacrifices in order to defeat internal or external enemies, invoking memories of previous struggles in heroic and mythical terms, and tapping the moral, physical, and intellectual reserves of the nation allowed the regime to survive the crunch between social expectations and economic realities. Politics became more than a hierarchical relationship between leaders and led, more than a means through which power is used in pursuit of either concrete or ill-defined goals. Rather, politics became a total, all-consuming activity demanding personal abnegation, group subordination to wider social ends, and national rather than parochial vision.

As I have argued up to this point, the politics of the revolutionary process mattered because of what the process of transformation promised. Abolishing the old class structure allowed new clienteles to enter into the political arena; that these elements failed to exercise control was not as important as the fact that, finally, they were invested with political significance. For the first time, many felt that they were a part of something big, without precedent, with great potential. One did not have to rationally comprehend what was happening in order to *feel* the pulse of the times. It was exciting, if not thrilling. A revolution. A nation beginning to feel what it meant to be in control of its destiny. The Yankees had been humiliated and were gone. Fidel was in charge, and he was very good. If this was socialism, so be it. Who could possibly have doubts about the future?

Confronting, not obviating, challenges is an indispensable part of the development process. Visions of what development, or socialism, would bring acted as powerful political magnets. Recognizing that motivation was a key not only to individual behavior but also to the attainment of gains, the Cuban leadership coped with potential disaffection through a combination of exhortation and social intimidation. Accordingly, "Cubans are constantly reminded that the titanic struggle between good and evil now being played out on the world stage can be found in microcosm in the factories, fields and offices where they work."[17] When framed in such epic terms, individual conduct is subject to peer review and constant evaluation and one's life becomes but part of a nebulously comprehended design. In sum, a psychocultural dilemma involving the transformation of individual attitudes into something manipulable and malleable occurs when those seeking order through change clash with those seeking to preserve order at the expense of change. In Cuba's case, the surrender of individual prerogatives on behalf of a higher purpose effected necessary transformations but did not lead to a benign order or to a benevolent state. This, however, was not readily apparent at the time.

RULING, CASTRO-STYLE

Loyalty, revolutionary commitment, proper conduct, and most of all, unabashed zealousness were valued more than one's prerevolutionary pedigree. If such values prevailed, establishing Castroite control over critical areas reduced the probability that factionalism would threaten the regime's stability. Allowing for the "conversion" of unreconstructed Stalinists into docile Castroites also minimized friction in the ranks without total self-denigration and loss of previous allegiances. What mattered was not to what one ultimately belonged, but how personal wishes conformed with the leader's designs. Castro acknowledged his preeminent position but maintained that no cult of personality existed in Cuba and that his roles did not necessarily confer power. For instance, when asked in 1965 why he held all of the important posts, he gave a formalistic reply, namely:

> The office of Commander in Chief is held by all constitutional heads of state, and most of the administrative tasks related to the armed forces here are carried out by the Minister of the Armed Forces. . . . And my office as Prime Minister is not strictly administrative, but a political office. The general administrative responsibility belongs to the President of the Republic.[18]

Castro's view of the proper role of the Communist party also contradicts empirical reality, in light of the fact that, as has been discussed, the PCC did not exist until October 1965 and that in terms of its composition it was far from being a representative or aggregator of workers' and peasant interests. Interviewed by a U.S. journalist in 1965, Castro asserted that the Party's organization was moving along well and that plans had been made to hold its first congress in 1967. "Later on," he said, "we will be in a position to promulgate the constitution of the Socialist State." The PCC did not, however, hold its first congress until 1975, and the Constitution of the Socialist State went into effect in 1976. The quintessentially Castroite bias against "ceremonies and institutions of a formal type," along with the expanded Soviet influence in Cuba's internal affairs that a legitimately recognized ruling Communist party would bring, probably explains the ten-year gap between thought and action. Castro, grandly overstating the Party's role and accomplishments, and suggesting that in the near future it would surely become the leading political organization in Cuba, in 1965 offered the following assessment of the Party and its functions:

> First it is the revolutionary vanguard, the political organization of the workers who, manifesting the power of the state, mobilize the masses to the accomplishments of the tasks and functions of the Revolution. It educates them, it organizes them, it directs and controls the administration, it draws up the plans of work and controls the carrying out of those plans. It is in short, the political power. There is no duality, neither of powers nor of factions.[19]

A number of themes emerge from the above discussion on the relationship among regime consolidation, the exercise of autocratic leadership, and organizational efforts. First of all, consolidation depended more on Castro's ability to maximize popular support through direct appeals, as well as on growing mobilizational capabilities, than on coercive mechanisms or other antipopular policies.[20] Second, as Castro's power expanded—he was also president of INRA, for example—mobilization served immediate political aims rather than pressing developmental needs. In other words, the stress on voluntarism and collective effort often inhibited economic gains but produced demonstrable political dividends. This feature, incidentally, would persist. Third, achieving internal order without subordinating the course of the Revolution either to the demands of the Soviet Union or to orthodox interpretations of what path to socialism Cuba would take preserved internal autonomy and left developmental choices wide open. Lastly, the survival of the Revolution up to that point showed that typical Latin American *personalismo* (personalism), rather than institution building, served the regime's political needs. Not surprisingly, unrestrained personal leadership was both a cause and a consequence of the failure to create viable institutions with legitimate and specified governing functions, as a multiplicity of ad hoc procedures and provisional guidelines affected policymaking.

Cuba's revolutionary dictatorship defied conventional prescriptions. It was concerned more with control than bargaining, it was characterized by a diffuse ideological orientation, it was resistant to efforts to organize the political process, and it relied on a "governing formula in which policies were set from above by Fidel and his most trusted subordinates and then communicated to the masses below."[21]

ECONOMIC POLICIES AND SOCIAL CHANGE

Following the transition to socialism and the beginnings of a planned economy in the 1960–1961 period, Cuban economic policymakers hoped to embark on a policy of growth through industrialization. The plan was to expand nonsugar exports, achieve self-sufficiency in food production, eliminate economic bottlenecks and scarcities resulting from the shift of nonmarket forces of supply and demand, and reduce Cuba's historic dependence on sugar, while maintaining sufficient sugar production to sustain consumption levels and not increase unemployment in the interim. From this standpoint, agricultural diversification and industrial development would improve Cuba's foreign trade earnings, as well as its ability to meet its own needs, especially in foodstuffs and light consumer durables. New markets would be found for Cuba's goods, and investment in nontraditional areas would break the pattern of monocultural agriculture that, presumably, kept the country underdeveloped. Without deviating substantially from developmental thinking along the lines advocated by the Economic Commission for Latin America (ECLA), Cuban planners envisioned industrial development based on the installation of a "wide range of new import substituting industries, including metallurgy, chemical products, heavy engineering and machinery, transportation equipment and even automotive assemblage."[22]

Cuban officials, out of a romantic notion of socialist solidarity, expected substantial Soviet technical and financial assistance in pushing forward these ambitious development projects and were therefore prone to grossly overestimate goals and output when discussing immediate and long-term economic goals. Planners, unaware of market limitations, the difficulties inherent in moving from a private to a planned economy, obstacles stemming from new and distant sources of supply, and the impact that the loss of skilled manpower would have, anticipated dramatic improvements in performance and demand satisfaction. For example, Regino Boti, the minister of economy and head of the Central Planning Board (JUCEPLAN), said in 1961 that "the total material production of Cuba would grow in 1962–65" somewhere between 10 and 15 percent annually and that consumption would rise dramatically. Similarly unrealistic assessments were made regarding other sectors.[23]

Not surprisingly, difficulties in administration, planning, and production soon affected economic performance. Rationing was introduced in 1962, long lines appeared at stores and commercial establishments, shortages and scarcities of basic goods soon led to widespread black market activities, and persistent delays and bottlenecks plagued the internal distribution and delivery systems. Labor mobilization, originally conceived to be a major productive asset, turned out to be detrimental, since volunteers were often unskilled, poorly motivated, and unprepared for their assigned tasks.

Such problems were attributable to the rapidity of the shift from a dependent capitalist economy to one in which planning and state control over the means of production prevailed. The creation of "command" bureaucracies (those with almost absolute authority to make decisions) failed to enhance administrative efficiency and retarded the drafting of rational macroeconomic plans. The political leadership itself was largely ignorant of economic matters, and its insistence on politicizing decision making alienated the few competent technocrats who were left. In short, politics reigned supreme, and development goals were set with political criteria in mind.

In many cases, the opposite of the official predictions came true. Sugar production dropped to 4.81 thousand metric tons (TMT) in 1962 and 3.82 TMT in 1963 (5.29 and 4.2 thousand tons) from a high of 6.76 TMT (7.44 thousand tons) in 1961; it would not reach 1961 levels again until 1970.[24] Total agricultural output fell 16 percent between 1960 and 1962, dropping another 13 percent in 1963. Overall, following years of moderate growth in 1959–1961, "the 1962–63 attempt to apply the Soviet pre-economic reform model resulted in a loss of at least 7 percent in total growth, or 12 percent per capita."[25]

Losses in sugar or agricultural production were not made up for by rising industrial output. As a matter of fact, industrial production fell short of expectations, showing a decreasing rate of growth in 1962 and 1963 compared to 1960 and not improving substantially in the years immediately following.[26] Inevitably, poor economic performance affected foreign commerce, Cuba's balance of trade, and export earnings. Between 1961 and 1967, Cuba's negative trade balance with the socialist countries reached $1.4 billion, some $1.1 billion with the Soviet Union itself. Imports were higher than exports every year between 1959 and 1967, with food, manufactures, and machinery making up a substantial part of Cuba's imports. Ironically, exports of sugar and sugar by-products fluctuated between 80 and 85 percent of total exports in the 1960–1967 period, maintaining the high sugar export dependence the development policies had presumably set out to alter.[27] Partly subsidized by credits and aid from various socialist countries, Cuba's poor performance nonetheless increased its external debt and constrained its overall development; the extent to which increasing indebtedness affected nondevelopmental matters such as foreign policy will be dealt with in Chapter 7. In summation, Cuba's realignment of trade away from traditional U.S. and capitalist markets improved neither its earnings nor its foreign trade structure and added tremendously to its external debt due to the shortfall between earnings and aid. Cuba's external payments position between 1960 and 1967 was "characterized by a widening trade gap, the consequence of stagnation, and even decline, in export values and a persistent rise in commodity exports."[28]

Several factors account for the failure of Cuba's economy to perform as predicted. First, the idealism, zealousness, and undue optimism generated by political conquests seeped into economic decision making, led to an overestimation of the practical contribution that the socialist bloc would make, and grossly underestimated the impact of the U.S. embargo. Second, the migration of hundreds of thousands of upper-class, middle-class, and professional Cubans, including technicians, sugar *peritos* (experts), engineers, and other skilled personnel, crippled the economic system precisely at the time when technical and managerial expertise were needed. There is little doubt that the radical political measures and climate of ideological hostility directed against the middle class raised the economic costs of moving from capitalism to socialism, though from a doctrinaire standpoint, that was the price the Revolution chose to pay in order to defeat its class enemies. Third, reliance on extensive labor mobilization and volunteer workers for often-complicated production or administrative tasks reduced the quality of goods produced while affecting the repair and maintenance of plants and equipment, raising the costs of training and on-site education, and—ultimately—necessitating coercion in order to impose labor discipline.

Fourth, as unused capacity was utilized and pressure on resources mounted, an essentially U.S.-made and -supplied infrastructure and production complex suffered from stresses and dislocations that could not be quickly remedied. This was particularly true in transportation and the sugar industry, in which the unavailability of spare parts and machinery led to breakdowns, lost time, and inefficiency. In other words, once the conventional sources of supply were cut off, difficulties multiplied, scarcities appeared, plant and equipment upkeep suffered, and the new types of raw materials imported did not always prove to be the best available. Costs of freight and transportation rose, since goods had to be brought from distant and unfamiliar markets; these new markets were ill prepared to cope with the developmental needs of a "sugar island" whose political economy had been uniquely shaped by monocultural capitalism. Fifth, what Archibald Ritter calls "transitional organizational difficulties," especially in agriculture, compounded purely economic dislocations. For example, the Second Agrarian Reform of October 1963 "reduced the number of private holdings and increased the proportion of state owned land to 60 percent, broadening the scope of the central administration and undoubtedly creating new transitional problems of an institutional nature."[29]

Sixth, close adherence to Soviet-style organizational and administrative procedures increased centralization and rigidity in planning efforts; additionally, as communist cadres assumed positions in the economic bureaucracies and ministries, labor relations worsened and workers' input was stifled, creating "obstacles to all original research on the role of the trade unions and on rank and file participation in the control and management of the economy."[30] According to Carmelo Mesa-Lago, the unions became "transmission belts"—captive organizations grouped under the state-sponsored Confederation of Cuban Workers (CTC), without the power to assert demands or act as bona fide representatives of working-class interests.[31] Finally, the failure of the industrialization strategy to produce

tangible benefits in the expected time frame retarded developmental priorities; capital as well as physical and human resources were used up in
trial-and-error fashion—that is, less than efficiently and consequently, quite
unproductively.

In sum, from the standpoints of economic growth, diversification,
industrialization, and reduction of external dependence, not much was
accomplished between 1961 and 1965. Social gains were relatively equalized
and qualitative improvements registered in the standard of living of the
poorer sectors, but at considerable cost and with enduring sacrifices.
Structural factors such as small market size, a poorly developed industrial
base, Cuba's position in the international division of labor, and contradictions
between "Cuba's resource endowments and objectives" led to intense
reassessment and eventually a new course for the balance of the decade.[32]

SOCIAL GAINS

Economic development, in the broadest sense, stems from a society's
rational and efficient allocation of its resource base, since in order to
maximize resources, capabilities for creating wealth have to be improved.
A second aspect of economic development involves how and what portion
of a society's wealth is to be used for different purposes, a process that
involves setting priorities and selecting among competing choices. Thus,
distributional questions, often derived from ideological preferences, assume
critical importance even in contexts in which growth is limited by a host
of different factors. In Cuba's case, developmental socialism held the promise
of achievement in several interrelated areas, namely growth, distribution,
quality of life, internal autonomy, and external dependence. Abolishing
capitalism would mean expanded social choices, new opportunities, and
a concomitant improvement in Cuba's ability to fend off harmful external
economic forces. As capitalism had brought dependence and an onerous
relationship with the United States, ending it would—for the first time in
history—bring economic sovereignty to Cuba.

Improvements in the quality of life and standard of living would
result once the structure of domination perpetuating backwardness was
successfully challenged; consistent gains generated by autonomous productive forces would be distributed according to collective rather than
individualistic goals. Committed to an order in which egalitarianism
superseded private interests, and demanding extended sacrifices in order
to foster an acceptable, collectivist notion of the public good, the revolutionary dictatorship transferred resources into social areas out of ideological as well as practical motivations. The purposes of such policies were
quite clear, namely, to strengthen the regime's popular base, foster political
consciousness, and gradually reshape the political culture.

Education

Cuba's educational system underwent profound transformations in
both purpose and function; its principal mission would now be to foster

revolutionary attitudes, rather than simply instructing or transmitting knowledge. Political socialization—or resocialization—are keys to any revolution, and a primary objective of education is to instill new values and beliefs.

Revolutionary leaders viewed education as a means through which social consciousness could be fostered and elitism abolished. They also wanted education to exalt national virtues and national deeds, strengthen the people's patriotism, and encourage their cultural and technical sophistication.[33] Education was crucial to nation building and development; its content could not therefore be left to private or parochial interests. Interpretations of the past also mattered, so the state saw to it that its view of Cuba's history and political economy prevailed.

Religious and private education was abolished, and the state assumed responsibility for education from kindergarten through the university and the professions. In turn, the massive literacy campaign of 1961 produced positive scholastic results, increasing the number of literates by 707,000 and reducing illiteracy to roughly 4 to 5 percent. Though the quality of instruction left much to be desired and pedagogy served blatant political purposes, the effort on the whole "if not an overwhelming and unquestionable triumph from the scholastic point of view, was nevertheless seminally important in the evolution of the institutional life and political culture of the revolution."[34] Inescapably, the content of education reflected the regime's political views and its Marxist-Leninist interpretation of history. As was evident, "students are required to devote school time to three types of work: educational, productive, and socially useful,"[35] combining work with political discussions that seek to instill a tripartite commitment to *estudio, trabajo y fusil* (study, work, and the rifle).

Stressing revolutionary duty, communist civic-mindedness, militancy, obedience, and discipline as well as technical competence or expertise heightens students' understanding of revolutionary goals and anchors their political loyalties. In the words of then PCC Secretary for Organization and currently Minister of Culture Armando Hart: "The objective of socialist education is the ideological, scientific and technical formation of whole generations capable of actively constructing socialism and communism."[36] Study (mental work) serves social ends, aiding in the development of consciousness (*conciencia*) as well as in the acquisition of skills. Since social transformation involves attitudinal as well as structural changes, education too must be subordinated to the attainment of nationally defined goals without frivolous excesses or "petit-bourgeois" interference. Accordingly:

The only way to overcome underdevelopment and to build the socialist society is with work and *conciencia*. It seems that the puritanic ideology of the Protestant ethic has finally arrived in Latin America. In this case, however, the fruits of labor are not a symbol of individualistic achievement and justification, but of self realization in the collectivity.[37]

Cuban schoolchildren crowd around the entrance to their school in Santiago—a building with historical significance. The Castro regime has converted military barracks into schools, and this school was once the Moncada Barracks, the site of Castro's first abortive uprising in 1953. The advances in education, particularly the proliferation of schools and the elimination of illiteracy are among the accomplishments of the regime.

In terms of resources allocated to this sector, Cuba's educational system expanded at all levels during the 1960s. According to Nelson Valdés, "from 1961 to 1969 the Cubans spent, on the average, about 275 million pesos yearly in education, or four times as much as ten years before."[38] In terms of facilities and enrollments, as shown in Table 5.2, the number of primary schools doubled between 1958 and 1968, as did the number of students. Equally impressive advances were registered in secondary education, technical and vocational training, and to a lesser degree, university enrollments.

Unquestionably, revolutionary policies created educational opportunities for sectors that might otherwise have been deprived of them. The emphasis on technical and scientific training has already paid off developmentally and in Cuba's foreign policy as well, since Cuban missions to Third World countries are made up of doctors, nurses, construction personnel, engineers, technicians, and teachers in addition to political and military personnel. According to Castro, "no country has as many doctors as Cuba working in the Third World, and in such a variety of countries. Cuba alone has more doctors than the World Health Organization working

Table 5.2. Number of Schools, Teachers, and Students in
            Public Education in Cuba: 1958, 1962, 1968

	Primary Schools			Secondary Schools		
Year	Schools	Teachers	Students	Schools	Teachers	Students
1958	7,567	17,355	717,417	184	2,580	63,526
1962	13,780	36,613	1,207,286	335	7,380	123,118
1968	14,807	48,994	1,460,754	434	10,703	186,358

Source: Adapted from Ronald G. Paulston, "Education," in Revolutionary Change in Cuba, ed. Carmelo Mesa-Lago (Pittsburgh: University of Pittsburgh Press, 1971), Table 1.

in the Third World"; over one thousand out of some two thousand health-related personnel working outside of Cuba are doctors.[39]

One should not view Cuba's educational achievements uncritically, however. Quantity often comes at the expense of quality, training does not encourage critical thinking, and state control reinforces discipline, obedience, and subordination rather than independent inquiry. Moreover, especially at higher levels, "political correctness" rather than aptitude determines career pursuits, advancement, and professional placement. Observers have also noted that poorly trained teachers, the uneven quality of curriculum, ideological heavy-handedness, and widespread resistance to cultural change—often manifested through high dropout rates—adversely affect educational progress.[40]

In summary, educational reform was one of the first priorities of the Revolution. The training of individuals for developmental, political, and even military tasks has been an integral part of building socialism and of instilling a sense of duty, mission, and loyalty among the young while redefining Cuba's national identity as an internationalist, Marxist-Leninist society. In the 1980s, educational policies continue to stress technical training and ideological firmness.

Health and Social Services

Health and social services have received considerable attention in Cuba during the past two decades. Resources have been allocated for the construction of hospitals, clinics, and health centers and for the training of medical personnel. In particular, health education programs in the rural areas have improved the quality of care available irrespective of status or ability to pay.

On the other hand, the quality of medical services in prerevolutionary Cuba was not as abysmally poor as is the case in the typical underdeveloped country. According to one source, the modest revolutionary achievements in the field owe much to the facts that in 1958 Cuba already had a good program, that migration has affected care and health delivery systems, and that the Revolution's own rural development program leaves much to be desired.[41] Migration clearly affected both quality and training, since many of those who left had been teachers at the universities and medical schools. Training replacements in Eastern Europe, the Soviet Union, and Cuba itself took time and often involved unfamiliar procedures and techniques, as past training had been heavily influenced by U.S. standards and practices. The number of hospitals and *policlínicos* (health centers) increased in comparison with prerevolutionary levels, as did the number of beds available, but the ratio of beds per one thousand population fluctuated close to prerevolutionary levels for most of the 1960s. That, however, may be due to the emphasis on preventive medicine and outpatient services rather than hospitalization as a means of taking care of health problems. Infant mortality rates went up from 33.7 per 1,000 live births in 1958 to 44.7 in 1967, though that was probably due to economic deterioration in general rather than poor medical services.[42] By the early 1980s, this indicator had shown dramatic improvement, and Cuba compared favorably with more advanced countries in Latin America and elsewhere. With an infant mortality rate of 17.4 per 1,000, a life expectancy of seventy-three years, and a low child death rate, Cuba's health indicators have improved considerably since 1959. Not surprisingly, according to Overseas Development Council figures, Cuba had the third highest index of Physical Quality of Life (PQLI) in 1978, surpassed only by Argentina and Uruguay in all of Latin America.[43]

The success rate in combating infectious and other diseases during the 1960s appears to have been mixed. The quality of services in nonurban areas has improved, but other areas such as nutrition and housing have not fared as well and Cuba has often sacrificed "quality of medical and paramedical personnel for the sake of quantity."[44] Nonetheless, medical education continues to have broad developmental and foreign policy significance. Through 1981, some 16,017 doctors had graduated, including 579 in 1978, 683 in 1979, and close to 1,000 by 1982, allowing Cuba to send hundreds of these abroad in "internationalist" missions.[45]

SUMMARY

Internal and external challenges posed continuing dilemmas for the revolutionary regime through the mid-1960s. Castroite control of a restructured Communist party demonstrated that the Cuban path to socialism depended more on the interaction between a larger-than-life, charismatic figure and the masses than on orthodox notions demanding that social forces be aligned under a single party organization. Authority exercised without constraints permitted Castro to interfere in various aspects of decision making simply because he, as the *máximo líder* (maximum leader), commanded absolute loyalty without having to demonstrate expertise in any given policy area. A mobilizational regime anchored by a personalist dictatorship was in fact consummated.

Regime consolidation came about through sustained mobilization, direct exhortation, top-to-bottom direction of an ongoing revolutionary process, and the leadership's ability to maintain political legitimacy in the face of deteriorating economic circumstances. Having dealt successfully with organized internal opposition by the mid-1960s, the regime maintained tight political control over individual and group activities, relying on the mass organizations and its own internal security apparatus to detect early signs of popular dissatisfaction. Daily life became intensely political.

Rewards and sanctions were utilized to elicit compliance with revolutionary goals, but care was exercised not to alienate key sectors in the working class, peasantry, and urban proletariat. This was not always possible, and a "brain drain" resulted that crippled the economic system. Definitions of acceptable political behavior stressed obedience and commitment to collective efforts rather than articulation of exaggerated socioeconomic demands. Organizations such as the CDR, UJC, CTC, ANAP, and FMC, whose combined membership totaled several millions, assumed exhortatory, integrative, and communicative functions; participated in various campaigns designed to stimulate voluntarism; and set standards of proper revolutionary conduct. Broadly speaking, the shaping of a new ethos demanded militancy, uncritical acceptance of the leadership's developmental goals, and moral righteousness; intensified conflicts between enduring norms and emerging values; and presaged deeper social resistance in the future.

Finally, the creation of numerous ad hoc organizations and parainstitutions—such as the popular tribunals—without a corresponding legal or institutional foundation led to a veritable bureaucratic anarchy in which the sources of authority and responsibility were hardly identifiable. As a result, social gains were partly overshadowed by declining economic performance and the stage was set for a strategic reversal and new radical orientations.

NOTES

1. The year 1961 was designated as "The Year of Campaigning Against Illiteracy"—"*El Año de la Alfabetización.*" Hundreds of thousands of people, including teachers, young people, committed adults, and paraprofessionals, were mobilized in order to locate illiterates and, presumably, instruct them in basic reading and writing skills. For an excellent overview and analyses, see Richard R. Fagen, *The Transformation of Political Culture in Cuba* (Stanford, Calif.: Stanford University Press, 1969).

2. CDR, Committees for the Defense of the Revolution; FMC, Federation of Cuban Women; UJC, Communist Youth Union; ANAP, National Association of Small Farmers; CTC, Confederation of Cuban Workers.

3. Edward Gonzalez, *Cuba Under Castro: The Limits of Charisma* (Boston: Houghton Mifflin, 1974), p. 46.

4. Maurice Zeitlin, *Revolutionary Politics and the Cuban Working Class* (Princeton, N.J.: Princeton University Press, 1967).

5. Irving Louis Horowitz, "The Political Sociology of Cuban Communism," in *Revolutionary Change in Cuba*, ed. Carmelo Mesa-Lago (Pittsburgh: University of Pittsburgh Press, 1971), p. 128.

6. Fagen, *Transformation of Political Culture*, p. 105.

7. K. S. Karol, *Guerrillas in Power* (New York: Hill and Wang, 1970), p. 191.

8. Richard R. Fagen, "The Integrated Revolutionary Organizations," in *Political Power in Latin America: Seven Confrontations*, ed. Richard R. Fagen and Wayne A. Cornelius, Jr. (Englewood Cliffs, N.J.: Prentice-Hall, 1970), pp. 357–358.

9. Ibid., pp. 359–370; speech also appeared in *Revolución*, March 27, 1962.

10. Maurice Halperin, *The Rise and Decline of Fidel Castro* (Berkeley: University of California Press, 1972), p. 155.

11. Jorge Domínguez, *Cuba: Order and Revolution* (Cambridge, Mass.: Belknap Press, 1978), pp. 323–324.

12. The account here relies heavily on Maurice Halperin, *The Taming of Fidel Castro* (Berkeley: University of California Press, 1981), pp. 26–70. Fascinating in all of their complexity, emotion, and intrigue, Castro's interrogation of Rodríguez and each one's testimony are particularly revealing.

13. Andrés Suárez, *Cuba: Castroism and Communism, 1959–1966* (Cambridge, Mass.: MIT Press, 1967), p. 209. Pages 201–209 offer this author's account of the trial and its ramifications.

14. Domínguez, *Cuba*, p. 312.

15. Hans Magnus Enzensberger, "Portrait of a Party: Prehistory, Structure and Ideology of the PCC," in *The New Cuba: Paradoxes and Potentials*, ed. Ronald Radosh (New York: William Morrow, 1976), p. 128.

16. For a balanced and useful assessment of economic conditions and policies during the mid-1960s, see David Barkin, "Cuban Agriculture: A Strategy of Economic Development," in *Cuban Communism* 4th ed., ed. Irving Louis Horowitz (New Brunswick, N.J.: Transaction Books, 1981), pp. 47–82. Data indicate lagging sugar production in 1962–1965, as well as drops in per capita income and other indicators of overall economic performance.

17. Richard R. Fagen, "Mass Mobilization in Cuba: The Symbolism of Struggle," in *Cuba in Revolution*, ed. Rolando E. Bonachea and Nelson P. Valdés (Garden City, N.Y.: Anchor Books, 1972), p. 221.

18. Lee Lockwood, *Castro's Cuba, Cuba's Fidel* (New York: Vintage Books, 1969), p. 176. Osvaldo Dorticós was president until 1976.

19. Ibid., p. 154.

20. These are not to be underestimated. In this interview, Castro admitted that close to twenty thousand political prisoners were held by the regime. Exile estimates have consistently been much higher; several thousand were still incarcerated through the 1970s. For a brief assessment, see Carlos Alberto Montaner, *Secret Report on the Cuban Revolution*, trans. Eduardo Zayas-Bazán (New Brunswick, N.J.: Transaction Books, 1981), pp. 209–215. Periodicals like *Of Human Rights* (Georgetown University) regularly monitor conditions in Cuban jails, prisoner releases, violations of human rights, reports of torture, and other seldom-publicized activities. The *Miami Herald* also provides excellent coverage of Cuban affairs.

21. Gonzalez, *Cuba Under Castro*, p. 94.

22. Archibald R. M. Ritter, *The Economic Development of Revolutionary Cuba* (New York: Praeger Publishers, 1974), p. 135.

23. An excellent overview and analysis of conflicting goals, planning and production difficulties, dwindling resources, and various aspects of economic policy-

82 THE POLITICS OF SURVIVAL

THE POLITICS OF SURVIVAL

making in the 1960–1962 period can be found in Edward Boorstein, *The Economic Transformation of Cuba* (New York: Monthly Review Press, 1968).

24. See G. B. Hagelberg, "Cuba's Sugar Policy," in *Cuban Communism*, ed. Horowitz, pp. 141–162.

25. Carmelo Mesa-Lago, *The Economy of Socialist Cuba* (Albuquerque: University of New Mexico Press, 1981), p. 176.

26. James O'Connor, *The Origins of Socialism in Cuba* (Ithaca, N.Y.: Cornell University Press, 1970), pp. 271–275.

27. Eric N. Baklanoff, "International Economic Relations," in *Revolutionary Change in Cuba*, ed. Mesa-Lago, pp. 259–269 and Tables 1 and 5.

28. Ibid., p. 272.

29. Ritter, *Economic Development of Revolutionary Cuba*, p. 148.

30. Karol, *Guerrillas in Power*, p. 235.

31. Carmelo Mesa-Lago, *Cuba in the 1970s*, rev. ed. (Albuquerque: University of New Mexico Press, 1978), p. 82.

32. Ritter, *Economic Development of Revolutionary Cuba*, p. 159.

33. See Ronald G. Paulston, "Education," in *Revolutionary Change in Cuba*, ed. Mesa-Lago, pp. 375–397.

34. Fagen, *Transformation of Political Culture in Cuba*, p. 55.

35. Nelson P. Valdés, "The Radical Transformation of Cuban Education," in *Cuba in Revolution*, ed. Bonachea and Valdés, p. 433.

36. Armando Hart, "Objectivos de la educación secundaria en Cuba," *Boletín de la Universidad de Chile* (June 1965):26. Quoted in Jaime Suchlicki, *University Students and Revolution in Cuba, 1920–1968* (Coral Gables, Fla.: University of Miami Press, 1969), p. 105.

37. José A. Moreno, "From Traditional to Modern Values," in *Revolutionary Change in Cuba*, ed. Mesa-Lago, p. 484.

38. Valdés, "Radical Transformation of Cuban Education," p. 439.

39. *Granma Resumen Semanal*, March 28, 1982.

40. Lowry Nelson, *Cuba, The Measure of Revolution* (Minneapolis: University of Minnesota Press, 1972), pp. 139–140, offers an assessment of primary and secondary education through the early 1970s.

41. Ibid.

42. Ricardo Leyva, "Health and Revolution in Cuba," in *Cuba in Revolution*, ed. Bonachea and Valdés, pp. 490–491.

43. The Physical Quality of Life Index (PQLI) is a composite measure of life expectancy, literacy, and infant mortality rates. For rankings and comparisons, see Montaner, *Secret Report*, pp. 180–181.

44. Domínguez, *Cuba*, p. 223.

45. *Granma Resumen Semanal*, March 28, 1982.

6

The Cuban Model: Idealism and Coercion

Cuba's economy and political culture underwent major reshaping during the second half of the 1960s. The period was characterized by massive mobilization, ideological experimentation, social radicalism, and economic dislocation. Changes in the productive system, in the forms of ownership, in the country's efforts to preserve distributive gains without discouraging production, and in the army's domestic role, as well as in the role and functions of the Communist party, created new dilemmas even as long-standing problems were confronted. Believing that a society's material base shaped its cultural, ethical, and political outlook, the leadership framed social goals in nonutilitarian terms. Collectivist themes were constantly articulated, and efforts to deepen mass revolutionary consciousness were earnestly pursued. Militancy was stressed in politics, culture, state-labor relations, and Party development. Coercive measures were employed against ideological nonconformists and others whose behavior deviated from revolutionary norms.

In this chapter, I focus on the normative features spawned by the chosen development strategy and the dominant ideology, examining how building an ethos of collectivist beliefs, values, and norms became part of a major political experiment. I also examine how feelings of euphoria and utopianism clashed with the reality of a low-growth, agriculturally dependent economy, and how the all-consuming drive to harvest 10 million tons (9.07 million metric tons) of sugar by 1970 led to a major crisis and subsequent policy reassessments.

THE SETTING: DEFINITIONS, CONTRADICTIONS, AND GOALS

During the mid-1960s, efforts to move ahead with development plans reversed the prior commitment to a strategy of industrialization, agricultural diversification, and de-emphasis on sugar. As was briefly mentioned in Chapter 4, the purposeful de-emphasis on sugar production stemmed from the conviction that in order to expand the society's material base and, consequently, its social wealth, major investments in nonsugar development were needed. Discarding the notion of comparative advantage, some economists and planners argued that such a theory simplified the relationship between small producers of raw materials and external market forces to an unhealthy degree. In addition, under the impact of the U.S. embargo, the concomitant loss of markets meant that major surpluses in sugar production could adversely affect world prices. The vagaries of the international market were also well known to the leadership. On the other hand, since the benefits of industrialization and agricultural diversification would not be realized in the short term, the government faced a serious dilemma, namely, how to find new markets while making inroads into the structure of dependence.

Castro's trip to the Soviet Union in 1964, during which the latter agreed to purchase some 24 million tons (21.8 million metric tons) of sugar in the 1965–1970 period, partially contributed to the reversal of policies pursued in the 1963–1964 period. With a guaranteed market and with the prospects of Soviet assistance in hand, Castro now argued that Cuba's development could be accelerated through increasing sugar production.[1] Logically, that goal required a cutback in those crops such as rice, corn, and cotton that had been expanded during the diversification phase, and some domestic needs were to be satisfied through imports.[2] Finally, in a euphoric moment, Castro declared that producing 10 million tons (9.07 million metric tons) of sugar by 1970 would set Cuba on a path of sustained development, usher in an era of unprecedented prosperity, and eliminate the vestiges of underdevelopment.

From cultural and ideological standpoints this was a period of intense controversy over economic policymaking, the pace of cultural change, and the adaptability of Marxism-Leninism to Cuba's unfolding experiments. Retrospectively, it is clear that as the Revolution moved forward, efforts to integrate the masses occurred alongside deepening changes in the political culture. Contradictions emerged that often divided the leadership regarding the appropriateness of the planning system, the extent to which some market forces could be preserved, and the role of the Party and the mass organizations. In fact, despite the socialist features of the country's political, economic, and class systems, a process of experimentation, if not improvisation, ensued. Indigenous elements were combined with characteristics of the Soviet or the more radical Chinese model, insofar as some held the Chinese experience to be somewhat similar to Cuba's. For instance, as efforts to develop the rural areas intensified, and voluntary work was encouraged, some felt that "mixing among the rural masses" had a salutory effect, especially on urbanites. The city, in fact, represented the decadent, capitalist past.[3] The future was in the countryside among the peasants and the laborers. Having won the "hearts and minds" of the common people, that is, those whose sense of belonging to the nation had seldom been taken into account, the Revolution now focused on turning converts into loyal political militants.

Divisions in the leadership between cautious bureaucrats and radicals slowed the revolutionary process; doctrinal legitimacy conferred power, so those whose ideas were ultimately accepted clearly gained in influence. As is often the case in highly politicized situations, each "camp" resorted to its ideological arsenal, to the sacred texts of Marx, Lenin, and Mao, or to the experience of other socialist countries in order to improve its credentials, impress higher-ups (including Castro), and make its case invulnerable against politically motivated charges. In a context in which doctrine, reputation, and political longevity were linked, casualties occurred. Neither foreign (Soviet) sponsorship nor past behavior counted as much as calculating which way the wind might shift, that is, where Castro's thinking was likely to end up. The latter, given to spontaneity rather than to debate and less concerned with ideological rigor than with practical matters, made his own decisions on policy questions.

No longer threatened domestically, or directly by the United States, the leadership anticipated that the regime's long-term survival depended on its ability to foster militancy and sustain political support. The leadership knew that economic conditions were harsh and that its ability to deliver social goods suffered from dwindling resources. That realization focused the need to frame a viable political strategy, one that would allow the leadership to maintain its momentum. As James Malloy pointed out, the revolutionary elite sought to allocate costs in a manner that strengthened its control but minimized social costs. Consequently, "the ongoing need for mobilization in an environment of scarcity" became crucial;[4] that, of course, fit in with the *fidelista* style of direction from above.

ECONOMIC POLICY AND ORGANIZATION

A great debate set the stage for a renewed commitment to development by expanding sugar production. This was to be a campaign of several years' duration in which the masses, the revolutionary organizations, labor, and, subsequently, the armed forces would be involved. Millions of people would participate in the "battle for the ten million" (tons) by 1970; in the interim, economic priorities were rearranged to maximize the resources available in the sugar sector. The other, more critical side of the debate involved models of economic organization and management; that is, through what methods would the economy be run—those emphasizing quasi-capitalist means or those calling for a highly centralized, planned approach.

According to Carmelo Mesa-Lago,[5] on one side were Minister of Industry Guevara and his associates, who advocated centralized control of state enterprises, extensive planning, complete collectivization of the means of production, and the gradual phasing out of money and other material incentives. Guevara was not an economist by training and he viewed revolutionary change as a process by which the nourishment of consciousness (*conciencia*) was just as important as promoting growth and efficiency; he contended that "what we are seeking is a more efficient way to reach communism." Insisting that one could not reach communism using market mechanisms, Guevara held that a radical abolition of market forces induced essential transformations in individual attitudes and, over time, in mass behavior.

In order to reduce the probability that vestiges of the profit motive and desires for personal gain would retard the emergence of consciousness, Guevara proposed a budgetary system of financing, relying on moral rather than material stimuli. For instance, under that system, profitability would not necessarily be the overriding goal of enterprises; their contribution to the *national* plan would be more critical. Accordingly, "the budgetary system of financing is based on centralized control of the enterprise's activities. Its plan and its economic functioning are controlled by central organs in a direct way. The enterprise has no funds of its own, nor does it receive bank credits."[6]

Guevara was concerned with the totality of revolutionary change and was convinced of the unethical as well as economic evils of capitalist practices in a society presumably moving toward full social equality, without class distinctions; he felt that pragmatism and socialist reformism would undermine authentic socialist consciousness. Attitudes and values, in his opinion, mattered more than economic performance, though a society's aggregate wealth clearly sustained its distributive expectations. But Guevara's belief that socialism would be perverted if the economic model relied on costs, profits, output, and returns revealed either profound ignorance of economic realities or an absolutist's passion for utopia. Criticizing those who did not accept the view that consciousness without development was preferable to development without consciousness, Guevara disdained the "temptation to follow paths of material interest" as a means of spurring growth. In sum, Guevara ridiculed his opponents' view that market socialism and self-financing approaches for economic enterprises were proper remedies for Cuba's poor situation. That approach, he said, "runs the risk of not seeing the forest for the trees. In chasing the chimera of achieving socialism with the rusty arms inherited from capitalism, one may end up on a dead-end road . . . In the meantime, the economic basis chosen has eroded the development of consciousness."[7]

THE NEW MAN

Considering the structural and cultural transformations under way in Cuba from the middle to late 1960s, questions of political socialization raised during the Campaign Against Illiteracy became central to the revolutionary process. The leadership, including Guevara and his disciples, believed that in order to succeed in the building of socialism, political attitudes and individual consciousness must reflect a new ethos. Accordingly, it is what goes on in one's mind that principally decides one's political positions; if the "right" set of ideas and values could be embedded into the political culture, socialization as well as the natural transmission processes would lead to new attitudes. Castro appeared to agree with Guevara's ideas when he stated that "we want the coming generations to receive the heritage of a very different attitude toward life, to receive the heritage of an education and a formation that is totally devoid of selfish sentiment, that is totally devoid of the sentiments appropriate to a man of the jungle."[8] Castro clearly understood the political implications of socialization efforts intended to create "a new socialist man" motivated not by greed but by a desire to serve the Revolution.

Changes effected in the superstructure, that is, through the nationalization measures, abolition of most forms of private property, and socialization of the means of production, should be followed by deepening consciousness of what else socialism entails. In dialectic fashion, attitudes, values, and behavior must gradually reflect a new reality, namely, that those private, selfish motives that determine behavior under capitalism are obsolete when collective social welfare is the stated goal. In fact, one's ability to acquire new values, such as a sense of duty and sacrifice, voluntarism, selflessness, and a willingness to subordinate personal aims to group goals, determines the "correctness" of one's attitudes. Unwillingness to move with the new currents leads to marginality or apathy; a predisposition to subject one's outlook to larger influences may lead to either critical awareness or docility. In short, though remnants of the old society and its "bourgeois" vices may exert influence, especially among older cohorts, socialization processes, educational campaigns, and unceasing official sloganeering designed to create a "new man" proceed on all fronts. Schools, factories, neighborhood committees, the work place, and other units become agents of socialization; peer pressures to either change or risk being left out strongly manifest themselves. As much as in any other field, the success or failure of the Revolution is to be determined by the acquired values and sense of commitment to the new social order of present and future generations; insofar as various forms of "contamination" penetrate, these threaten the established value system.

In his famous essay "Man and Socialism in Cuba"[9] Guevara illustrated the difference in motivation and outlook between people in a capitalist society and individuals committed to socialism, even during a transition period. Drawing on the ideas of the "young Marx," Guevara argued that under capitalism "man is guided by a cold ordinance which is usually beyond his comprehension. The alienated human being is bound to society as a whole by an invisible umbilical cord: the law of value. It acts upon all facets of his life, shaping his road and destiny." This is a restatement of the Marxist view that under capitalism, man is but a commodity; as such, the value of his labor determines his personal worth and social status.

One of the ways through which consciousness is affected is by doing away with the law of value and the market forces that it regulates. Recognizing that "the flaws of the past are translated into the present in the individual consciousness" means "constant efforts must be made to eradicate them." Moral stimuli, social pressures, direct education, ideological training, and if necessary, "rehabilitation," are some of the means utilized in the struggle against the pull of the old society. Once the dominant modes of production and the system of economic organization stress moral criteria over selfish ones, social good over private gains, planning over the anarchy of the market, and voluntarism over individuality, "we can see the new man who begins to emerge in this period of building socialism." In short, a selfless, committed, highly motivated citizen willing to immerse himself totally in shaping a new order without those bourgeois prejudices regarding who is in control of the new order and whose interests it best serves.

The debate between the pragmatists (Carlos Rafael Rodríguez, National Bank president Marcelo Fernández, and others) and the Guevarists regarding the economic model and the question of incentives created a problem for the political leadership. A crossroads was reached demanding forceful action by the final arbiter of ideological, organizational, and political disputes— Fidel Castro. Further divisions and factionalism (a cardinal sin in communist regimes) could erupt if binding decisions were not forthcoming. Political embarrassment and ostracism would follow, especially for those on the losing side. Nonetheless, Castro sided squarely with Guevara, launching nothing short of a cultural and economic revolution, adopting the ideas concerning the creation of the "new man" and criticizing those obsessed with monetary calculations.[10]

THE CUBAN MODEL

The idea that political gains would result from commitments to a development model stressing obedience, altruism, and sacrifice appealed to the leadership. Policies designed to promote social goods over individual ones would strengthen loyalties, deepen political consciousness, and generate mass support for the regime's domestic foreign policies. From a developmentalist perspective, sacrifice and hard work make up for the obvious deficiencies in the resource base.

Intrigued by the notion that communism could be reached through promoting an intense and radical brand of egalitarianism, the government instituted a series of measures designed to further erode class distinctions. Wage scales, work quotas, and labor norms in effect since 1964 were partially neglected while the principle of "socialist emulation"[11] was enhanced. Socialist emulation replaced the naked competition of market economies, and the idea of working harder in order to benefit oneself was censured. Rather than trying to beat one's coworkers in order to receive some material reward, one would be satisfied in the knowledge of having done a good day's work. Moral rewards and recognition rather than bonuses, higher pay, or material goods would be more than adequate compensation. According to one study, "as the official attitude towards material incentives became more and more negative, the approach for bonuses for overfulfillment [of quotas] also changed," disappearing altogether by 1970.[12]

With increasing centralization, unions, peasant organizations, and obviously individual enterprises became captive organizations incapable of influencing decisions affecting them. In assessing the overall impact of the central planning system on labor organization, wages, and the functioning and relative independence of farmers' and workers' associations, observers concluded that "power is concentrated in a small coterie, which allows little or no mass participation in decision-making." The notion of sectoral representation is absent, since these associations "function as agencies that mobilize the membership in the direction of facilitating the acceptance of already-made decisions and the execution of already-made plans."[13] In short, concentration of power in the revolutionary elite, and the widespread use of mobilization in order to further centrally defined aims, were basic features of the Cuban model during this period.

The shift in 1966 to the radical model produced neither satisfactory economic gains, prudent resource allocation, increased labor productivity nor *lasting* political consciousness. Cuba's economic system deteriorated rapidly, a victim of improvisation and mismanagement, Castro's own "microplans," and bureaucratic snafus. Sugar output fell short of planned targets from 1966 through 1970. Production of tobacco, the second cash crop, dropped as did the production of major food crops, such as beans, yucca, and a tuber, *malanga*. Citrus production failed to improve markedly during the four-year period, and declines in the production of vegetables such as tomatoes were also registered. Pork and chicken production fell, and between 1967 and 1970 milk production went from 565 to 520 thousand metric tons.[14]

Some declines in key agricultural commodities, sugar, livestock, pork and other items can be attributed to bad weather, poor inputs (such as lack of fertilizer or lack of knowledge of soils), or unskilled labor; nonetheless, much of it resulted from poor planning decisions, incompetent management of state farms and enterprises, inexperience, and a tendency to overestimate labor's effective contribution. By 1969, labor absenteeism itself was a major problem, especially in industry and manufacturing. A Workers' Dossiers Law was promulgated that year establishing a "Labor File and a Work Force Control Card as compulsory measures for all workers in the country, whatever be their activity."[15]

Losses in production were ultimately reflected in the total value of goods and services (gross material product, or GMP). Between 1965 and 1970, GMP went from 4.137 million pesos to 4.204 million, a less than 1 percent increase in the five-year period.[16] Table 6.1 gives a more complete account of the economy's performance during the period in which the "moral economy" was in effect, demonstrating that increased investments led neither to greater aggregate wealth nor to more efficient administration.

Explanations for the failure of the radical model range from Mesa-Lago's view that idealistic expectations regarding the disappearance of

Table 6.1.   Selected Indicators of Cuba's
              Economic Performance, 1965-1970

Year	GMP[a]	State Investment[b]	Sugar Production[c]
1965	4.137	827	6.156
1966	3.985	909	4.537
1967	4.081	979	6.236
1968	4.352	1.240	5.164
1969	4.180	--	4.459
1970	4.204	--	8.538

[a]gross material product in million pesos
[b]in million dollars
[c]in thousand metric tons

Sources: Carmelo Mesa-Lago, The Economy of Socialist Cuba (Albuquerque: University of New Mexico Press, 1981), p. 34.   Speeches
by Fidel Castro reproduced in Cuba in Revolution, ed. Rolando E.
Bonachea and Nelson P. Valdés (Garden City, N.Y.: Doubleday and Co.,
1972), pp. 305-356.

"economic man" were overstated—leading to economic chaos—to arguments focusing on Castro's antiorganizational style and "guerrilla approach,"
to views asserting that no society can disregard basic economic principles
and still hope to expand production and social wealth.

On the other hand, the ideas surrounding the "new man" were not
solely concerned with his economic abilities. Much more, motivation and
a willingness to adopt a new style of revolutionary conduct were what
counted. The argument that idealism is bound to clash with remnants of
the traditional mentality is insufficiently appreciative of what revolutionaries
aim to do: destroy in order to create. Excesses, waste, arbitrariness, and
violations of life and limb are a natural though disgusting aspect of that
process. The extent to which coercion is used to force a change in behavior
divides repressive regimes from more traditionally authoritarian ones. In
Cuba, those who for a variety of reasons refused to go along with the
values sustained by the new order bore (and bear) the brunt of the regime's
psychological pressures, as well as the disdain of their peers. Forcing
individuals to become "new men" (through socialization) may to some
appear to be degrading, perhaps involving a process of recanting one's
values and upbringing. To others, it is a necessary condition for any
revolution aspiring to change the essence of the mind as well as conduct.

TWO CRISES

Private property, such as individually owned small businesses, vending
stands, bars, shops, restaurants and cafes of various kinds, and other street-

type commerce existed in the nonagricultural sector of the socialized economy. Largely, the regime had tolerated this because it alleviated scarcities in some foods and consumer goods, it created employment and subemployment for thousands who would otherwise look for employment with the state, and because it really did not constitute a major antiregime source of economic power. It is probable that some individuals involved in this kind of commerce were also involved in black market activities such as selling rice, beans, meat, and other basic items often unavailable in the cities or the larger towns. The black market itself had always existed in one form or another since rationing had been imposed in 1962. Depending on the circumstances, the regime has either tolerated such "illegal transactions," looking the other way, or clamped down harshly on black marketeering.

On the other hand, the social and ideological contradictions stemming from such "petty capitalism" were not lost on the leadership, especially at a time when hardship and sacrifices were demanded. Castro would subsequently charge that owners of various establishments profited from the general austerity, insofar as some of them charged high prices for the goods and services provided. More important, the permanence of a profit-motivated class of small proprietors whose values and behavior were at odds with those of the "new socialist man" constituted a sore and a social contradiction. These activities went mostly unregulated and lay beyond central planning mechanisms. Thus the regime had little or no control over them, which was politically significant.

The Revolutionary Offensive

In 1968 the government decided that economic benefits accruing from this sector were not sufficient to outweigh the social and ideological costs generated by this "petty bourgeoisie growing in the heart of the socialist economy."[17] In one swift stroke, Castro launched a "revolutionary offensive," announcing the immediate takeover and socialization of some 57,000 individually owned and operated units. From this point on, responsibility for the administration and functioning of numerous small businesses fell to the state; included among these were shoe shops, bars, and auto repair shops as well as metal, lumber, and other industries. Almost overnight, Cuba became the most socialized economy in the world, eliminating the vestiges of small-scale urban capitalism and leaving only a small portion of agriculture in private hands.

Castro's motivation was neither sinister nor hidden from the public. In essence, the offensive was intended to demonstrate that no one was immune from sharing in hardships and difficulties, that profiteering was considered a major evil in a socialist society, and that even if legitimate services were now abolished, the political gains to the Revolution justified such actions. According to K. S. Karol, the "major aim was to inspire the productive enthusiasm of the workers."[18] Castro himself put it in the following terms:

Gentlemen, we did not make a Revolution here to establish the right to trade! . . . When will they finally understand that this is a revolution of socialists, that it is a revolution of communists? . . . Clearly and definitely, we must say that we propose to eliminate all manifestation of private trade, clearly and definitely . . .

Once again, the regime's actions during the offensive demonstrated its ability to move quickly and convincingly against potential sources of economic and social opposition. Castro's harsh characterization of these "parasitic" elements left no doubt regarding the treatment meted out to the Revolution's ideological enemies. The fact that this sector did not constitute a political opposition as such mattered less than the lessons that were taught, namely that defiance was costly, that the new norms of revolutionary conduct would be enforced, and that laxity and a carefree attitude made one suspect. This was serious business of the highest order, and one should not doubt the willingness or the ability of the regime to forcefully carry out its self-assigned responsibilities.

At the same time, additional burdens were placed on an already poorly administered economy plagued by inefficiencies, labor problems, low productivity, and little growth. Former owners and employees became salaried workers on the state payroll, but their disgruntlement only compounded a worrisome labor situation. The swift statization of the private sector and the proletarianization of its members converted a somewhat independent class into a dependent one, enlarging the public sector without increasing the availability of goods. But the swiftness with which the regime moved and the scope of the "offensive" was typically *fidelista:* dramatic and with little regard for long-term consequences. More important was the fact that the regime now reached deeper into the social fabric, since many who owned, administered, or worked at these establishments came to depend on the state for their livelihood. According to an article in *Granma* on March 31, 1968, the revolutionary offensive rooted out "nests of parasites, hotbeds of corruption, illegal trading and counterrevolutionary activity," but it can also be viewed as one more effort to effect changes in attitudes and personal behavior through coercion.

The Microfaction Affair

As was noted in Chapter 4, tension and suspicion characterized relations between former PSP members and Castroites during the period of "sectarianism" and through the Marcos Rodríguez trial. Those conflicts were partially settled in the 1962 purge of the ORI and the exile of Aníbal Escalante. The latter returned to Cuba in 1964 but did not assume any politically sensitive position, remaining officially isolated from decisions— as was generally the case with most members of the reconstructed PCC.

Upon his return, Escalante activated a network of old PSP loyalists. In not-so-clandestine meetings and reunions, the group began to criticize the Revolution's radical turn in foreign and domestic policies, considering the former adventurist and pro-Chinese and the latter ill conceived, wasteful, and totally unorthodox. The "microfaction" (as it became known) also questioned the class origin of revolutionary leaders, expressed alarm at Castro's freewheeling governing style, and sniped at the poor ideological preparation of revolutionary cadres. To Escalante and his followers, the Revolution was led by harebrained incompetents who could only lead the country to disaster.

The group hoped to capitalize on some of its members' close ties to the Soviets in order to impress upon Castro that the Kremlin was not totally unaware of goings-on in Cuba. Most of Castro's tirades were public and even in revolutionary Cuba there were few secrets. On the other hand, it is not inconceivable that the group sought to reestablish a foothold for orthodoxy in what it perceived to be an unrestrained regime. Frozen out of influential circles and decision-making positions, some individuals may also have been motivated by ambition or a desire for political revenge.

The government's intelligence services became aware of the group's activities in 1966 and subsequently monitored contacts between the group and Soviets and Eastern Europeans. Presumably, damaging information on the poor state of the economy and on the misuse of Soviet aid was being passed to the Soviets. Most important, according to Raúl Castro, the group had approached officials and Communist party members from the Soviet Union and Eastern Europe "in an attempt to make known their views opposing the PCC line and to influence opinion in the leadership of these parties favorable to their own position."[19] In short, they had attempted to discredit the PCC's "revolutionary" line in the eyes of more mature and established Communist parties.

In January 1968, Raúl Castro presented to the PCC's Central Committee a report on the group's activities that included documentary evidence of the microfaction's conspiratorial ways, especially its criticisms of the Party and the leadership. Punishment was swift and forceful. In condemning the microfaction the report focused not on the merit of the accusations, but on the behavior and attitude of those involved; it charged them with a "tendency to lie and combine slander with criticism," distorting the history of the revolutionary process, and holding "malicious, petty and treasonous aims." Subsequently, the Central Committee (in which the influence of "old" communists was nil) resolved that the microfaction should be expelled from the party and recommended that legal measures be taken against Escalante and others.

The purge of the microfaction quashed potential divisions in the Party, demonstrated that fealty to Moscow did not necessarily translate into influence within the regime, suppressed efforts to force deviations from the established line, and reasserted Castroite supremacy over the direction and objectives of the regime's foreign and domestic policies. In addition, it defined once and for all the limits of debate within the regime, proscribing certain types of conduct even if that conduct was motivated by political loyalty to Moscow. Since then, no overt challenges to Castro's authority over intraparty affairs have arisen. Then as now, the balance of power within the Party and ruling elite decidedly favors proven and loyal Castroites, though new cadres are starting to move upward.

The resolution of the affair in terms that were unfavorable to Moscow and its local allies also demonstrated that Castro's defiance would, on occasion, sting the Soviets. The need for Soviet economic assistance and military protection dampened neither Castro's radicalism nor his persistent intrusion into economic policymaking. In fact, if the Cuban leadership failed to behave as a client is expected to do, it was because Cuba's ties to the Soviets were *not yet* those of a weak client deferring to the wishes of its powerful patron. Cuba was not Poland, and Castro was not Gomulka. Rather, a more symmetrical relationship was in effect, one in which Cuba was vulnerable to Soviet pressures while exercising limited leverage itself.

"THE TEN MILLION ARE ON THE WAY"

Castro's decision to reach the arbitrary and entirely unrealistic goal of harvesting 10 million tons (9.07 million metric tons) of sugar in 1970 revealed the prime minister's poor knowledge of economic affairs, his penchant for grandiose campaigns, his view that nature would conform to the will of one man, and his belief that enormous sacrifices are justifiable on behalf of necessary goals. In a sense this would be the "harvest to end all harvests," the all-consuming drive to show the world what Cubans are made of, the one promise that would be met no matter what the cost. The harvest was no less than an epochal event around which national energies were to be concentrated; it was, in short, a sustained push that would liberate Cuba, make future development viable, and usher in an era of socialist comforts.

It is probable that the leadership also calculated the political aspects of the drive, either as a way of revitalizing slackening revolutionary fervor and discipline or as a means through which the collectivist principles associated with the "new man" could be tested. Thus the campaign must be seen in its economic, political, and moral dimensions, and its outcome judged accordingly.

Though the commitment was made years in advance, and the regime had already a proven record of inaccuracy in its economic forecasts, the goal was absolute. Any deviation was considered a sign of weakness, something not insignificant in a very Latin culture. Moreover, since it was Castro's idea that the effort get under way, questioning it could pose serious political problems. Official reservations, if any, were sotto voce.

Cuba's largest harvest had been 7.2 million tons (6.5 million metric tons) in 1952, a year of exceptionally good yields. In the mid-1960s production had fallen to between 4 and 5 million tons (3.6 and 4.5 million metric tons); nevertheless, Castro stated that even "9,999,999 tons" would constitute a "moral defeat." The regime's prestige, the credibility of its leaders, the pride of the nation, and the rosy expectations of the future—if not the very vindication of the development strategy followed in the late 1960s—were at stake.

Unquestionably, the society's energies were concentrated on the sugar drive to an unprecedented degree, surpassing prior efforts against illiteracy and bureaucratization. A regime characterized by its ability to stretch mass support to the limit geared up its organizational and mobilizational apparatus once more. This was its litmus test. Peasant organizations such as ANAP, the CDR, the women's federation, unions, professionals, and bureaucrats were enjoined to participate. Voluntarism, exhortation, social pressures, and messages via the controlled media encouraged involvement. Apathy was frowned upon, and one's political mettle was determined by one's contribution.

By early 1970 it had become clear that the goal would not be met, though Castro continued to believe that intensifying efforts would ultimately make the campaign successful. There is little doubt that he was personally involved in various aspects of the harvest, citing statistics, making technical reports, traveling across the island ceaselessly, and taunting foreign observers. As Carlos A. Montaner remarked, this was Castro the overseer of a huge cane plantation, "sticking his Hellenic nose into everything and enjoying it. Power is fun, and if it is absolute, it is absolute fun."[20]

Warning signs that production was slackening in industry, nonsugar agriculture, and manufacturing were noted, but these were considered logical and expected side effects, to be remedied in the following years. Neither the structural distortions caused by all-out mobilization in the sugar sector nor the damage done to the infrastructure was fully appreciated. Cane was wasted due to bottlenecks in the transportation system, the lack of skills in voluntary brigades affected *future* planting of cane, and equipment was overworked. In the end, despite the massive economic, moral, and psychological investment, the long grinding season, and the all-out drive, the harvest totaled 8.5 million tons (7.7 million metric tons), a 15 percent shortfall. In Mesa-Lago's words, "the 1970 sugar harvest set a historical output record, but it turned into a Pyrrhic victory achieved by depleting resources from other sectors of the economy, which in turn suffered output declines offsetting the increase in sugar output."[21]

A few statistics indicate the necessity of obtaining full optimality of resources in order to reach the goal of 10 million tons (9.07 million metric tons) of sugar. Respectively, from 1967 to 1969 Cuba produced 6.23, 5.16, and 4.46 thousand metric tons (6.23, 5.16, and 4.46 thousand tons) of sugar; in order to fulfill the 1970 target, production would have had to double. In addition, taking or shifting resources away from agriculture meant lower production for an economy that was nowhere near self-sufficiency in various basic crops. For instance, lands that would have been planted with vegetables, tubers, or other crops were utilized for sugar cane; the sucrose yield of that cane was not always the highest, because as experts in sugar production know, cane depletes the soil quickly and cannot be planted everywhere.

The transportation system suffered under the impact of prolonged mobilization. Machinery, vehicles, and other units were placed at the disposal of the army or the Ministry of Sugar in order to extract maximum capabilities. In many instances, breakdowns, waste, and inefficiency resulted; it is also probable that some industrial sabotage such as the wrecking of equipment occurred, especially toward the end. Scholars have also noted the "militarization of agriculture" characteristic of the period. Soldiers, reservists, and militiamen worked the fields, drove trucks and tractors, and supervised some aspects of production and administered others. Their practical inexperience in such tasks created chaos and disorder, but in situations in which the lines of responsibility were often blurred, one could not always determine who was at fault. Ironically, the military was perceived as the solution to disorganization, lack of discipline, and absence of skilled cadres. The French agronomist Rene Dumont asserted critically that "in an environment of generalized disorder, the Army appears as the only solution," adding that undue haste "caused so many errors that by now one should have known how to prevent them in the future."[22] Not surprisingly, the military model proved incapable of matching resources to needs, nor was it able to extract the labor discipline necessary. If anything, militarization created rigidities in the economic system that took time to overcome. The use of military personnel in productive tasks probably affected its morale, since cutting cane is not as prestigious an occupation as "defending the fatherland."

Recrimination and scapegoatism were mild by conventional standards, but such a colossal failure could not be swept under the rug. Technical reasons were given for failing to reach the goal. In his Report to the People, Castro at one point concluded that "we have lost the battle of the ten million because of the problem of the sugar yield," i.e., poor sucrose content in cane stalks.[23] To its credit, the regime did not ascribe the failure entirely to weather-related troubles, the imperialist blockade, flagging militancy, or poor Soviet-made equipment. Gradually, the accepted explanation came to be that the original decision itself was flawed and that the leadership had attempted too great a rise in production in too short a time. The people were ultimately absolved when Castro recognized that "we, we alone—are the ones who have lost the battle. The administrative apparatus and the leaders of the Revolution are the ones who lost the battle."[24] In any case, a major economic miscalculation cut severely into the regime's legitimacy, dealt a final blow to the "moral economy," and produced a generalized feeling of injured national pride.

AFTERMATH AND ASSESSMENT

Castro's speeches on 26 July of any year are generally policy statements, either looking back on the state of the Revolution, pointing to needed improvements, making some dramatic new announcement, or setting a new course. With uncharacteristic humility Castro soberly assessed the state of things in July 1970, acknowledging defeat in a memorable effort to contain the domestic and foreign fallout. Since the 10-million-ton (9.07-

million-metric-ton) harvest had been the battle that would have decided Cuba's future for the next decade, the setback invariably had a profound impact on the leadership, its foreign sponsors, and Castro himself. Caught in the contradiction of having publicly blamed himself for the failure but needing to make the best of a bad situation, Castro acknowledged that errors had been committed, that zealousness and good will were no substitutes for competence, that ignorance and idealism had been too costly, and that future expectations needed some rethinking. In short he admitted that the dilemma of how to make headway against underdevelopment could not be solved through infantile subjectivism, half-baked ideas, ill-conceived impulses, or permanent experimentation. Why? Because for the future, "we want the people to gird themselves for battle. This is because our problems will not be solved by means of miracles performed by individuals or even by groups of individuals. Only the people can perform miracles."[25]

In one of the few instances in which the regime or its leaders have admitted that they are not entirely unaccountable for their behavior, Castro added that "the people can replace us whenever they wish—right now if you so desire!" since the leaders' learning process had been too slow, their style (and his) too reckless, and their blunders unnecessarily costly. On the other hand, one could only attribute so much to inexperience or zealotry. In the final analysis, it was the system's "neurotic fixation with production" that failed, that "raving atmosphere of goals, emulations, production tables and ghostly fights against imperialism that in Cuba reaches its highest mark."[26]

From the standpoint of sheer political survivability, the regime's ability to ride out the deepest crisis in a decade suggested that even if its development strategy proved disastrous, its mass appeal and its political capital were not entirely used up. There is little question that the regime's political strength was at a low point, with discontent rampant and spirits low. How, then, did it endure and live to fight another day?

Maurice Halperin has suggested that "there have been few, if any, examples in recent history of the head of a government who could survive a crisis of comparable dimensions without resort to drastic measures of repression,"[27] but more than Castro's political skills were involved. Granted that his public *mea culpa* had a cathartic effect, and that his blunt assessment played uncharacteristically well to a people unaccustomed to uncontrived public criticism; it was Castro's defiance of conventional risk taking that ultimately saved the day, and the public plaza became his confessional. Neither cynically repudiating the ideas that led to the errors nor wallowing in self-pity, through paternalistic manipulation and a steeled force of will, Castro turned the crisis into a political crucible out of which unspent energies were subsequently drawn.

It is also true that no institutional means existed through which popular will could force a change in the leadership. Neither the party, nor the military, nor the discredited bureaucracy, and certainly not the Soviets could exert decisive pressure to oust the Castroites and move in a new team. The regime retained a monopoly over the instruments of coercion; old fashioned Latin-style conspiracies were unlikely to succeed against Castro, who was himself the consummate conspirator. No opposition existed that could present a viable new alternative. In sum, the regime endured because its leader's reading of the people's near-limitless capacity for sacrifice was right, because a return to the prerevolutionary status quo was inconceivable, and because a feeling of nationhood had been forged through struggle and defeat.

SUMMARY

It is generally accepted that 1970 marks a critical threshold in Cuba's revolutionary development. A radical period of experimentation and improvisation gave way to a more structured style of decision making and to improvements in economic management. Cuba's unconventional brand of socialism, characterized by efforts to create an order in which satisfaction of one's material needs was not determined exclusively by one's talents, ran up against the limitations of a dependent economy unable to generate sufficient wealth. Rethinking among the political leadership, planners, and the managerial elite led to the view that a radical brand of egalitarianism pervaded the social fabric, mistakenly equating desires for self-improvement with the wrong kind of political consciousness. Guevara's romantic legacy, elevated to popular mythology, spawned numerous contradictions and sharpened internal debate regarding what future course to take. Gradually, a new pragmatism replaced the spontaneity and zeal of the 1960s.

New dilemmas stemming from the palpable absence of restraining mechanisms emerged, confronting as always Castro's central political role, his inability to delegate effective authority, and his charisma. At this point, the "Cuban political system could be characterized as a variant of the charismatic model, in which ideology and party play a minimal role, in which the process of institutionalization is very weak,"[28] and whose legitimacy is at a low point. Processes of genuine democratization characterized by effective popular participation were not in evidence. The political autonomy of the mass organizations, as well as their ability to directly influence the revolutionary elite, was practically nonexistent. Insofar as these processes strengthen the relationship between the few and the many, deepen the system's legitimacy, and institutionalize restraint, their absence demonstrated the regime's essentially authoritarian nature.

On the other hand, socialization processes encouraging uniformity in behavior and political attitudes reinforced traditional norms supportive of strong leadership, paternalism, and political docility. The new ethos, aiming to sustain a form of collective spartanism was not yet fully developed, nor had the process of *concientización* (deepening consciousness) eradicated individualism, political apathy, or various forms of social resistance. A new generation of communists had not yet been formed.

Lastly, changes in the political culture nurtured national consciousness, aggregating previously unfocused feelings of nationhood. But the failure of the *zafra* (sugar harvest) meant that idealism and commitment had been dealt a heavy blow. As Castro correctly sensed: "Our enemies say we have problems, and in reality our enemies are right."[29] Defeat tasted bitter, and many realized that more struggles lay ahead. Feelings that additional sacrifices would be borne kept the system from collapsing entirely, but it was unclear where new departures might lead.

NOTES

1. See Maurice Halperin, *The Taming of Fidel Castro* (Berkeley: University of California Press, 1981), pp. 13–14; or Hugh Thomas, *Cuba, The Pursuit of Freedom* (New York: Harper and Row, 1971), p. 1438.
2. Leo Huberman and Paul M. Sweezy, *Socialism in Cuba* (New York: Monthly Review Press, 1969), p. 80.
3. See Susan Eckstein, "The Debourgeoisement of Cuban Cities," in *Cuban Communism*, 4th ed., ed. Irving L. Horowitz (New Brunswick, N.J.: Transaction Books, 1981), pp. 119–140.
4. James M. Malloy, "Generation of Political Support and Allocation of Costs," in *Revolutionary Change in Cuba*, ed. Carmelo Mesa-Lago (Pittsburgh: University of Pittsburgh Press, 1971), p. 26.
5. Carmelo Mesa-Lago, *Cuba in the 1970s*, rev. ed. (Albuquerque: University of New Mexico Press, 1978), pp. 6–8.
6. Quoted in Donald C. Hodges, *The Legacy of Che Guevara, A Documentary Study* (London: Thames and Hudson, 1977), p. 95.
7. Ibid., p. 96.
8. Quoted in Richard R. Fagen, *The Transformation of Political Culture in Cuba* (Stanford, Calif.: Stanford University Press, 1969), p. 13.
9. Reproduced in John Gerassi, ed., *Venceremos! The Speeches and Writings of Ernesto Che Guevara* (New York: Macmillan, 1968), pp. 387–400.
10. See Fidel Castro's speech, *Granma*, September 28, 1966.
11. According to Bernardo, such opposition "was to be fraternal, marked by nonsecrecy, a spirit of camaraderie about the whole process and willingness to share one's superior methods." The regime created a National Emulation Commission charged with selecting winners (the most selfless and productive workers) and handing out prizes. For a thorough discussion, see Robert M. Bernardo, *The Theory of Moral Incentives in Cuba* (University, Ala.: University of Alabama Press, 1971), pp. 56–64. See also Joseph A. Kahl, "The Moral Economy of a Revolutionary Society," in *Cuban Communism*, ed. Horowitz, pp. 95–115.
12. Roberto E. Hernández and Carmelo Mesa-Lago, "Labor Organization and Wages," in *Revolutionary Change in Cuba*, ed. Mesa-Lago, p. 229.
13. Nelson Amaro and Carmelo Mesa-Lago, "Inequality and Classes," in *Revolutionary Change in Cuba*, ed. Mesa-Lago, p. 371.
14. See Archibald R. M. Ritter, *The Economic Development of Revolutionary Cuba* (New York: Praeger Publishers, 1974), pp. 188–191. For a different interpretation, see Arthur MacEwan, *Revolution and Economic Development in Cuba* (New York: St. Martin's, 1981), pp. 95–153.
15. Law Number 1225 appears in *Cuba in Revolution*, ed. Rolando E. Bonachea and Nelson P. Valdés (Garden City, N.Y.: Doubleday, 1972), pp. 417–420. Under

this law, "anyone guilty of falsification, loss, or total or partial destruction of the Labor File and Work Force Control Card shall be charged with a criminal offense, and referred to the proper judicial authorities for issuance of a penalty."

16. See Carmelo Mesa-Lago, *The Economy of Socialist Cuba* (Albuquerque: University of New Mexico Press, 1981), p. 34.

17. Huberman and Sweezy, *Socialism in Cuba*, p. 137.

18. K. S. Karol, *Guerrillas in Power* (New York: Hill and Wang, 1970), p. 443.

19. The Report on the Microfaction issued by the PCC's Central Committee and Raúl Castro's Report of the Investigative Committee appear in *Political Power in Latin America: Seven Confrontations*, ed. Richard R. Fagen and Wayne A. Cornelius, Jr. (Englewood Cliffs, N.J.: Prentice-Hall, 1970), pp. 373–380. See also Thomas, *Cuba, The Pursuit of Freedom*, pp. 1468–1469.

20. Carlos A. Montaner, *Secret Report on the Cuban Revolution*, trans. E. Zayas-Bazán (New Brunswick, N.J.: Transaction Books, 1981), p. 53.

21. Mesa-Lago, *Economy of Socialist Cuba*, p. 26.

22. Rene Dumont, *¿Cuba Es Socialista?* (Caracas: Editorial Tiempo Nuevo, S.A., 1970), pp. 117–118. Dumont was later accused by Castro of working for the CIA and since the early 1970s has been on Havana's Blacklist of Foreign Intellectuals. See Montaner, *Secret Report*, pp. 126–127.

23. The all-important yield is the ratio of sugar produced to the weight of cane milled. A yield of 12 *arrobas* (1 *arroba* equals 25 pounds) of sugar from the milling of 100 *arrobas* (2,500 pounds) of cane is good and anything above that is excellent. For 1970's harvest, the yield was 10.7 *arrobas* (267.5 pounds), by far the lowest since 1958.

24. Fidel Castro, "Report on the Sugar Harvest," in *Cuba in Revolution*, ed. Bonachea and Valdés, p. 296.

25. Speech by Fidel Castro, 26 July 1970, reported in *Cuba in Revolution*, ed. Bonachea and Valdés, pp. 317–356. Quote on p. 317.

26. Montaner, *Secret Report*, p. 99.

27. Halperin, *Taming of Fidel Castro*, p. 325.

28. Andrés Suárez, "Leadership, Ideology and Political Party," in *Revolutionary Change in Cuba*, ed. Mesa-Lago, pp. 15–16.

29. Speech by Fidel Castro, 26 July 1970, reported in *Cuba in Revolution*, ed. Bonachea and Valdés, pp. 317–356. Quote is on p. 329.

7

Revolutionary Foreign Policy: Activism and Clientelism

Revolutionary governments often stake their legitimacy on demonstrating political will in times of crisis or stress, realizing stated social or economic goals, or advancing causes abroad that link domestic objectives to foreign policy goals. A country's foreign relations, intended to maximize its international standing and its degree of influence abroad, are subject to both domestic pressures and external constraints. Indeed, vigorous involvement in foreign affairs may be intended primarily to maximize domestic goals, or to turn attention away from these when they appear unattainable.

By definition and through their overt behavior, revolutionary regimes such as Cuba's challenge the international order; they are often compelled to do so for ideological reasons, in order to obtain conventional foreign policy advantages, or simply to ensure the survival of revolutionary rule.[1] In the case of Cuba mutually supportive linkages exist between the regime's domestic policies and its foreign policy goals, though the internal set of constraints shaping its external behavior is entirely different from those found in democratic or most authoritarian regimes.

On the other hand, convinced that revolutions cannot prosper in isolation, and shrewdly mindful that proximity to the United States is politically advantageous but not entirely risk-free, Havana views the prospects of revolution elsewhere as a means through which its influence can be extended, its own security enhanced (paradoxically), and its domestic values reaffirmed.

In this chapter, I focus on (1) the sources of the regime's foreign policy and the themes on which it is waged; (2) the methods by which Havana pursues its objectives; (3) Cuba's continuing conflicts with the United States; and (4) how clientelism (dependence, Cuba's pro-Soviet behavior) affects Havana's cultivation of allies in the Third World and its foreign policy autonomy.

101

SOURCES AND MOTIVATION

Cuba's foreign policy has since the Revolution been characterized by a revolutionary messianism. Havana, infused with ideological romanticism and a desire to rid the Caribbean Basin of corrupt, personalist dictators like Trujillo, sent expeditions to the Dominican Republic and other countries following the revolutionaries' victory. At that point, no grand strategy had yet been developed. Cuba was quite preoccupied with its internal security and had yet to acquire the capability or political stability necessary to extend its influence. In other words, until the mid-1960s, "the objective was to mobilize support for Cuba within the established order rather than pursue a coherent strategy to export the revolution."[2]

As the conflict with the United States heated up, leading to suspension from the OAS and regional isolation, Havana developed a counter-strategy of its own, stemming largely from its leaders' guerrilla experience. The regime learned to exploit geopolitical rivalries for its own purposes, garnering Soviet support and deriving useful political capital from its periodic confrontations with the United States.

The country's historical legacy, especially its record of anti-imperialist struggles in the 1930s and the deeds or writings of heroes like Maceo, Martí, and Gómez, sustains Havana's image of a nation seeking to control its own destiny. Cuba's own ethnic and cultural heritage, heavily influenced by black Africa through slavery, is now viewed as a major asset, since Cuba can rightly claim that its culture and population have not lost sight of their African roots. Thus nonsystemic factors and even affective influences that are part of Cuba's national character shape its activist policies.

A prudent realization of Havana's own capabilities, a complex assessment of Cuba's national interest, and Castro's driving force constitute additional elements. In particular, Castro's own temperament, shrewdness, unrepentant anti-imperialist convictions, and episodic megalomaniacal outbursts shape Havana's policies in nonbureaucratic, noninstitutional ways. Much evidence suggests that Castro is not a grand strategic thinker but is quite good at assessing trends and calculating options. His decisions still carry the day. Crises and challenges provide him with a comfortable operational milieu. His style is that of the consummate actor, and his ability to turn disasters into short-term foreign policy victories is by now legendary.[3]

Havana's foreign policy is also shaped by the official ideology, Marxism-Leninism. By defining its believers' world view, reconciling tactical behavior with longer-term strategic aims, and providing a proven method of political warfare, Marxism-Leninism serves a variety of purposes. Castro's speeches and known policy positions, Guevara's legacy and his writings on the theory and method of revolutionary warfare, and powerful nationalistic feelings provide additional impetus. Simply stated, "Marxism-Leninism has been grafted onto Cuban nationalism," shaping perceptions and partly defining "the nature of the international political game, the natural adversaries faced by Cuba, and the friends it should support through internationalist solidarity."[4]

In sum, the sources of Havana's foreign policy are found in the geopolitical rivalry between East and West, in the ideological struggle between radical movements and status quo forces, in Castro's manifest desire to play a global role, and in Cuba's own cultural makeup and anti-imperialist legacies. Once this perspective is established, the regime's policies, from the early expeditions to Caribbean Basin countries through its commitment to create "one, two, three or many more Viet Nams," its African campaigns, and its extensive involvement in regional affairs, can be properly examined.

CONTINENTAL REVOLUTION: "THE DUTY OF EVERY REVOLUTIONARY IS TO MAKE THE REVOLUTION"

Cuba saw itself surrounded by covert and overt threats for most of the 1960s.[5] It had been suspended from the OAS, branded as a regional troublemaker by the United States, and subjected to a then little-known "secret war" by the Kennedy and Johnson administrations, carried out by the CIA and Cuban exiles. The conflict with the United States acquired regional dimensions and was responsible for a period of deep hostility between Havana and most Latin American governments. Cuba perceived itself as a pariah. At the same time, Cuba challenged the notion that U.S. hegemony over Latin America was permanent or inevitable, repeatedly lambasting area governments for their alleged subservience to Washington while redirecting its own military and security ties to the Soviet bloc. In short, feeling threatened, probably unsure of Soviet commitments, unable to move against the United States directly but seeking to fend off some of the pressures, the regime took a radical turn and adopted a confrontational outlook.

In the Second Declaration of Havana, Castro argued that class oppression, economic exploitation, and oligarchical domination by pro-U.S. repressive regimes made revolution inevitable in Latin America and that Havana sympathized with such prospects. According to Castro, small countries in the front lines (those in confrontation with U.S. imperialism), feeling the brunt of imperialist aggression, could not compromise with the enemy, nor could the policy of "peaceful coexistence" (then supported by the Soviets) lead to anything but a weakening of revolutionary fervor. Thus Castro called for armed revolution throughout Latin America in order to overthrow regimes whose dependence on Washington was total and that characteristically repressed the peasantry, the working class, and the important, potentially explosive, and viscerally anti-U.S. radical intelligentsia. Uttering his famous line that "the duty of every revolutionary is to make the revolution,"[6] Castro unequivocally denounced comrades sitting "in the doorway of their homes to watch the corpse of imperialism pass by," setting the stage for the subsequent emergence of guerrilla *focos* (places in rural areas where guerrilla activities begin) in several Latin American countries.[7]

In calling for armed revolution on a continental scale, Castro lent his undisputed talents and charisma to earlier pronouncements by Guevara, long thought to be a theorist of guerrilla strategy. Guevara's writings on armed struggle and his hatred of U.S. imperialism continue to inspire legions of Latin American and Third World radicals mesmerized by the life and martyrdom of "the heroic guerrilla." In 1961, Guevara offered Cuba as an example of a country that had successfully defeated hunger, imperialism, and the "great landed propertied classes." Cuba's path, he asserted, "is now scientifically confirmed" for all Latin America in a matter of time. "Missing in America," contended Ché, "are the subjective conditions of which the most important is the awareness of the possibility of victory over the imperial powers and their internal allies by taking the violent road," adding that "armed struggle helps to foresee and clarify the inevitability of change."[8] In short, there is no authentic revolution without armed violence.

Such core ideas on revolutionary warfare lent focus and substance to Havana's foreign policy for most of the 1960s. Contacts between the regime and radical movements in other countries were initiated, partly as a result of Cuban diplomacy in international conferences as well as Guevara's trips to Africa in 1964 and 1965. In Latin America itself, the Revolution's demonstration effect was dramatic. The Colombian ELN, the Revolutionary Armed Forces and FALN in Venezuela, and the Guatemalan MR-13 received training, subsidies, and other forms of assistance from Havana, indicating the regime's penchant for intervention in its neighbors' internal affairs (see Table 7.1). According to Cole Blasier, "the guerrillas of the 1960s [also] sought to overthrow governments of a reformist democratic persuasion" in Guatemala, Venezuela, and Colombia, partly out of a belief that "reformism had failed, that the United States had opposed and would continue to oppose needed social change, and that the Cuban Revolution demonstrated that radical strategies can succeed."[9] A second reason was (and is) the fact that radical movements fear moderate reforms, since these often take away the revolutionaries' banners. Havana also gave military assistance to the Algerian National Liberation Front (FLN) in 1960, sent a battalion of combat troops to help in that country's dispute with Morocco in 1963, trained several revolutionary leaders in Zanzibar in 1964, collaborated with rebel forces in the Congo in 1965, and sent troops to Syria in 1973.

Revolutionary movements in Latin America blended indigenous elements with Marxist-Leninist ideas and Castroite methods. Their strategies included various forms of guerrilla warfare, such as a prolonged people's war, foquismo (the strategy of establishing focal points for guerrilla activity in the countryside), urban violence, lightning terrorist attacks, assassinations, and political kidnappings. Guerrilla leaders and their intellectual mentors, along with their uncritical followers, believed that they could successfully

Table 7.1.   Latin American Revolutionary Movements, 1960s

Country	Name	Year Founded
Perú	APRA Rebelde (later reorganized as MIR)	1959
Perú	National Liberation Army (ELN) Frente de Izquierda Revolucionaria	1962
Venezuela	Movimiento de Izquierda Revolucionario (MIR)	1960
Venezuela	Fuerzas Armadas de Liberación Nacional (FALN)	1962
Guatemala	Revolutionary Armed Forces	--
Guatemala	13th of November Revolutionary Movement (MR-13)	--
Nicaragua	Frente Sandinista de Liberación Nacional (FSLN)	1961
Colombia	National Liberation Army (ELN)	1964
Chile	Movimiento de Izquierda Revolucionario	1965
Bolivia	National Liberation Army (ELN)	1966

Source: G. Pope Atkins, Latin America in the International Political System (New York: The Free Press, 1977), pp. 146-149.

create "another Cuba" in their respective countries. They were dogmatically convinced of the need for revolution, they made wild assumptions about the "readiness of the masses," and they routinely underestimated the repressive capabilities of local armies. These movements were (and are, in the case of Central America) led by urban intellectuals and others of middle-class origins—educated individuals alienated from the squalor and corruption of their societies who willingly took up guns out of a perennial Latin American reverence for political drama and heroics. Ideology was also involved. Ultimately, doctrinal and tactical divisions, feuds with pro-Soviet Communist parties, failure to generate mass support, repression, and personal intrigues among leaders often led to the demise of these movements, as well as to a reassessment of the viability of guerrilla warfare and the doctrine of armed struggle.[10]

Havana's encouragement of Latin American and Third World revolutionary movements is characterized as (1) an effort to create troubles for governments supportive of United States policies, (2) an attempt to legitimize Cuba's own experience on a continentwide scale, (3) a means through which Havana distances itself from the Soviet Union and increases its influence in the Third World, and (4) as commitments made out of genuine principles that in turn serve Havana's real interests.[11] Havana's own initiatives were effective at a time in the 1960s when the Soviets reestablished diplomatic relations with governments hostile to Havana, granting trade and credit concessions to strongly anticommunist authoritarian regimes such as Brazil's. In addition, the Soviets' support of traditional

Communist parties, their unwillingness to challenge the United States in areas deemed vital to the latter's security, their view that Latin America was not ripe for revolution, their belief that adventurism and romanticism were incompatible with Marxist-Leninist discipline, and their cautious policy of peaceful coexistence contradicted Castroite positions. For a good part of the 1960s, Havana's foreign policy deviated substantially from the Soviets'. Havana was not the obedient, loyal client that the Soviets may have expected, nor was Castro's behavior comparable to that of the docile, unpopular communist leaders of Eastern Europe. The full impact of clientelist politics was not yet felt by Havana. Prior to 1968, Cuba was not fully integrated into the socialist bloc, Moscow's pressures were at times effectively resisted, and Cuba's status as a Soviet client had yet to be defined and formalized.[12]

THE TRICONTINENTAL AND OLAS CONFERENCES

Castroite radicalism took shape and demonstrated its potential influence among assorted movements in the mid-1960s. The Tricontinental and Organization of Latin American Solidarity (OLAS) conferences held in Havana in 1966 and 1967 brought out the essence of Castroism—action, defiance, ideological controversy and the primacy of subjectivism over long-term interests—ultimately confirming the view that "armed struggle was the primary path for revolution in Latin America to which all other forms must be subordinated."[13]

Delegates from Asia, Africa, and Latin America met in Havana in January 1966. The First Conference of Solidarity of the Peoples of Africa, Asia, and Latin America, (informally named "The Tricontinental") included official delegates from the Soviet Union, the People's Republic of China (PRC), North Korea, North Vietnam, and other countries, as well as an assortment of anti-imperialist movements of differing Marxist persuasions.[14] Havana acted as the host government, playing a key role in selecting delegates, framing the issues, organizing debate, and leading discussions. As chairman, Castro delivered the final speech.

Three issues dominated debate, namely, whether or not "armed struggle" was to be the only strategy for liberating "oppressed" peoples from imperialist domination; to what extent was the doctrine of peaceful coexistence (the Soviets' position) compatible with the irreconcilable class struggle between capitalism and socialism; and under whose direction revolutionary movements would fall, that is, under Castroite control or that of more restrained Communist parties.

To a large extent, since Havana's views differed sharply from Moscow's, legitimating the former's positions would undermine Soviet claims as a leading world revolutionary power. It would also deepen the schism in an already deeply divided world communist movement and probably tip the ideological balance in favor of Peking, then the more radical government. The PRC's delegation, for example, lambasted Soviet soft-pedaling of the ultimate need for world revolution, continuing to characterize the Soviets as "revisionists."

Orthodox Communist parties did not escape unscathed. Their advocacy of mass action and temporary coalitions with various national bourgeoisies came under attack from radicals committed to the Castroite path. Of critical significance was the fact that the "advanced socialist countries," but especially the Soviet Union, were told that they had a *duty* "to aid liberation movements and liberated countries," a duty involving more than moral or ideological support.[15]

The conference's resolutions strongly supported Havana's views on armed struggle, its insistence on confronting imperialism head on, and its disdain for the strategy of peaceful coexistence. Not surprisingly, "the arch-villain and implacable enemy of the 'peoples' of the three continents was repeatedly identified as the United States, and their virtuous and dependable ally was the socialist camp," especially the radicals within it.[16] The resolutions strengthened Havana's position among Third World radicals and liberation movements. Subsequently, the PRC and Mao himself bore Castro's wrath, but on a largely bilateral (Cuba-PRC) dispute stemming from China's failure to live up to the terms of its rice agreement with Cuba.[17] With little doubt "the Tricontinental Conference marked a new and ultra militant tack on Castro's part," establishing Havana as the center of political radicalism and ideological deviationism and Castro as a major figure in world revolutionary politics.[18] The conference also increased the fragmentation of leftist forces in Latin America and elsewhere, reducing the Soviets' ability to manipulate radical forces for their own *national* ends and discrediting the willingness of Communist parties to compromise with permanent class enemies. Castro's contention that "the duty of every revolutionary is to effect the revolution in deed, not in word" undermined the parties' claim to lead (as a vanguard) peasant or proletarian struggles, challenging their leadership record, and asserting Havana's right to assist revolutionaries the world over. Havana remains committed to episodic confrontation with the capitalist world, especially the United States. This commitment is manifested in a variety of forms, including political support, training in guerrilla methods and urban terrorism, or through conventional military expertise. The ideas expressed at the Tricontinental and OLAS conferences have been modified to take account of tactical needs and new situations "in the field," but the notion of permanent revolution lies at the core of the regime's foreign policy.

The OLAS Conference was held in Havana in August 1967 and attended by some 158 delegates from Latin American countries, international organizations, socialist countries, and even special guests. The Conference signaled to some the birth of "a new International."[19] Among the more noteworthy participants were the Chilean socialist Carlos Altamirano; Clodomiro Almeyda, Allende's future communist foreign minister; Rodney Arismendi, then secretary general of the Uruguayan Communist party; Regis Debray (now among President Mitterrand's advisors on Latin American affairs); Carlos Marighela, the Brazilian radical and former leader of the terrorist National Liberating Alliance (ALN); and the American black power advocate Stokely Carmichael. The World Council of Churches, the World Federation of Youth, the Tricontinental Committee for Support to the People of Vietnam, and other selected international organizations were also represented. As was the case during the Tricontinental, Castroites dominated debate and organization; Fidel's closing speech was pointedly titled "Waves of the Future." Not unexpectedly, "most of the delegates were ultra-leftists and guerrilla fighters," with pro-Soviet and even pro-Chinese delegates in a distinct minority, unable to exercise much influence.[20] Ché Guevara, then having extreme difficulties in Bolivia (unknown to the delegates, or to the Cuban people) attempting to carry out his dream of continental revolution, was elected president of the conference in absentia.

Among the organization's purposes were (1) to develop and promote the unity of the anti-imperialist movement in each Latin American country; (2) to support by all means within its power, the peoples of Latin America struggling against imperialism and colonialism, especially those engaged in armed struggle; and (3) to coordinate the struggle against U.S. imperialism in order to form a united strategy.[21]

Cuban delegates argued that conditions of underdevelopment prevalent in Latin America forced revolutionaries to support a single line of attack—armed struggle—with less emphasis on how national peculiarities affected local options. Havana also took the view that Latin America "lacked the basis for a peaceful transition to socialism" due to the weakness of the working class, attacking the notion that transitory alliances between anti-imperialist forces and the national bourgeoisie could topple the unholy trinity of local oligarchies, the army, and the United States. Confirming once again Castro's insistence on revolution without boundaries, his delegates declared "that they were not merely well intentioned advisers to, but active participants in the Latin American revolution," unabashedly proud of their duty to provide material and other types of assistance to kindred souls.[22]

Castro's closing speech summarized Havana's position, reasserting the inevitability of revolution in Latin America. Castro insisted that guerrilla struggles instead of accommodationist options would ultimately prove successful, ridiculing "self-evident truths" (orthodox Marxist prescriptions) as "part of bourgeois philosophy."[23] Castro acknowledged that various paths to liberation existed, but that electoral options were never to be contemplated because the ruling classes would always retain instruments of control. Directing his comments at those favoring nonviolent approaches, he stated: "Those who believe that they are going to win against the imperialists in elections are just plain naive; and those who believe that the day will come when they will take over through elections are supernaive." Violent revolution, coordinated between the rural areas and the cities, is the basic path. Incidentally, it is a strategy that some revolutionary movements in Central America adopted in the late 1970s. The ideas can be traced in no small measure to Havana's line during the 1960s, and the "electoral dilemma" is one that radical movements with little popular support often confront.

To sum up, Havana's firm anti-imperialist posture, its commitment to *la lucha armada* (armed struggle), its willingness to challenge Moscow, Peking, and the Communist parties while defying the United States, and its efforts to centralize control over various guerrilla movements multiplied its options while creating several contradictions. Legitimation of the revolution appealed to radicals, but constant criticism of the Soviets was bound to clash with Havana's increasing economic dependence on them, as well as with its need for reliable military protection. A shrewd assessment of local conditions meant encouraging revolution without overt Cuban participation, which would endanger the Revolution itself. Thus, even though the political aims of the conference went unrealized, "Castroism was institutionalized as a regional force,"[24] expanding Havana's network of influence, creating a new set of security-related problems for the United States, and nourishing Cuba's hope of becoming a global revolutionary power.

GUEVARA IN BOLIVIA: A FINAL COMMENT

The acid test of Guevara's doctrines on guerrilla warfare, and of Castro's determination to turn the "Andes into another Sierra Maestra," came in Bolivia, where Guevara, along with local recruits and Cuban fighters, had started a guerrilla *foco*. Lack of support from the mostly illiterate Indian peasants, tactical disagreements with the Bolivian Communist party, poor logistics, and the superior force of CIA-trained Bolivian Rangers led to the guerrillas' military defeat and Guevara's ignominious execution.

In April 1967, belatedly, and probably with the knowledge that Guevara's unknown whereabouts fueled pernicious speculation regarding his personal safety, the Cuban government released a document from Guevara, "from somewhere in Latin America." Described as a message to the Tricontinental, the pamphlet condemned U.S. intervention in Vietnam, ridiculed then President Johnson's Great Society programs, stated dogmatically that monopoly capitalism exploits underdeveloped continents, and praised guerrilla leaders and active fronts throughout Latin America. The "message" pointedly echoed the political line taken by delegates at the Tricontinental, adding Guevara's stature to Castro's designs.

In his statement, Guevara described how the personal motivation of guerrilla fighters sustains them during crisis. Stripping away the veil of romanticism and idealism purportedly surrounding guerrilla struggles, Guevara bore in on the crucial element:

> hatred as an element of the struggle, a relentless hatred of the enemy, impelling us over and beyond the natural limitations that man is heir to and transforming him into an effective, violent, selective and cold killing machine.

Our soldiers must be thus; a people without hatred cannot vanquish a brutal enemy.[25]

Lastly, Guevara exhorted fellow revolutionaries to sacrifice on behalf of humanity, turning their "every action into a battle cry against imperialism, and a battle hymn for the people's unity against the great enemy of mankind: The United States of America."[26] It is a message taken to heart by a generation of Latin American youths committed to a dangerous doctrine that has not lost its relevance.

CUBA AND LATIN AMERICA IN A PERIOD OF RESTRAINT

The Soviet invasion of Czechoslovakia and the subsequent relaxing of East-West tensions induced by President Nixon's inauguration and the gradual phase-out of U.S. involvement in Vietnam directly affected Havana's foreign policy. Out of economic necessity and political realism, Castro supported the overthrow of Dubcek's reformist regime on the grounds that "it was marching toward capitalism and was inexorably marching toward imperialism,"[27] a total misrepresentation which, despite its transparency, served Kremlin interests. In effect, Castro accepted the legitimacy of the Brezhnev Doctrine, which held that the Soviet Union had the right to intervene in a socialist country in order to preserve its "revolution," but he wondered if similar actions would be taken if Cuba's security was ever severely threatened.

Castro's approval of blatant Soviet aggression carried political risks. By sanctioning the Kremlin's move against a friendly socialist state ruled by a Communist party, Castro demonstrated a high degree of subservience to the Soviets, which obviously challenged the notion that Havana was a maverick committed to an independent foreign policy.[28] Castro's explanation is also seen as sending a message "to his internal opposition that he would not hesitate to take similarly brutal measures to guarantee the survival of socialism in Cuba."[29] Carla Robbins also feels that Castro's capitulation "was not nearly as complete" as many observers suggest and that he was in fact reasserting Havana's right to "intervene against the regimes of Latin America."[30]

But by 1968, Castro's opponents did not need any more signals regarding what opposition to Castroite socialism would bring. That issue had been settled in the early 1960s. In addition, even if Castro's calculated defiance of the Soviets played well on the absolutist left, his obvious retreat from this stance alienated scores of fellow radicals who despised Moscow's high-handedness and conservatism and looked to Cuba for guidance and inspiration.

Dubcek's policies in Prague were intended to whittle away at the ossified bureaucratic socialism so characteristic of Eastern European "penitentiary" societies. The fact that moderate internal reforms were perceived by Moscow as a major threat to its security left little doubt that a socialist satellite's domestic affairs *were* Moscow's business and that history and geography aside, Havana's own conduct could presumably at some point be questioned. It is unlikely that Havana was unmindful of the implications of the Czech crisis in the context of its relations with Moscow, or on potential constraints on its foreign policy that would ensue if it endorsed Moscow's behavior. In other words, Havana's endorsement was a conscious one, since events in Prague forced a painful political choice. Thus, "Castro's speech on the Czech crisis proved to be a turning point in Cuban-Soviet affairs," followed by political reconciliation, increased economic assistance, "mutual concessions and new bonds of solidarity between the two countries."[31] Subsequently, Castro moderated his proguerrilla line, moved closer to Moscow's view that "local conditions" determine the nature of political struggles, and took the Soviets' side more and more in disputes with Peking. Peking itself maintained its revolutionary line for a few more years, until President Nixon's announcement in 1971 of his proposed trip to China and then his subsequent visit to China (1972) signaled a dramatic shift in China's radical foreign policy.

In sum, as Soviet pressures increased, the politics of clientelism and conventional bargaining gradually replaced Havana's freewheeling zealousness of the 1960s. The need for Soviet economic and technical assistance superseded lingering political reservations in Havana regarding Moscow's growing influence on Cuba's domestic and foreign policies. By 1976, Soviet assistance in the form of balance of payments aid and subsidies for sugar, nickel, and petroleum totaled $8 billion. Military assistance in turn came to $2 to 3 billion more, and the "grand total," including additional millions in scientific, cultural, and educational aid, approached $11 billion.[32]

Shifting geopolitical alignments surrounding Nixon's "China initiative," the Soviets' willingness to look the other way as U.S. military escalation in Indochina forced Hanoi to the peace table, and changes in the composition of several Latin American governments elicited further responses in Havana. Moscow's desire for stable relations with Washington was picked up in Havana; the latter could not afford to aggressively challenge U.S. interests in Latin America and elsewhere without risking rebuke from Moscow. This is not to say that Cuba's foreign policy aims were quietly subordinated to the Soviets', or that the latter had veto power over Castro's initiatives. More accurately, the overall East-West climate of reducing hostilities, defining areas of mutual interest, and relying on negotiation rather than confrontation conspired against Havana's aggressive impulses. In addition, setting its house in order (see Chapter 5) following the 1970 debacle required concentrated attention by the leadership. Ideology became less central to foreign as well as domestic policymaking, and Cuba became "increasingly compromising with the socio-economic political systems of other Latin American countries," neither challenging their legitimacy nor encouraging their radical adversaries.[33]

Cuba reestablished relations with important Latin American governments in the early to middle 1970s, partially breaking out of its isolation.

To many, it appeared that Havana was now willing to maintain conventional diplomatic ties with governments in the area, prudently scaling back its overheated political rhetoric. It would quietly await the revolutionary millennium. Castro's visit to Chile in 1971 following Allende's inauguration put to rest speculation that he had assumed the role of a proper statesman (Castro openly chided the Chileans for their bourgeois civility), but during his trip he also called on Latin Americans "to fight for the union of all our countries." Subsequently, Cuba resumed diplomatic ties with the "progressive" government of General Velasco Alvarado in Peru (1972), as well as with Jamaica, Barbados, Guyana, and Trinidad and Tobago. In 1973, Cuban-Argentine relations were reestablished, leading to a partial break in the economic blockade. Argentina granted Cuba $1.2 billion to be used to purchase vehicles, railroad equipment, and shipping goods; as a result, Cuba became Argentina's main trade partner in Latin America.

Lest it appear that Cuba was simply reacting to favorable changes elsewhere, for example, the replacement of an Argentine junta by *peronistas*, it should be noted that Cuba's relations with nonradical regimes changed drastically. Keeping up a trend that brought Havana official respectability, Cuba reestablished ties with the government of Panama in 1974. Headed by General Omar Torrijos, who became one of Castro's closer supporters until Havana's intrusions in Central America in the early 1980s threatened regional stability, Panama often sympathized with Havana's anti-Yankeeism. Relations with Venezuela resumed in 1974 prior to the inauguration of Carlos Andrés Pérez as president; his predecessor, Rafael Caldera, was instrumental in improving the climate between Havana and Caracas, at one point proposing that the principle of "ideological pluralism" be institutionalized in Basin countries' relations. When Cuba and Colombia resumed diplomatic ties in March 1975, the then Colombian foreign minister Indalecio Liévano called it another step toward "dismantling the Cold War in Latin America."[34]

On the other hand, U.S.-Cuban relations, as well as Cuba's posture vis-à-vis rightist authoritarian governments, especially Brazil's, Chile's, and Uruguay's, did not change. Havana perceived these governments, which severely repressed their domestic left, to be solidly pro-Washington. The same view prevailed toward the governments of Guatemala, Honduras, El Salvador, and Nicaragua. The Cuban press repeatedly characterized these regimes, especially Somoza's, as puppets of U.S. imperialism. A sign of the hostility that prevailed between Cuba and Nicaragua became clear in 1974 when Havana allowed Sandinista guerrillas to go to Cuba following their seizure of several Nicaraguan officials, who were released after $1 million in ransom was paid.

On numerous occasions, Castro made the issue of a government's independence from Washington the sine qua non of its rapprochement with Havana. Havana distinguished between maintaining formal diplomatic ties with the United States and capitulating to the latter's wishes. Even as relations were improving with several Latin governments, Castro said in 1972 that Cuba was prepared to live "five, fifteen, or even thirty years" without relations with the United States, reaffirming the view that Havana's priorities lay in its ties to the socialist bloc, some Western European countries, and with the Third World.

Efforts to bring Cuba back into the regional system and the OAS were not successful then or now. Havana has consistently characterized the OAS as Washington's "Ministry of Colonies." In August 1970, then Cuban foreign minister Raúl Roa described the organization as "an entity in an accelerated process of corruption and impudence."[35] Despite these hostile characterizations from Havana, member states attempted at various points in the 1970s to ease restrictions on Cuba in an effort to induce it back into the fold. U.S. initiatives supporting the suspension imposed in 1964 met resistance, especially from Venezuela and Mexico, which were beginning to assert their regional influence. As already mentioned, President Caldera's view that ideological pluralism must guide the mutual relations of Latin American governments influenced regional opinion and official policy.[36] After failing in 1972 and 1974 to lift diplomatic and economic sanctions against Cuba, thus continuing with the embargo, the OAS voted to end it in 1975. Putting aside major policy differences between member states and Havana, and taking stock of the fact that Castro had toned down his rhetoric, the organization felt that Havana's behavior could be influenced more directly through the resumption of formal collective ties rather than through bilateral pressures. The United States, not willing to alienate key governments at a time when negotiations between itself and Panama were continuing over the fate of the canal, prudently supported the OAS's decision. That vote and subsequent inquiries have neither changed Havana's position nor altered its unwillingness to reenter the OAS. In fact Havana's isolation cuts several ways, allowing it to operate free of regional constraints and to adopt a posture of injured innocence when it is left out of decision making, while minimizing direct pressures from the United States.

Paradoxically, several factors account for Havana's willingness to improve bilateral relations with area governments and yet curtail its multilateral entanglements. First of all, Havana's commitment to continental revolution had failed, but that policy had generated considerable animosity toward Cuba from governments mindful of the nonintervention principle. Cutting back on support of armed groups was one way in which Havana could regain political legitimacy and be able to diversify its trade and economic relations. Given the geopolitical climate and the absence of local struggles that could be exploited, Havana could de-emphasize armed struggle without repudiating it, maintaining low-profile contacts with the regional left.[37] Second, Soviet policies aimed at strengthening détente indirectly affected Havana's options, placing constraints on its desire to challenge U.S. interests in the region and probably encouraging Havana to renew some regional commercial and economic ties. For example, Cuba was involved in the formation of the Latin American Economic System (SELA) in 1975, a regional unit excluding the United States. Here Havana saw an opportunity to circumvent the U.S. embargo.

Third, the fact that several area governments challenged the "hegemonic presumption" of the United States indicated a new assertiveness on their part, something Havana welcomed and sought to encourage on the grounds of promoting Latin American unity. The notion that a united Latin America could achieve national autonomy and foreign policy independence appeals to Havana; restoring ties to influential Latin American nations brings diplomatic leverage and strengthens contacts with respected Third World members. Fourth, Cuba's security was presumably enhanced by diplomatic normalization and renewal of economic ties. Joint moves against Cuba would be unlikely from governments that openly admitted the value of bringing it back into the fold. By the same logic, aggressive impulses by the United States could be tempered through resistance from governments fearful of activating their own violence-prone left (with which Castro had, and maintains, solid ties) or unwilling to escalate tensions with a regime whose behavior they hoped to moderate. In sum, geopolitical, practical, and even historical factors account for the thaw in relations between Havana and some of its strongest adversaries in the 1970s. It took the revolutionary outbreaks in Central America, Havana's renewed encouragement of subversion and armed violence, its proven involvement in the domestic affairs of some of its neighbors, and its willingness to capitalize on their distress to reverse the accommodationist trends.[38] As it now stands, the likelihood of Cuba's reintegration into the regional system is at best remote, and its relations with influential governments have fallen into a cyclical pattern of improvement and hostility.

CUBA AND THE UNITED STATES

Relations between Cuba and the United States from the missile crisis of 1962 to the late 1960s remained frozen in a hostile mode. Havana's support for armed revolution in Latin America, its nonacceptance of the United States as a regional hegemonist, and its post-1968 rapprochement with the Soviets lay at the core of its struggle with Washington. The Johnson administration, fearing "another Cuba," intervened in the Dominican Republic in 1965, but there is a consensus now that Havana was not the principal instigator of the aborted rebellion. More important, the record shows that U.S. intelligence services in collaboration with anti-Castro groups mounted a "secret war" against Cuba in the 1960s involving raids, infiltration, and harassment. On several occasions attempts were made to assassinate Castro.

The Johnson and Nixon administrations maintained the U.S. economic embargo, hoping to frustrate Cuba's economic development and create domestic difficulties for the regime. But Cuba used the embargo as a rallying point at home and abroad, craftily depicting itself as a victim of U.S. economic aggression. Because some European allies of the United

States did not have the same interest in isolating Cuba that Washington had, Cuba was in fact able to circumvent some of the embargo's provisions.

In mid-1970, then Assistant Secretary of Defense G. Warren Nutter restated the prevalent view that "Cuba presents a potential double threat to United States and Caribbean security—the physical threat to United States or other national territory from strategic weapons which Cuba might obtain, and Castro's support for subversion and insurgency throughout the area."[39] Shaped by geopolitical considerations as well as by a desire "to contain the revolutionary virus" and cut Castro down to size, Washington's Cuban policy was a regional version of global containment. In the final analysis, Havana was not successful in exporting revolution, but the survival of the Castro regime and a Soviet strategic asset little more than one hundred miles from the United States constituted a major setback for Washington's policies.

From the 1970s to the present, U.S.-Cuban relations have gone through a phase of relative calm and mutual restraint (1970–1974); a period of increased tensions due to Cuba's African expeditions (1975–1976); a mild rapprochement during the first two years of the Carter administration; and deepening hostilities since then marked by flaming rhetoric, periodic challenges, and mutual bilateral attacks. Relations between the two countries have been described by one author as the "Madness of the Method,"[40] due to the volatility of the issues involved, the crisis-oriented approach preferred at times by both governments, the unwillingness of each side to move beyond the partial formalization of 1977–1978, and the failure to explore the possibilities that protracted bargaining might produce. Little has happened to improve an extremely tense climate. Both governments repeatedly characterize each other in vile epithets, an unabated propaganda war partly designed for domestic purposes fuels charges of communist or CIA-sponsored "conspiracies" and obscures signals that might suggest an opening, and the absence of an acceptable regional settlement precludes improvements in the bilateral context. Altogether, continuity and hostility, rather than fundamental changes, characterize the relationship.

The relaxation of the economic embargo by the United States in 1975, permitting trade with Cuba by subsidiaries of U.S. firms and visits by several U.S. senators, scores of businessmen, academics, journalists, and others, improved the climate of opinion and the prospects for normalization. Some felt that a reassessment was in order, since "the historic U.S. preoccupation with protecting military security in Latin America no longer made sense."[41] An integral part of that reassessment would be improving relations with a Cuba then less preoccupied with extending its influence and pursuing pragmatic policies. In other words, political differences such as Cuba's treatment of political prisoners, its unrenounced belief that revolution in Latin America was necessary, the status of the base in Guantanamo, the embargo, and Cuba's military relationship with the Soviet Union should be put aside in order to find some common ground on which to move the relationship forward. Comments by U.S. Secretary of

State Henry Kissinger in March 1975 that the United States was prepared to "move in a new direction" in its policy toward Cuba were followed by Castro's observation that President Nixon's resignation and the end of U.S. involvement in Vietnam improved the prospects for conciliation.

Yet no breakthrough was ever realized by either the Ford or Carter administrations. The process of mutual accommodation abruptly halted when in late 1975 Cuban expeditionary forces were sent to Angola in order to assist the Popular Movement for the Liberation of Angola (MPLA) in its fight against rival pro-Western factions.[42] At that point, Kissinger stated that Havana's involvement on behalf of a pro-Soviet liberation movement damaged prospects of improving relations with Washington. By early 1976, there were several thousand Cuban troops as well as Soviet and East European support personnel in Angola. Due to inadequate military preparedness, logistical problems, association with South Africa, and U.S. congressional bans on assistance to them, the MPLA's rivals could not sustain their effort. Stinging from what was perceived as a strategic defeat at the hands of Havana and Moscow, President Ford in February 1976 branded Havana's conduct as that of "an international outlaw," adding that his administration would "have nothing to do with the Cuba of Fidel Castro."

Havana saw things differently. In line with the regime's ideological convictions—which had not been repudiated—Havana felt compelled to "demonstrate revolutionary solidarity." From their standpoint, the MPLA was involved in a classic struggle against colonial powers and their local allies, and so it was in Havana's interests to assist that African liberation movement. Havana's credibility was at stake. Though its involvement in Africa dated back to the early 1960s, never had its commitment been so large, with thousands of troops actually participating in combat. A military victory over the Angolan elements (the National Union for the Total Liberation of Angola—UNITA—and the National Front for the Liberation of Angola—FNLA) allied to South African "reactionaries," Western imperialism, and the now "counterrevolutionary" Chinese could bring substantial payoffs. It could also show the Soviets themselves what the Cubans were made of, teaching them a lesson in true internationalism.[43]

Havana's decision to intervene militarily in African conflicts scuttled the opportunities for reconciliation with the United States at a propitious moment and suggested that Havana prizes a political victory over Washington more than submitting itself to a stable relationship that would invariably bring some form of U.S. leverage. Such a relationship could also compromise its revolutionary image at home and abroad. Havana is not ready to sacrifice its political commitments in the Third World for Washington's sake, is not about to cut its military ties to the Soviets, and has repeatedly informed the United States that linking its presence in Africa to the resumption of bilateral negotiations is unacceptable. Lastly, in a clear example of how a foreign policy crisis can serve its domestic ends, Havana reacted strongly to the threats against Cuba articulated by

President Ford. Advising the president to "study a bit of history" and draw the correct conclusions from its lessons, Castro riposted that

> they are not the first Yankee rulers who have used, to no avail, these intimidating tactics against our homeland. Eisenhower, Kennedy, Johnson, and Nixon all tried to intimidate Cuba. All without exception underestimated the Cuban Revolution; all were mistaken. Cuba cannot be intimidated by bellicose threats.[44]

Castro's blast underscored a major principle of Havana's foreign policy: defiance of the United States. In fact, Castro is fully aware that he has been the only Cuban leader to cast off and resist U.S. hegemonic pressures. That attitude is rooted in Cuba's struggle for autonomy, in the failed efforts of prior generations to create a society able to control its destiny. In this regard, Castro and the Revolution's foreign policy are a reaffirmation of national will.

The Carter Administration

The Democratic party's 1976 platform statement that the United States "can move [to normalize relations] if Cuba abandons its provocative international actions and policies" partly shaped the early outlook of the Carter State Department. Carter's first moves were influenced by his moralism, his disdain for the Machiavellian policies of the Nixon-Ford-Kissinger period, his belief that U.S. foreign policy should not be subject to "an inordinate fear of communism," and the view of some of his advisers that the country's Cuba policy had become obsolete. For example, the administration granted visas to selected Cuban citizens for visits to the United States, lifted the ban on travel to Cuba, permitted the resumption of charter flights between the two countries, cut back U.S. reconnaissance flights over the island, and concluded a bilateral agreement on maritime boundaries and fishing rights. Cuba released several U.S. political prisoners, permitted all U.S. citizens still in Cuba to depart along with their families, and guardedly welcomed the prospects of renewed trade with the United States. Political topics were purposely avoided. The then Cuban Foreign Commerce Minister Marcelo Fernández told a conference of U.S. businessmen in October 1977 that removing the embargo would lead to some $1 billion in exports to Cuba in three to four years. More important, interests sections opened in Havana and Washington in 1977, working out of the Swiss and Czech embassies respectively. These have been maintained; they constitute the only conventional channel of communications established since 1961, when diplomatic relations were broken. That they have not been upgraded since 1977 attests to the fact that neither government places high priority on full normalization of ties, even though periodic press reports speak of a willingness to enter into a more meaningful dialogue.

U.S. domestic politics regularly intrude into the foreign-policy-making process, and relations with Cuba are subject to pressure from various constituencies. The Cuban exile community, for example, remains opposed to any sort of rapprochement with the Castro regime. Some exile leaders and the community as a whole exercise some influence in the Republican party's conservative wing, but the community is no longer monolithic. Democratic presidents in particular also realize that making a unilateral move toward Castro is politically costly. On occasion, some U.S. firms have expressed a desire to reenter the Cuban market and have lobbied Washington to move away from its hard line, but their efforts have not been successful.

In any case, Havana's involvement in Ethiopia's war with Somalia over the Ogaden in 1978 soured an otherwise promising climate. Viewing it as a joint thrust by Moscow and Havana into a strategically sensitive region in which, ironically, the Carter administration was unwilling to take a stand, the administration nevertheless singled out Cuba for much of the blame. Soviet logistical support and military equipment airlifted into Ethiopia gave it a decided advantage. Some ten to thirteen thousand Cuban troops, under the command of Soviet generals, drove Somalia from Ogaden and restored Ethiopia's territorial integrity. By mid-March 1978, the "Soviet Union and Cuba, due to their massive mobilization of war material, armored vehicles, airplanes and Cuban troops had won the day."[45] In 1979, the State Department observed that such a presence "continues to impede progress toward normalizing United States–Cuban relations," adding that Washington refuses to make gestures "until there is convincing evidence, including troop reductions, of Cuban restraint in Africa."[46] Due to political instability throughout the Horn, continuing conflicts with secessionist rebels in the Ethiopian province of Eritrea, and because of the obvious geopolitical value to Moscow of a Cuban military presence there, Havana has not pulled out its troops. In effect, as seen in Table 7.2, Cuba's presence in Africa extends beyond its Angolan and Ethiopian armies of occupation, but the extent to which it can translate a military or advisory presence into effective and lasting political influence is subject to numerous indigenous factors.[47]

A more damaging incident occurred in 1979, when a Soviet combat brigade of some twenty-six hundred men was discovered in Cuba allegedly carrying out provocative maneuvers. Subsequent accounts revealed that it had been there for quite some time (it is still there) and that it was part of the overall Soviet military presence on the island. A major foreign policy crisis erupted as a result of publicity surrounding the brigade's capabilities and its potential uses in the region.[48] President Carter declared its presence "unacceptable"; others considered it a violation of the Kennedy-Khrushchev agreement signed in 1962 during the missile crisis. Calling the brigade a "training center," Castro refuted the charges that the unit had combat capabilities and that its presence threatened either U.S. security interests or regional stability. In fact, Castro accused President Carter, for whom he had previously expressed some regard, of being "dishonest, insincere and immoral," as well as of "deceiving the American people . . . by creating an artificial problem."[49]

Manufactured or not, the crisis acquired a life of its own. The president stated in a national broadcast that "the presence of Soviet combat troops in Cuba is of serious concern to us," constituting a "challenge to our determination to give a measured and effective response to Soviet competition and to Cuban military activities around the world."[50] Arguing that the brigade "is a manifestation of Moscow's dominance of Cuba," the president ordered measures to be taken by the United States to protect its security as well as that of others in this hemisphere. Surveillance of Cuba was stepped up; a permanent Caribbean Task Force was established at Key West, Florida; there were expanded U.S. military maneuvers in the region and increased economic assistance to friendly nations. To some, that was Carter's version of "big stick diplomacy," but neither Havana nor the Soviets flinched. The crisis ended when the Soviets reportedly provided assurances that the unit would not take on offensive capabilities and that it would not pose a threat to U.S. interests. Largely the product of U.S. domestic politics, the crisis deepened antagonisms between Havana and Washington and illustrated the Carter administration's penchant for sometimes talking tough without possessing the resolve needed to produce a favorable outcome. At the time, accepting a face-saving formula during the brigade incident "obscured both an old and a new reality of U.S.-Cuban relations. We have virtually no mechanisms for influencing Cuban behavior outside our policies toward the Soviet Union," something normalization would presumably remedy.[51]

Havana's exploitation of targets of opportunity in the Caribbean Basin in the wake of the 1979 Grenadan and Nicaraguan revolutions broadened its disputes with Washington. In addition, the massive exodus from the port of Mariel via the 1980 Freedom Flotilla revealed that hundreds of thousands of the Revolution's own generation preferred to live away from socialist Cuba. At this point, Havana turned a major domestic and foreign policy disaster into a successful confrontation with Washington by forcing individuals who had gone to Cuba in order to bring back relatives to return with hundreds of bona fide undesirables. Shouts of "Freedom!" and "Viva Carter!" were amplified by the international media at Key West while the boats streamed in. But the sense of drama was subsequently forgotten in the mindless violence that racked several refugee camps. The administration was caught off guard, underestimating the numbers willing to leave Cuba. President Carter's well-intentioned "open hearts, open arms" welcome opened the door to Havana's mischief, and Castro deflected some of the political damage surrounding the question of why so many risked life and limb in order to come out. Thus Washington lost a critical opportunity to portray Cuban socialism in demonstrably shabby terms or to lastingly tarnish the reputation of an image-conscious regime whose social achievements hide its politically oppressive nature.

Mariel was clearly a watershed, a crisis whose impact is likely to last well into the 1980s. These were the children of the Revolution—blacks, young men and women professionals, even some government officials. The charge that all 125,000 refugees were "social scum" is simply ludicrous, but the regime did *purposely* send criminals, convicts, homosexuals, and assorted undesirables along with those willing to leave for traditional reasons. As is the case with earlier refugees from Cuba, the *marielitos* (the Mariel refugees) sought economic opportunity and political freedom; from their point of view the future in Cuba promised neither.

The Grenadan and Nicaraguan revolutions sharpened Washington's perceptions that political instability in the region could severely affect its political, economic, and security interests. From Washington's standpoint, Havana and even Moscow were looking to penetrate "the American lake" for obvious geopolitical gains. Some also felt that an expanded Soviet-Cuban military presence in the region tested Washington's resolve to keep foreign intruders out of its immediate security zone. Two associated but opposite trends were at work in the region, namely, Havana's calculated opportunism and Washington's ability to react to an admittedly growing challenge. For instance, the director of Cuban affairs at the State Department pointed out in April 1980 that Cuba's involvement in the Basin demonstrates a capacity "to tailor their activities to local political realities and to make allowances for national and regional differences."[52] That sophistication, supported by a strong military relationship with the Soviet Union and solid political contacts with regional revolutionary movements, demands an effective response in both military and economic assistance.

When President Carter left office, the prospects of accommodation with Havana had disappeared. In January 1981, Salvadoran guerrillas, aided and abetted by Havana, mounted a "final offensive," which due to their own and Castro's miscalculations, failed to topple the ruling junta. President Carter, upon receiving intelligence reports on the offensive detailing Havana's role in organizing the guerrillas' command structure and in training, ordered a resumption of nonlethal military aid to the junta just prior to his leaving the White House.

Havana's meddling is not the principal cause of the revolutionary outbreaks in Central America, but there is no doubt that it is involved in promoting insurgencies. Former U.S. ambassador to El Salvador Robert White said in 1981, regarding Cuba's influence in the struggle: "That Cuba is involved there's no doubt. I think they've trained somewhere between 1000 and 2000 Salvadoran revolutionaries in Cuba. And they have undoubtedly sent some arms to the Salvadoran revolutionaries."[53]

There is no question that Havana supports the armed left in El Salvador and Guatemala and is deeply involved in Nicaragua's consolidation of a Marxist-Leninist dictatorship. In the wake of its tremendous setback in Grenada, Havana is once again attempting to use its political leverage to strengthen a regional bloc opposed to direct U.S. military intervention in Central America. Castro is also on record as favoring "a political solution" for the conflicts in Central America, but without specifying its terms or conditions, magnanimously reassuring area governments that "Cuban weapons will never pose a danger to them."[54] On the other hand,

Havana's talk of peace, of its willingness to participate in honorable negotiations seeking to resolve regional conflicts rings hollow in light of its track record and of Castro's revival of the "armed struggle thesis." In his speech on 26 July 1980 Castro declared that "the Guatemalan experience, the Salvadoran experience, the Chilean experience, the Bolivian experience, what have they taught us? That there is only one path: revolution. That there is only one way: revolutionary armed struggle!"[55]

Simply put, Havana is playing for the long run in Central America, fully aware that domestic pressures constrain any U.S. administration's ability to sustain an effective interventionist policy. Havana is under few constraints; its decision-making process is totally insulated from public pressures, and the number of policymakers involved in making crucial foreign policy decisions is small. Thus, the domestic costs of an interventionist policy are marginal, and the regime can fully manage them. If Havana supports negotiations and sues for peace, it is because of its conviction that the political balance has shifted in favor of its clients, because it can procure gains at relatively low cost, and because it needs to preserve or improve its relations with Mexico, Venezuela, Colombia, Spain, and nongovernmental organizations (NGOs) like the Socialist International.

The Reagan Administration

The Reagan administration, much more so than its predecessor, has no qualms in characterizing Havana as a regional aggressor bent on destabilizing governments through propaganda, subversion, and other forms of low-intensity political warfare. In addition, the administration perceives Havana as a Soviet proxy, whose foreign policy thrusts into the region ultimately serve larger purposes. Early in its tenure, then Secretary Alexander Haig's State Department released a White Paper detailing Havana's involvement in efforts to incite regional violence, especially in El Salvador.[56] The document spelled out Havana's (1) tutelary role in uniting the Salvadoran guerrillas; (2) its assistance and advice to them; (3) its role in transferring weapons to the insurgents; and (4) its related propaganda efforts. Citing evidence of Nicaraguan collaboration in shipping weapons to the Farabundo Martí National Liberation Front (FMLN), the report concludes that "the insurgency in El Salvador has been progressively transformed into a textbook case of armed aggression by Communist powers through Cuba."

The document has been challenged by a host of critics, who have raised serious doubts about the reliability of the information that went into it and the credibility of some evidence.[57] At a minimum, it appears to have been a case of bureaucratic bungling by overzealous staffers wanting to get on the "right" side of an incoming hawkish administration. It is also clear that more than the prevention of a communist revolution is at stake and that if structural problems remain unsolved, the prospects for democracy and social justice in El Salvador are grim.

On the other hand, when Hans Jurgen Wischinski, vice-chairman of the West German Social Democratic party (SPD) visited Cuba in early

1981, Castro confirmed to him that Cuba had indeed supplied arms and war materials to the Salvadoran guerrillas. Since then, additional evidence of Havana's involvement in the Salvadoran struggle has come from broadcasts on the guerrillas' Radio Venceremos that they solicit and obtain weapons from "friendly quarters," from congressional testimony, and from several defectors' accounts.[58] In short, denials of Havana's involvement in Central America's civil wars are not plausible. Even if the extent of Havana's activities is not taken as the sole reason for the region's turmoil and instability, its policies contribute to continuing—perhaps escalating—violence.

Cuba's influence in Nicaragua is also substantial, stemming from its sizable military role and its strong political and ideological ties to the Sandinista regime. At present, Cuba has several thousand nonmilitary personnel in Nicaragua—teachers, technicians, construction workers, and medical personnel. In April 1982, Cuba and Nicaragua "signed the most extensive economic cooperative agreement so far," with Cuba pledging some $130 million in financial assistance and additional nonmilitary personnel.[59] At the end of 1983, Cuba also had two to four thousand military and security advisers in Nicaragua, alongside contingents from other Soviet-bloc countries. High-level contacts between Havana and Managua are frequent; the Castro brothers have both visited Nicaragua, and Daniel Ortega, Tomás Borge, and other Sandinista leaders have gone to Havana.

It is very much in Cuba's interest that the Sandinista regime survive, especially in the wake of the humiliating setback Cuba suffered in Grenada in 1983 and the expulsion of Cubans from Suriname. Nicaragua is Cuba's only true ally left in the region, but Castro's declaration that Cuba would not send troops if an invasion threatened the Sandinista regime is bound to have a sobering impact on the more *fidelista* commanders among the Sandinistas, those who look up to Castro and listen to his advice. Castro's actions reveal that Cuba's own security remains his utmost concern, especially if the Soviet Union goes through a prolonged succession crisis. What was once perceived as Cuba's unconditional support for Nicaragua is now in question, and it will take some doing for Havana to recover its lost regional influence. In short, the political climate in the region is hostile to Havana, its probes have been partially contained, and it is increasingly isolated.

But pressures for negotiation among the combatants in El Salvador, and among the Central American countries themselves, are strong in the United States as well as in the region itself, and many have concluded that Havana cannot be excluded from any settlement. The assumption that political conflicts can be resolved through negotiation is ingrained in U.S. political culture, forcing policymakers to accommodate demands that in the long run might prove prejudicial but that require settling due to escalating domestic pressures. Havana, regularly playing for time, is neither reckless nor infallible, but it is able to circumvent constraints that would paralyze a less confident actor. Through intrusion and intimidation, Havana's foreign policy combines boldness with tactical prudence. Havana's policies, although not risk-free and certainly vulnerable to a firmly pursued counterstrategy, will continue to have an impact on regional affairs.

NONALIGNMENT AND INTERNATIONALISM

Havana's role in the Non-Aligned Nations Movement (NAM), its commitment to proletarian internationalism, and its sustained activism in Third World affairs do not stem only from messianistic impulses, convictions, and well-thought-out political calculations. Cuba also draws on a legacy built from historical U.S. hegemony. As a developing nation besieged by "imperialist aggression," and as a society whose domestic achievements are often emulated, Havana fashions a foreign policy that is adaptable to the mainstream demands of most Third World states. Havana sustains levels of good will and political acceptability despite being aligned to and partially satellized by the Soviet Union. This is accomplished by capitalizing on contacts often dating back to the 1960s, cultivating good relations with liberation movements such as the Southwest Africa People's Organization (SWAPO) or the PLO, and by portraying itself as an unflinching enemy of "oppression, colonialism, racism, and Zionism." But Havana's claim that it belongs in the NAM because it does not belong to any military pact (even the Warsaw Pact) belies its obsequious repetition of the Soviet line at NAM meetings, especially the Algiers Summit in 1973 and the Sixth Summit in Havana in 1979.

Havana's role in the NAM expanded in the 1970s as relations with Third World countries were consolidated; Soviet views did not interfere with Havana's interests and Western countries went on the defensive. On the other hand, Havana's high-handed ideological manipulation at the Sixth Summit, Castro's insistence that developing countries are the "natural allies of the socialist bloc," his challenge to founding members of the movement like Yugoslavia and Egypt, and his provocative anti-Western tirades unnecessarily brought divisions to the surface.[60] Havana's abuse of the powers of the chairmanship at the summit, its subsequent refusal to condemn the Soviet invasion of Afghanistan (a member Muslim state), and its ineffective leadership in other matters led the NAM into a period of inertia. One year later the NAM remained "immobilized, frustrated and uncertain—its potential for concerted action undercut by deep divisions on regional and ideological issues."[61] Castro gave up the chairmanship at the summit in New Delhi in 1983. At that meeting, his remarks were not provocative or blatantly pro-Moscow as they had been in Havana, but included passionate anti-U.S. statements.[62] The loss of the chairmanship of NAM reduces Havana's ability to frame its political agendas. For some time now, a number of pro-Western (Egypt) or truly nonaligned (Yugoslavia) countries have perceived Cuba as the very antithesis of nonalignment, little more than a Trojan horse for the socialist superpower.

Havana's natural association with anti-U.S., anti-Western interests and causes is reinforced by its multifaceted presence in several Third World countries. Contingents serving abroad include military personnel, construction brigades, doctors and other health specialists, economic technicians, and teachers (see Table 7.2). Units carry out a variety of development-related tasks, from literacy campaigns in Nicaragua, to improving the health delivery and care systems in Tanzania, Guinea, and several African countries, to building roads and bridges in Ethiopia. Cuba's state-owned enterprise Unión de Empresas Constructoras Caribe (UNECA) is involved in construction projects in several Third World countries; it contracts out work to others, retaining a fee itself and thus generating valuable foreign exchange. Cuba also provides scholarships for Third World students who are brought to Cuba to study medicine, science and technology, agricultural development, engineering, and other mostly technical subjects. Political and ideological instruction is also offered, rounding out the formation of thousands who presumably are destined for future leadership positions. According to official figures, some 19,604 students were on scholarship in Cuba during 1982–1983, with an additional 5,600 scholarships available in 1983–1984, including 1,440 specifically for countries in the Caribbean Basin.[63]

Differing explanations of Havana's extensive overseas commitments involve the revolution's ideology and its nationalist fervor, legitimate political interests whose protection is important, ties to the Soviet Union that prove valuable if Havana's help is solicited, and Castro's megalomania. Michael Erisman adds that Cuba also recognizes "the developing nations' fear of Western colonialism, presenting itself as their David challenging the U.S. Goliath" in order to reaffirm its own leading role.[64] These forces converge into Havana's view of proletarian internationalism, involving more than superficial expressions of solidarity or mere political opportunism.

The relationship between proletarian internationalism and Havana's global policies was clearly defined in the foreign policy platform of the PCC's First Congress, held in 1975. "Cuba's foreign policy," states the document, "has as its starting point the subordination of Cuban positions to the international needs of the struggle for socialism and for the national liberation of the peoples." Adding that proletarian internationalism is expressed through the "cohesion and firmness of those who *in all areas of the world* [my emphasis] have espoused the banners of Marx, Engels and Lenin," the Party goes on to condemn "any attempt at weakening the unity of the communist forces in the international sphere," denouncing efforts to slander "the glorious role that the Communist Party of the Soviet Union (CPSU) has played in contemporary history."[65] Thus Havana feels duty bound to pursue foreign policy goals that do not contravene the inevitable struggle between capitalism and socialism, defining its broad national interests in line with those of the international communist movement but retaining political and military flexibility.

On occasion, fulfillment of internationalist duties often leads to confrontations with status quo powers (as in Africa) or with those not resigned to accept socialism's "inevitable" triumph (as in the eastern

Table 7.2.   Cuba's Overseas Presence

Country	Military Personnel (troops and technicians)	Economic Technicians
Africa		
Algeria	170	250
Angola[a]	20,000	6,500
Congo	950	--
Ethopia[a]	15-18,000	1,000
Guinea	280	125
Guinea-Bissau	50	--
Libya	3,000	5,000
Madagascar	--	50
Mozambique	1,000	1,000
Other (Africa)	--	760
Other		
Afghanistan	100	100
Iran	--	3,500
Iraq	2,200	--
South Yemen	800	150
Nicaragua[a]	2-4,000	4-6,000

[a]Best estimates that I have found.   In late 1982, Cuba increased its troop strength in Angola by some 10,000.   The size of its military advisory presence in Nicaragua also varies.   Some 2,000 Cubans left Nicaragua in late 1983, including military personnel, but many have returned.   Between 750 and 800 Cubans once in Grenada and 100 or so in Suriname are no longer there.

Sources: Ruth Leger Sivard, World Military and Social Expenditures, 1982 (Leesburg, Va.: World Priorities, 1983); U.S. Department of State, "Soviet and East European Aid to the Third World, 1981" (Washington, D.C.: Bureau of Intelligence and Research, 1983).

Caribbean). Havana is fully cognizant of that fact and is careful in utilizing military means in order to enforce its values or principles. It has not sent combat troops to Central America, preferring instead to leave any fighting to local forces. It certainly has not lost any respect for the power of the United States, but it welcomes a political confrontation rather than a military one. Its tone is ever-defiant and often chauvinistic, and moralistic. Accepting no ambiguities in world politics, refusing to adopt a neutral stand wherever "progressive forces" are driving for political power, and unabashedly characterizing non-Marxist forces as allies of bourgeois reaction, Castro makes Havana's position crystal clear: "There are two paths in the world: that of reaction and that of progress. A choice must be made; neutrality is impossible."[66]

Cubans taken prisoner by U.S. Marines during the invasion of Grenada in October 1983.

In summary, Havana's pursuit of vigorous internationalism, its still considerable influence among NAM radicals, its problematic but essential membership in the socialist bloc, and its ability to mount successful political and military ventures make it a not insignificant force in world politics. Perceived as Moscow's loyal client, as a resilient and defiant problem child for Washington, as an international maverick or agent provocateur, the Castro regime exults in its expanded global role. Fully conscious that military power, political will, doctrine, and strategy must be integrated in order to sustain a successful foreign policy, the regime passes off hard calculations as righteous morality, claiming to defend absolute principles and roundly convinced that history is on its side.

CONCLUSIONS

Havana's foreign policy has been characterized by a revolutionary messianism since the first years of the Revolution, tapering off in the early 1970s only to reemerge in striking fashion. Infused with ideological romanticism as well as hard-nosed realism, the regime draws on Cuba's struggles against Spain and the United States in order to fuse nationalism with Marxism-Leninism. In keeping with changes in the domestic order, from the early radical measures to more regularized processes in the 1970s and 1980s, Havana sustains an activist role legitimated with internationalist principles. In doing so, Havana is mindful of how the global correlation of forces impinges on its ability to successfully extend its influence. Perceived weaknesses on the part of its adversaries are exploited, but restraint is exercised when its intrusions threaten to (or do) elicit a convincing response.

The instruments in Havana's foreign policy arsenal include militant rhetoric, experienced leadership tested in numerous confrontations, proven military capabilities, a penchant for turning setbacks or miscalculations into manageable retreats, and a unity and singlemindedness of purpose that is able to overcome otherwise crippling limitations. Its foreign policy thrusts, especially in Africa and the Caribbean Basin, have been preceded by painstaking cultivation of forces Havana believes will someday become critical political contenders. But the regime is also prone to blunder, as the disintegration of Maurice Bishop's regime in Grenada shows.[67] By identifying with the themes of anticolonialism, antiracism, and anti-Zionism that dominate the Third World's political agenda, Havana has skillfully carved out its place among the more radical developing countries. Its African policies, for instance, appeal to black African states that see Cuba as an ethnic ally that has not discarded its rich nonwhite heritage.

On the other hand, Havana's multifaceted relationship with the socialist bloc, its economic and military dependence on the Soviet Union, its unwillingness to deviate sharply from Soviet policies, and its challenges to the United States in periods when restraint might be more productive perpetuate its unnatural isolation and client status. As long as adversaries and lukewarm friends perceive Havana as nothing more than a surrogate for Soviet imperialism, its image will be tarnished. Also, its leadership in the NAM, its attempts to win over neutrals, and its insistence on preserving anti-Western unity at all costs in the Third World will be resisted. In sum, the central Cuban foreign policy dilemma in the 1980s stems from its contradictory status as a Soviet client aspiring to ease out of that orbit in order to maximize its foreign policy effectiveness and enhance its autonomy.

NOTES

1. Jorge Domínguez wrote in 1978 that "Cuban foreign policy may, in fact, be the outstanding success of the Cuban Revolution," citing the regime's ability to survive in the face of "implacable and multifaceted U.S. opposition." With some reservations, that judgement is accepted here. See Jorge Domínguez, "Cuban Foreign Policy," *Foreign Affairs* 57, 1 (Fall 1978):83–108.

2. Ernesto Betancourt, "Exporting the Revolution to Latin America," *Revolutionary Change in Cuba*, ed. Carmelo Mesa-Lago (Pittsburgh: University of Pittsburgh Press, 1971), p. 114.

3. Two examples can be cited: Castro's defiant defense of Cuban sovereignty during the 1962 missile crisis, resisting U.S. and Soviet efforts to allow on-site inspection of missile sites, and his confrontation with President Carter during the 1980 Mariel crisis.

4. W. Raymond Duncan, "Cuba in the Caribbean and Central America: Limits to Influence," in *Colossus Challenged: The Struggle for Caribbean Influence*,

ed. H. Michael Erisman and John D. Martz (Boulder, Colo.: Westview Press, 1983), p. 88.

5. See B. E. Ayer, *The War That Never Was* (Indianapolis, Ind.: Bobbs-Merrill, 1976); Senate Select Committee to Study Governmental Operations with Respect to Intelligence Activities, *Final Report*, 94th Cong., 2d sess. (1976). See also Arthur M. Schlesinger, Jr., *Robert Kennedy and His Times* (Boston: Houghton Mifflin, 1978), Chapters 19–23.

6. Fidel Castro, "Second Declaration of Havana," February 1962, cited in *Verde Olivo* (Havana), 1 September 1968, pp. 21–30.

7. M. Michael Kline, "Castro's Challenge to Latin American Communism," in *Cuba, Castro and Revolution*, ed. Jaime Suchlicki (Coral Gables, Fla.: University of Miami Press, 1972), p. 196.

8. Donald C. Hodges, *The Legacy of Che Guevara* (London: Thames and Hudson, 1977), p. 83.

9. Cole Blasier, *The Hovering Giant* (Pittsburgh: University of Pittsburgh Press, 1976), p. 243.

10. An excellent appraisal is John D. Martz, "Doctrine and Dilemmas of the Latin American 'New Left,'" in *The Dynamics of Change in Latin American Politics*, ed. John D. Martz (Englewood Cliffs, N.J.: Prentice-Hall, 1971), pp. 179–207.

11. See Edward Gonzalez, "Relationship with the Soviet Union," in *Revolutionary Change in Cuba*, ed. Mesa-Lago, pp. 86–87.

12. For discussion, see Carla Anne Robbins, *The Cuban Threat* (New York: McGraw-Hill, 1983), pp. 150–168; and Leon Goure and Julian Weinkle, "Soviet-Cuban Relations: The Growing Integration," in *Cuba and Revolution*, ed. Suchlicki, pp. 146–157.

13. Kevin Devlin, "The Permanent Revolutionism of Fidel Castro," *Problems of Communism* 27 (January-February 1968):7.

14. Good accounts are found in D. Bruce Jackson, *Castro, the Kremlin and Communism in Latin America* (Baltimore: Johns Hopkins University Press, 1968), pp. 68–94; Andrés Suárez, *Cuba: Castroism and Communism 1959-1966* (Cambridge, Mass.: MIT Press, 1967), pp. 230–237.

15. Jackson, *Castro, the Kremlin and Communism*, p. 84.

16. Maurice Halperin, *The Taming of Fidel Castro* (Berkeley: University of California Press, 1981), p. 192.

17. See K. S. Karol, *Guerrillas in Power* (New York: Hill and Wang, 1970), pp. 304–306. At one point in the dispute, Castro called Mao "a senile idiot and invited his own compatriots not to put up with leaders who had passed the sixty mark." If his comrades take Fidel's advice, his leading role would end in 1986. Short of death or an accident, it is extremely unlikely to come to pass.

18. Kline, "Castro's Challenge to Latin American Communism," p. 129.

19. See John Gerassi's sympathetic account, "Havana: A New International Is Born," in *Latin American Radicalism*, ed. Irving L. Horowitz et al. (New York: Vintage Books 1969), pp. 532–542.

20. William E. Ratliff, *Castroism and Communism in Latin America 1959-1976* (Washington, D.C.: American Enterprise Institute, 1976), p. 201.

21. Ibid., p. 202.

22. Karol, *Guerrillas in Power*, p. 371.

23. Most of the speech is found in *Latin American Radicalism*, ed. Horowitz et al., pp. 543–579, including Castro's bitter denunciations of the "rightist" leadership of the Venezuelan Communist party.

24. Devlin, "Permanent Revolutionism of Fidel Castro," p. 7.

25. "Message to the Tricontinental: Create Two, Three . . . Many Vietnams," in John Gerassi, ed., *Venceremos! The Speeches and Writings of Ernesto Che Guevara* (New York: Macmillan, 1968), p. 422.

26. Not by coincidence, the Sandinista anthem includes similar terminology, namely, "The sons of Sandino, Don't sell themselves nor give up. Ever! We fight against the Yankee, Enemy of Humanity."

27. Speech by Fidel Castro, 23 August 1968, in Carlos A. Montaner, *Secret Report on the Cuban Revolution*, trans. Eduardo Zayas-Bazán (New Brunswick, N.J.: Transaction Books, 1981), pp. 25–28.

28. For a good appraisal, see Foy D. Kohler, "Cuba and the Soviet Problem in Latin America," in *Cuba, Castro and Revolution*, ed. Jaime Suchlicki (Coral Gables, Fla.: University of Miami Press, 1972), pp. 119–143.

29. Robbins, *Cuban Threat*, p. 171.

30. Ibid., p. 172.

31. Gonzalez, "Relationship with the Soviet Union," p. 95.

32. Cole Blasier, "COMECON in Cuban Development," in *Cuba in the World*, ed. Cole Blasier and Carmelo Mesa-Lago (Pittsburgh: University of Pittsburgh Press, 1979), pp. 225–255.

33. Carmelo Mesa-Lago, *Cuba in the 1970s*, rev. ed. (Albuquerque: University of New Mexico Press, 1978), p. 118.

34. Lester A. Sobel, ed., *Castro's Cuba in the 1970s* (New York: Facts on File, 1978), p. 86.

35. Ibid., p. 60.

36. For discussion of how this affected Caracas's regional policies, see John D. Martz, "Venezuelan Foreign Policy Toward Latin America," in *Contemporary Venezuela and Its Role in International Affairs*, ed. Robert D. Bond (New York: New York University Press, 1978), pp. 156–198. For trends and changes since then, see John D. Martz, "Ideology and Oil: Venezuela in the Circum-Caribbean," in *Colossus Challenged: The Struggle for Caribbean Influence*, ed. H. Michael Erisman and John D. Martz (Boulder, Colo: Westview Press, 1982), pp. 121–148.

37. For background, see W. Raymond Duncan, "Caribbean Leftism," *Problems of Communism* 27 (May-June 1978):33–57.

38. Cuba's renewed activism in the Basin is analyzed from various perspectives in *The New Cuban Presence in the Caribbean*, ed. Barry B. Levine (Boulder, Colo: Westview Press, 1983). See also Juan M. del Aguila, "Cuba's Foreign Policy in the Caribbean and Central America," in *Latin American Foreign Policies*, ed. Elizabeth G. Ferris and Jennie K. Lincoln (Boulder, Colo.: Westview Press, 1981), pp. 211–222.

39. U.S. Congress, House, Committee on Foreign Affairs, *Cuba and the Caribbean, Hearings Before a Subcommittee of the House Committee on Foreign Affairs*, 91st Cong., 2d sess., 1970, p. 103.

40. Enrique A. Baloyra, "The Madness of the Method: The United States and Cuba in the Seventies," in *Latin America, the United States and the Inter-American System*, ed. John D. Martz and Lars P. Schoultz (Boulder, Colo.: Westview Press, 1980), pp. 115–145.

41. Abraham F. Lowenthal and Albert Fishlow, "Latin America's Emergence," *Headline Series 243*, Foreign Policy Association (February 1979), p. 30.

42. The literature on Cuba's expeditions to and continued presence in Africa is substantial. Much of it is designed either to substantiate Havana's claims that it acts out of principled conviction or to analyze Havana's policies from neostrategic premises. See, among others, *Cuba in Africa*, ed. Carmelo Mesa-Lago and June S.

Belkin (Pittsburgh: Center for Latin American Studies, 1982); Wolf Grabendorff, "Cuba's Involvement in Africa: An Interpretation of Objectives, Reactions and Limitations," *Journal of Interamerican Studies and World Affairs* 22, 1 (February 1980):3–29.

43. See Nelson P. Valdés, "Revolutionary Solidarity in Angola," in *Cuba in the World*, ed. Blasier and Mesa-Lago, pp. 87–117.

44. Speech given in Havana in April 1976, in Michael Taber, ed., *Fidel Castro Speeches* (New York: Pathfinder Press, 1981), p. 94.

45. Nelson P. Valdés, "Cuba's Involvement in the Horn of Africa: The Ethiopian-Somali War and the Eritrean Conflict," in *Cuba in Africa*, ed. Mesa-Lago and Belkin, pp. 65–94.

46. "US-Cuban Relations," *Gist* (Washington, D.C.: Bureau of Public Affairs, Department of State, November 1979).

47. Gerald J. Bender, "Comment: Past, Present and Future Perspectives of Cuba in Africa," in *Cuba in Africa*, ed. Mesa-Lago and Belkin, pp. 149–159.

48. For an excellent analysis, focusing on how U.S. domestic politics shaped Washington's response, see Gloria Duffy, "Crisis Mangling and the Cuban Brigade," *International Security* 8, 1 (Summer 1983):67–87.

49. "Search for a Way Out," *Time*, 8 October 1979, p. 24.

50. U.S. Department of State, Bureau of Public Affairs, *President Carter, Soviet Troops in Cuba*, Current Policy No. 92, 1 October 1979.

51. Alfred Stepan, "The United States and Latin America: Vital Interests and the Instruments of Power," *Foreign Affairs, America and the World (1979)* 58, 3 (1980):686.

52. U.S. Department of State, Bureau of Public Affairs, *Cuban-Soviet Impact on the Western Hemisphere*, Current Policy No. 167, 17 April 1980.

53. Jeff Stein, "The Day of Reckoning Is Coming: An Interview with Robert E. White," in *El Salvador: Central America in the New Cold War*, ed. Marvin E. Gettleman et al. (New York: Grove Press, 1981), p. 357. Ambassador White was otherwise critical of the Reagan administration's policies in the area, especially of the conclusions drawn in the State Department's White Paper.

54. *Granma Resumen Semanal* 17, 9 (February 1982), p. 1; *Granma Resumen Semanal* 18, 4 (January 1983), p. 12, contains a statement by Foreign Minister Malmierca calling once again for a negotiated settlement. In July 1983, Castro essentially restated Havana's willingness for a settlement.

55. Taber, *Fidel Castro Speeches*, p. 326.

56. U.S. Department of State, Bureau of Public Affairs, *Communist Interference in El Salvador*, Special Report No. 80, 23 February 1981. This theme continued to be articulated by Reagan administration spokesmen, as well as the president himself in major national addresses. The administration has grudgingly come to the view that local factors and historical neglect contribute to the region's turmoil, but points out that the evidence of external involvement must be taken into account before lasting solutions are achieved. See Jeane J. Kirkpatrick, "A Communist Central America Is Sought," *Miami Herald*, 24 April 1983, 4E; U.S. Department of State, Bureau of Public Affairs, *Central America: Defending Our Vital Interests*, Current Policy No. 482, 27 April 1983; "Excerpts from the President's Speech to Long-shoremen on Central America," *New York Times*, 19 July 1983, 4Y.

57. For severe criticisms of the White Paper, see James Petras, "Blots on the White Paper: The Reinvention of the Red Menace," in *El Salvador: Central America in the New Cold War*, ed. Gettleman et al., pp. 242–253; and Robbins, *Cuban Threat*, pp. 267–276. Some scholars who tend to view the information in the White Paper

with less skepticism are Jiri Valenta, "Soviet and Cuban Responses to New Opportunities in Central America," in *Central America, International Dimensions of the Crisis*, ed. Richard E. Feinberg (New York: Holmes and Meier, 1982), pp. 127–159. See also Duncan, "Cuba in the Caribbean and Central America," pp. 92–93.

58. Cuba's strategy is assessed in "Cuba's Strategy of Unification at Work," Panel III Subcommittee Report, in *Western Hemisphere Stability—The Latin American Connection*, ed. R. Daniel McMichael and John D. Paulus (Pittsburgh: World Affairs Council of Pittsburgh, 1983), pp. 95–112.

59. William LeoGrande, "Cuba and Nicaragua: From the Somozas to the Sandinistas," in *The New Cuban Presence in the Caribbean*, ed. Barry B. Levine (Boulder, Colo.: Westview Press, 1983), p. 48.

60. See Michael Erisman, "Cuba and the Third World: The Nonaligned Nations Movement," in *The New Cuban Presence in the Caribbean*, ed. Levine, pp. 149–170.

61. John A. Graham, "The Non-Aligned Movement After the Havana Summit," *Journal of International Affairs* 34, 1 (Spring/Summer 1980):159.

62. Coverage of the summit, including the complete text of Castro's address, is found in *Granma Resumen Semanal* 18, 12 (March 1983):1–4.

63. *Granma Resumen Semanal* 18, 27 (July 1983):11.

64. Erisman, "Cuba and the Third World," p. 167.

65. *First Congress of the Communist Party of Cuba* (Moscow: Progress Publishers, 1978), pp. 242–243.

66. Taber, *Fidel Castro Speeches*, p. 55. The phrase comes from Castro's speech on 26 July 1978, commemorating the twenty-fifth anniversary of the attack on the Moncada barracks.

67. Havana's view is found in "Declaración del Partido y el Gobierno de Cuba Sobre la Intervención Imperialista en Granada," *Granma Resumen Semanal* 18, 44 (October 1983):1. Havana defends its noninterference in Grenada's internal affairs but speaks of the "gross errors of the Grenadian party and the tragic deeds which occurred due to these." Havana also says that during the crisis the Grenadian government twice sought its assistance, but that "Cuba simply could not send new troops" (*enviar refuerzos*) once U.S. naval and land forces approached the island.

Part 3
Performance and Prospects

8

The Politics of Stable Rule: Government and Institutions in the 1970s and 1980s

Upon entering its third decade, revolutionary rule assumed a distinct neo-institutional character, deviating substantially from the chaotic processes of the 1960s. Fundamental changes in government became evident, especially in the manner in which central authority was exercised, in Castro's role as the chief decision maker, in the institutional scope of the Cuban Communist party (PCC), and in the relationship between social forces and the central organs of the state. A gradual process of "building socialist legality," begun in the early 1970s, led to the creation of formal institutions charged with specific legal, political, and administrative duties.[1] Party congresses in 1975 and 1980 strengthened the PCC's hegemonic role. The party itself was viewed by Raúl Castro as "the supreme organ of our society's revolutionary vanguard," whose duty and responsibility would be to establish principles and objectives "bearing on the future course of our Revolution."[2]

Economic policies designed to make better use of the country's resources have been instituted, and the new Economic Management System seeks to reconcile the need for greater productivity and efficiency with the commitment to central planning. Lastly, ideological rigor continues to shape the cultural ethos, educational policies, and the management of intraparty affairs. "Deviationism" in either personal behavior or political attitudes is deemed detrimental to social goals; political passivity is in turn encouraged and largely obtained through controlled participation.

In this chapter, I focus on the internal political changes that occurred in the 1970s, arguing that the establishment of formal institutions enhanced the system's stability without democratizing the political process. In particular I will explain the vanguard role of the PCC and why the marginal expansion of the political elite has not effectively curbed the power of top decision makers. As is the case in other "institutionalized" communist systems, the interpenetration of party, government, and administrative organs is ensured by investing a few individuals with multiple roles.

REVOLUTION OR INSTITUTION BUILDING: OPTIONS AND CHOICES

Cuba's revolutionary leadership faced critical choices in the early 1970s. These were forced upon them by the economic debacle (see Chapter 6) of the 10-million-ton (9.07-million-metric-ton) sugar harvest, the need to transform a personal dictatorship into an institutional one, and Soviet pressures. In no small measure, decisions regarding the future pattern of revolutionary development required an early commitment to a "stable technocracy," thus reducing a penchant for experimentation. It also meant looking for new arrangements through which popular participation could be counted on without increasing the prospects that challenges to the leadership might arise. In effect, some felt that the instrumentality of participation and the design of new national institutions might overcome the flagging militancy and political inertia spawned by a serious legitimacy crisis. The system had never been closer to breakdown. On the other hand, if judgments regarding its nonviability were more frequently heard, a sense of gloom and despair did not lead to a catastrophic political paralysis.

Debate ensued along the following lines. Some felt that the unbridled spontaneity of the 1960s had been damaging, causing unnecessary economic dislocations, political uncertainties, ideological confusion, and social discontent. What was now mandatory, it was held, was rational management of available assets, a definite political course centered on viable "socialist institutions," social order, and ideological rigor. Greater efforts were required in the area of popular organizations in order to convert diffuse support into enduring communist loyalty, necessitating a redefinition of political objectives in order to enhance the socialization process. Much of the rhetoric regarding the robustness of the "people's revolutionary consciousness" became suspect, increasing the need for more formal training in "scientific and materialist" Marxism-Leninism. In order to achieve that, the populace must be given a respite from the "moralistic," zeal-filled campaigns of the past and must be shown that stability was not unwelcome.

A second view asserted that in order to legitimize claims that "the foundations of socialist legality" were being laid, the PCC needed rehabilitation, and some of its leaders needed more central roles. The party had atrophied during the late 1960s, worker participation in its ranks was poor, and total membership in 1969 was only fifty-five thousand. Well-known communists like Carlos Rafael Rodríguez and Blas Roca did not hold important policymaking positions, nor did the PCC function as the system's linchpin. There is also reason to believe that Soviet pressures influenced the revolutionary leadership's acceptance of greater authority for the PCC, even if Fidel Castro resisted that outcome.[3]

A third view held that conditions for institutionalization existed in the late 1960s and that bureaucrats and managers who had been pressing for more "rational" approaches to economic policymaking should be listened to. From this perspective, the manner in which central authority was exercised needed restructuring, and the "charismatic" tendencies restrained. In short, the need to institutionalize was evident in the late 1960s, but the types of institutions to be created had not been determined, and bureaucratic assignments not defined.[4]

If the contemplated necessary changes were to be made, the role of the charismatic maximum leader would be directly affected. Institutional rule might curb Castro's political hegemony as well as his known disdain for organizational and bureaucratic procedures. Up to that point, unconstrained by either institutional demands, popular pressures, or dissident cliques, Castro's power was nearly absolute. Any attempt to restructure lines of responsibility in order to establish where personal leadership clashed with competent policymaking was bound to affect the prime minister's dominant position.

Emerging demands for order and predictable regularity were framed in terms of improving the system's mobilizational capabilities, not in the hope of curtailing these. Efforts to increase popular participation in local affairs were deemed essential if future policies were to have strong support from the masses; discussion and consultation were now thought to be more effective than direct exhortation. On the other hand, the impact of popular participation would be diluted through mediating structures, so the net effect would not be increased accountability.

In sum, dilemmas were faced involving (1) maintenance of a proper balance between rational economic management and expanding social needs; (2) the institutional character of the socialist state, including the central role of the PCC; (3) Castro's overarching power; and (4) the scope and direction of popular participation.

THE PROCESS OF INSTITUTIONALIZATION: A BRIEF DISCUSSION

Successful revolutions invariably come to a phase during which the rapid pace of political, economic, and sociocultural change reaches its limits, giving way to more stable processes dependent on a higher degree of organizational maturity. At some point—induced by a major political crisis or perceived economic failure—societies compel leading elites to look inward and chart a new political or developmental course. For example, Brinton dates the period of War Communism in Russia, during which political and economic extremism prevailed, as the embryo of the crisis that in 1921 produced an abrupt tactical shift leading to Lenin's New Economic Policy.[5] That reversal ushered in a "Thermidorean reaction," namely, a period in which intraelite factionalism was atypically restrained while policy options were reassessed. Somewhat analogously, Lázaro Cárdenas's aggressive reformist policies in Mexico during the late 1930s created a legacy for the Mexican Revolution that subsequent administrations chose not to reverse, even though a qualitatively different political and economic model ensued after Cárdenas left office. More recently, the post-Mao leadership in China has set a new course, one that deemphasizes Mao's revolutionary spirit in favor of very pragmatic policies. The Chinese leaders' recognition that Mao's overarching powers and dramatic policy shifts stunted China's development is partly a repudiation of the view that revolutionary fervor is a major asset in nation building.

In Cuba, the exercise of authority became less arbitrary and coercive as institutionalization proceeded, but the radical legacy was retained as a political symbol and tool by the leadership. It is a pervasive element in the country's political culture. Thus, one can view the process of institutionalization as an attempt to build on the legacy of the past, enhance stable rule, and preserve the privileges of the revolutionary elite. Structuring the Cuban state in a way that guarantees the political hegemony of the Communist party is in line with the political model found in the socialist bloc, so it satisfies the Soviets and is congruent with Marxist-Leninist ideological demands.

The need to get the economy on a long-term path of growth required policies that depended on the skills of technocrats and "socialist managers," because even in a planned economy objective criteria could not be systematically disregarded. As has been noted, there was reason to believe that essential Soviet economic aid would not be forthcoming, or might be cut back, if Cuba failed to initiate more "rational" policies, that is, adopt measures that Soviet planners and advisers recommended. According to Cole Blasier, Castro was willing to "rationalize the economy largely along the lines of the Soviet model" not only because of fear of retribution, "but also because hard earned experience taught him that the new Soviet-sponsored arrangements were better suited to his regime's long term interests."[6] The new model de-emphasized moral incentives, encouraged decentralization in decision making and in the implementation of centrally planned policies, stressed output and efficiency over revolutionary militancy, valued "pragmatic assessments" of Cuba's economic prospects over "utopianism," and did not push aside consumer demands or labor's expectations.[7] For instance, in order to comply with the leadership's wishes that labor be given a greater role in economic affairs, the Confederation of Cuban Workers (CTC) ordered in October 1970 that union officials be elected, intensified its recruitment efforts, and presumably began to take greater stock of rank and file interests.

On the other hand, unions remained controlled, dependent on the state, and unable to assert independent political influence. At the Thirteenth Congress of the CTC in 1973, the unions ratified government-sponsored resolutions that confirmed labor's political role but did not recognize its right to strike or decide on critical issues affecting members; the measures assigned an essentially supportive role to labor. Since then, the unions' objectives have been to "support the revolutionary government, participate in national vigilance and defense activities, cooperate to improve managerial performance, strengthen labor discipline and fight any violations of it, and raise the political consciousness of their affiliates."[8] At the First Party Congress in 1975, Castro praised the CTC for "advancing the revolutionary consciousness of our working class," and for fostering in it a "new, collectivist attitude to work and social property." It thus appears that the regime is satisfied with labor's politically subordinate and passive role, though top policymakers, including CTC General Secretary Roberto Veiga, constantly remind the workers of their political obligations and of the need for increased productivity.

Broader changes in the structure of government, in the bureaucracy, and subsequently at local levels established clear lines of responsibility among state and administrative organs. In November 1972, seven cabinet ministers were promoted to vice-premier and charged with broad responsibilities, including the supervision of several ministries and state agencies. In effect, entire sectors would fall under these vice-premiers' authority, centralizing decision making in an executive committee composed of the Castro brothers and then President Osvaldo Dorticós. As intended, the "change improved coordination within sectors, and established the bureaucratic leadership that the Prime Minister alone had previously been unable to provide," while insulating some bureaucracies from Castro's direct intervention.[9] Prominent among the new vice-premiers were Major Ramiro Valdés (construction and related agencies); Major Guillermo García (communication, transportation); Major Pedro Miret (basic industries); and three other military men. A civilian, Carlos Rafael Rodríguez, took charge of the Foreign Ministry, signaling his reentry into the top inner circle and facilitating the ongoing integration of Cuban and Soviet foreign policies. It would be wrong to conclude that these changes moved Cuba closer to a collective leadership model or that they imposed lasting constraints on Fidel Castro's decision-making prerogatives. Rather, delegating authority to trusted associates in subordinate positions meant a more concrete designation of responsibilities at the top of the hierarchy. At the ministry level, the reorganization added to the burdens of individual ministers and heads of state agencies and institutes in that assigning clearer duties improved their chances of getting blamed (or purged) for inadequate performance.

Extensive judicial reforms were effected in 1973 that created a new court system composed of a People's Supreme Court, People's Provincial Courts, and at the local level, People's Basic Courts. Under the Law on the Organization of the Judicial System, whose draft was strongly influenced by the Communist party, the judiciary was integrated into the politico-administrative apparatus, supervised by the Council of Ministers.[10] At that point, the popular tribunals were abolished in order to streamline the judicial process, establish clear jurisdiction, and define the criteria for the selection of judges and paralegal personnel, which had been quite politicized. The judicial reforms and the creation of the super cabinet paved the way for subsequent efforts in institution building.

THE LIMITS OF CULTURAL FREEDOM: AN ILLUSTRATIVE CASE

Relations between critical intellectuals and the regime, which had fluctuated during most of the 1960s depending on the political climate, worsened in the late 1960s and reached a crisis point in 1971. In 1968, the poet Heberto Padilla and the playwright Antón Arrufat were reprimanded for writing "counterrevolutionary" literature even though an international jury had awarded each one literary prizes. Padilla's case attracted much attention. His collection *Fuera del Juego* (Out of the Game) was denounced by officials of the Writer's Union (UNEAC) but was published nonetheless. One of Padilla's poems pointed to why "The poet . . . always finding something to object to" is singled out for cultural ostracism and political censure, something that touched a raw nerve among cultural officials.

It is not hard to see why the poem(s) offended those who view poetry as nothing but an expression of the writer's political "clarity" or as a measure of his willingness to subordinate his work to ongoing social struggles. Writers who stood aside and bickered, or who raised difficult ethical or philosophical themes, were suspect. In any case, Padilla's work depicted the poet as "the summer malcontent," who

> sings the "Guantanamera" through clenched teeth.
> But no one can make him talk.
> No one can make him smile
> each time the spectacle begins.[11]

Padilla continued to work, but was the subject of attacks in several publications. In March 1971 he was arrested, some of his work was confiscated by the authorities, and he was put through interrogation and forced to admit in public that he had committed "serious transgressions" against the Revolution.[12]

Padilla's arrest and the public spectacle of his "confession" created an international incident. Latin American and European intellectuals, among them Jean-Paul Sartre, Mario Vargas Llosa, and Carlos Fuentes—who up to that point had been more or less supportive of Castro and the Revolution—condemned the incident. As a group, they saw in the Padilla affair contempt for human dignity comparable to the worst Stalinist practices; they saw no reason why Padilla's ideas suddenly posed a mortal threat to the Revolution. To them, persecution of someone for expressing certain views was morally repugnant and politically objectionable.

Castro's vituperative response came at the closing of the Congress on Culture and Education, held in April 1971. Characterizing his critics as "brazen pseudo leftists," "intellectual rats," and "agents of the CIA," Castro asserted that they would no longer be allowed to visit Cuba. According to Castro, those "who have never felt the fever of a Revolution" and who lived comfortably in capitalist societies did not have the moral strength to criticize Cuba. Cuba was in the front lines, a small island besieged by imperialist aggression. Anyone whose loyalty and solidarity were not absolute was, consciously or otherwise, giving aid and comfort to the enemy. The Revolution was putting them on notice. In such a struggle, there is no middle ground.

The congress itself, in its statement on cultural activities, rejected "the presumption of the pseudo leftist intellectual bourgeois mafia of becoming the critical consciousness of society," adding that while "charlatans will be against Cuba, the truly honest and revolutionary intellectuals will understand the correctness of our position." Because "culture, like education, is not and cannot be apolitical or impartial," the congress concluded that "the ideological formation of young writers and artists is a most important task for the Revolution. To educate them in Marxism-Leninism, to supply them with the revolution's ideas and to make them technically competent is our duty."[13]

Castro's views and the congress's statement set the cultural policy that has since prevailed, ratified at PCC congresses in 1975 and 1980. With little doubt, art, literature, cinema, and other forms of "culture" must conform to official views, largely shaped by "socialist realism" and the Party line. The regime views culture as a weapon, hence the emphasis on ideological firmness and vigilance against harmful foreign influences and various forms of capitalist "decadence."[14]

THE POLITICS OF SOCIALIST LEGALITY

A central question faced by nondemocratic systems is the extent to which genuine participation is desirable in order to sustain legitimacy derived from partial demand satisfaction. In revolutionary regimes of the charismatic type, rule through mobilized consent runs the risks either of having charismatic authority discredited or of never resolving the "participation dilemma." Before efforts to broaden participation can lead anywhere, mechanisms must be established that guarantee the political elite's control, because the elite ultimately desires to institutionalize itself.

In systems in which no viable opposition exists, or in which the prospects that anti–status quo forces would organize and forge compelling coalitions are nonexistent, defining the rules of the game freezes the political process and suspends the potentially democratic option. In such cases, the process of institution building does not lead to genuine liberalization, or to the expansion of effective participation; instead, and quite purposely, it leads to the politics of controlled participation and one-party hegemony. Control from above is exercised even as indirect participation is regularized, since the overriding political objective is to suppress potential antielite or antisystem forces. Thus, the context in which "elections" take place, for instance, is characterized neither by genuine competitiveness (a bourgeois concept) nor by a recognition that the system offers means through which genuine accountability is encouraged. Rather, the system is designed with self-perpetuation in mind, containing popular pressures that might conceivably challenge monolithic ruling institutions and their associated political elites. With this in mind, one can proceed to analyze the specific context of "socialist constitutionalism" that surfaced in Cuba in the mid-1970s, a process that foreclosed conceivable democratic options.

"Laying the foundations of socialism," or "building socialism," encompasses efforts to create governing bodies at local, regional, and national levels as well as to promulgate and adopt a socialist constitution. Beginning in 1974 under Raúl Castro's guidance, an experiment in "elected" local government began in Matanzas province, where residents elected individuals who then chose members of municipal assemblies. Once chosen, the 1,114 municipal representatives elected 150 regional delegates, who in turn elected 68 provincial representatives. The process was closely monitored by the leadership, known opponents of the regime could not be nominated, and "effective competition was sharply restricted because there was no campaign, no public discussion of issues, disputes, problems, differences or programs."[15] More than an effort to expand mass participation, this experiment in *poder popular* (popular power) was designed to improve public administration through limited decentralization and to offer residents greater involvement in local affairs.

Discussion of the draft of a new constitution began in 1975 following its approval by top government leaders. Blas Roca, then a member of the PCC's Central Committee and a former PSP secretary general with orthodox Marxist views, headed the committee that drafted the document. The draft declared that Cuba was a "socialist state of laborers, peasants and other manual and intellectual workers," with maximum power exercised through local assemblies and with the Communist party being "the superior force in the society." In the area of political and civil rights, the draft guaranteed the "freedom and inviolability of the individual," as well as freedom of speech, press, and religion, as long as these conform to "the goals of socialist society" and do not propagate "faiths or beliefs" contrary to those of the Revolution. Throughout 1975 the draft constitution was widely discussed in labor councils, local assemblies, CDR meetings, and in the media, where it received strong approval and where minor changes were suggested. Subsequently, the revised document—in effect the constitution that is still in place—received overwhelming support from those voting in secret-ballot elections held in February 1976.[16]

On the surface, the large turnout and the solid approval for the constitution vindicated the regime's strategy. The regime used the controlled media effectively, saturating the nation with messages encouraging approval of the document in a major political campaign. Noninvolvement would be seen as detracting from the event's importance and therefore potentially costly. Also, it is probable that many saw the enactment of the constitution as a milestone, not as an ordinary political rally, and felt compelled to vote. Others may genuinely have believed in its ideas.

The constitution was based largely on the Soviet Constitution of 1936; it paid homage in its preamble to past generations of Cuban patriots and recognized both the contributions of those who "spread socialist ideas and founded the first Marxist and Marxist-Leninist movements" and the leadership of Fidel Castro. The document framed the principles of state power, citizenship, and family; in addition, it defined fundamental rights, duties, and guarantees, gave the state the power to regulate the activities of religious institutions, established state ownership over the mass media, and laid out the institutional framework of national and local government. It guaranteed citizens the right to work and to receive health care and education provided by the state; it gave the state exclusive powers over foreign trade, the exploitation of domestic resources, and national economic planning. In language that remained intact from that of the draft, "the socialist state bases its activity and educates the people in the scientific materialist concept of the universe" and can punish those who on grounds of conscience or religion manifest beliefs contrary to the Revolution. No one, in other words, may exercise rights and freedoms "contrary to the existence and objectives of the socialist state, or contrary to the decision of the Cuban people to build socialism and communism" (Article 61). Finally, the constitution legitimized the PCC as the "highest leading force of the society and the state," thereby subordinating the country's institutional character to the party's guidance.

THE GOVERNMENTAL FRAMEWORK

The Council of Ministers

Cuba's highest-ranking executive and administrative organ is the Council of Ministers (CM), composed of the head of state and government, several vice-presidents, the president of the Central Planning Board, ministers, and "others that the law determines." Fidel Castro is president of the council as well as the formal head of state and government, thus holding Cuba's top executive and administrative positions. His brother Raúl is the council's first vice-president.

According to the constitution, the council is accountable to the National Assembly and has powers to "organize and conduct the political, economic, cultural, scientific, social and defense activities outlined by the Assembly." The council is empowered to conduct foreign relations and trade, maintain internal security, and draw up bills for submission to the National Assembly. Vice-presidents and members of the CM are appointed or removed by the assembly at Castro's initiative. The council has an Executive Committee whose members control and coordinate the work of ministries and other central organizations. For example, the Central Planning Agency (JUCE-PLAN) and formal ministries (education, defense, domestic trade), as well as institutes such as the Cuban Institute of Friendship with Peoples (ICAP) fall under its jurisdiction. In practice, the CM is subordinate to the Council of State, but it centralizes top bureaucratic authority in a cabinetlike structure.

Table 8.1. Composition of Cuba's National Assembly, 1981-1986

Deputy Characteristics	Number	Percent
Occupation		
Workers, technicians, administrative/service workers, professors, teachers	191	38.0
State and administrative leaders	160	32.0
Political & mass organization leaders	99	20.0
Military men & members of Ministry of Interior	38	7.0
Peasants	8	2.4
Students, retired	3	0.6
Total	499	100.0
Education		
Completed primary school or worker/peasant education	37	7.0
Secondary school, technical school, or worker/peasant secondary school	135	27.0
Preuniversity, technical institutes, or worker/peasant preuniversity	155	31.0
University	172	35.0
Total	499	100.0
Sex		
Male	386	77.3
Female	113	22.7
Total	499	100.0

Source: Granma Resumen Semanal, 10 January 1982, p. 3.
Flavio Bravo was elected president of the Assembly; Jorge
Lezcano, also a member of the PCC's Central Committee, was
elected as vice-president; José Arañaburo, a newcomer to
national politics, was elected as secretary.

The National Assembly

The National Assembly of People's Power (NA) is the only national
body invested with constituent and legislative authority. It is elected for
a five-year period (1976–1981; 1981–1986) but holds only two brief annual
sessions. During the 1976–1981 period, the assembly had 481 deputies
elected from Cuba's 169 municipal assemblies, which cover the island's
fourteen provinces. In the 1981–1986 *quinquenio* (five-year term) it has 499
deputies, roughly one for each 20,000 inhabitants. Deputies are *not* directly
elected by the people. They "serve part time, are not full-time professional
legislators and lack the autonomy that direct elections may have conferred."[17]
In addition, the composition of the assembly is quite elitist, with peasants,
workers, and women underrepresented. For the 1981–1986 period, workers
will make up 37 percent of the 499 deputies, with the rest of the membership

drawn from the military, the intelligentsia, and the socialist technocracy. Of the 499 deputies only 23 percent are women. A large proportion will be appointed as deputies (see Table 8.1).

The underrepresentation of workers and peasants and of women in general suggests that these groups have not transformed enhanced status into political influence. Altogether, these three are not as powerful as the military, the Party, or the bureaucracy. They fail to assert decisive influence, and their views are subordinated to the intelligentsia's, in whose favor lies the distribution of power within the regime. In fact, institutionalization has legitimated this structure of political cleavages.

Specifically in the case of women, the idea of sexual equality may be more accepted, but it has yet to lead to women exerting equal political influence. As the data in Table 8.1 make abundantly clear, the typical deputy is a fairly well-educated, probably white, male who is either a full-time *apparatchiki* (lower-level party bureaucrat) or other white-collar employee.

The deputies elected in 1981 were seated in December and proceeded to elect high government officials, ratify executive and administrative appointments, and choose assembly officers. Castro was elected as a deputy from Oriente province and was duly elected by the assembly as the formal head of state once again. Subsequently, the assembly approved the leadership's choices for the Council of State and the Council of Ministers.

Among its formal powers, the assembly can decide on constitutional reforms, discuss and approve (but not disapprove) the national budget as well as plans for economic and social development, declare war, approve the general outlines of foreign and domestic policy, and elect judges of Cuba's Supreme Court and its attorney general. In practice, legislative initiative is not exercised, votes are unanimous or nearly so, partisan bickering is nonexistent, debate is unpolemical, and the assembly is subordinated to the will of *higher* state and party organs. It does not in any substantive sense resemble democratic parliaments or congresses. Neither individual deputies nor the assembly as a whole is likely to contradict, challenge, or rebuff policies decided at higher levels, since the selection of deputies is tightly controlled by the Party and the concepts of separation of powers and legislative autonomy are not operative. The assembly does serve as a forum for citizens' grievances against the bureaucracy and deputies may on occasion propose slight modification to bills that will later become laws. Deputies may also render constituent services, though notions like "representing district interests" or even functional representation are hardly contemplated. As is very much the case with "parliaments" in communist countries, the National Assembly is really an ancillary institution, controlled by the Party and the political leadership. Membership confers some prestige, and is an indicator of one's political mobility, but in no way is the average deputy an influential political actor.

Deputies can and have made inquiries of ministers and may call for explanation or information about economic or nonsensitive matters. They are also constitutionally bound to "explain state policies to their electors" and "periodically render accounts to them of the result of their activities." This has in fact taken place.

In sum, the National Assembly is neither a policymaking institution nor an equal branch of government except in a meaningless, formalistic sense; it is inconceivable that the assembly would defy or overrule policies initiated and desired by the political leadership. It reacts, listens, and ratifies, offering a vacuous sense of individual participation to its members and a largely symbolic sense of representation to the masses.

The Council of State

The Council of State (CS) functions as the Executive Committee of the National Assembly between the assembly's sessions. It is modeled on the Presidium of the Supreme Soviet in the Soviet Union and is comparable though not analogous to the Permanent Commission in countries like Mexico and Venezuela. It has no counterpart in the United States. Its president is head of state and head of government; for international purposes he is the highest representative of the Cuban state.

The CS can issue decree laws on its own, exercise legislative initiative, decree general mobilization if warranted, replace ministers, and issue general instructions to the courts. Although decisions of the council are formally adopted by simple majority, its president, Fidel Castro, can assume direct control and supervise ministries and other agencies, as well as assume command of the Revolutionary Armed Forces (FAR), making him in effect commander in chief. For example, reacting to major problems in sectors of the Cuban economy, transportation, and internal security systems, Castro assumed direct control of the interior and defense ministries in late 1979, which he gave up in 1981. Since then a new team has been in place. It is probable that Castro's views prevail even when a crisis is not at hand.

The enactment of the 1976 constitution meant a functional delineation of Cuba's national executive, administrative, and legislative institutions; in addition, their powers have been specified and limited by legal parameters. The need to centralize, however, has been legitimated by the new structures; bureaucratic and administrative differentiation has not produced a dispersion of power but its very antithesis. Consequently, as the Interamerican Commission of Human Rights has found, "in practice the principal organs of the State and the Communist Party have been controlled by a small group since the very beginning of the current Cuban political process. Within this group, the role played by President Fidel Castro, who in effect and in the last instance exercises power in Cuba, stands out clearly."[18] In sum, conforming to Leninist organizational theory and incorporating proven centralizing mechanisms that draw on strains in the Latin American tradition, Cuba's process of institutionalization has in effect cloaked dictatorial one-man rule with an institutional facade in the process of constructing socialist legality (see Table 8.2).

Institutionalization has preserved Castro's political roles, legitimated the existence of monolithic political institutions, and thus established the

Table 8.2.   The Cuban Leadership: 1984

	Position			
	Party			State/Government
Name	Political Bureau	Secretariat	Central Committee	
Fidel Castro	Member	First Sec'y	Member	Head of State President (CM)[a] Commander in Chief
Raúl Castro	Member	Second Sec'y	Member	First Vice-President (CS)[b] Minister of Defense General of the Army
Juan Almeida	Member		Member	Vice-President (CS) Major of the Revolution
Guillermo García	Member		Member	Vice-President (CS) Vice-President (CM) Minister of Transportation
Ramiro Valdés	Member		Member	Vice-President (CS) Vice-President (CM) Minister of the Interior Major of the Revolution
Carlos R. Rodríguez	Member		Member	Vice-President (CS) Vice-President (CM)
Blas Roca	Member		Member	Vice-President (CS)
José R. Machado	Member		Member	Member (CS)
Pedro Miret	Member		Member	Member (CS) Vice-President (CM)
Armando Hart	Member		Member	Member (CS) Minister of Culture
Sergio del Valle	Member		Member	Member (CS) Minister of Public Health
Osmany Cienfuegos	Member		Member	Vice-President (CM) Secretary (CM)
Jorge Risquet	Member	Member	Member	
Julio Camacho	Member		Member Party Sec'y --Havana	
Joel Domenech			Member	Member (CS) Vice-President (CM) President, National Energy Commission
José R. Fernández			Member	Member (CS) Vice-President (CM) Minister of Education

Table 8.2 (cont.)

Name	Party			State/Government
	Political Bureau	Secretariat	Central Committee	
Armando Acosta	(alternate)		Member	Member (CS) CDR[c] National Coordinator
Diocles Torralba			Member	Member (CS) Vice-President (CM) Minister of Sugar Industry
Flavio Bravo			Member	Member (CS) President of National Assembly
Antonio Pérez	(alternate)	Member	Member	
Vilma Espín	(alternate)		Member	National Director, FMC Member (CS)
Miguel Cano	(alternate)		Member Party Sec'y --Holguín	
Jesús Montané	(alternate)	Member	Member Chief, Dept. of External Relations	
Roberto Veiga	(alternate)		Member	President, CTC[d]
José Ramírez	(alternate)		Member	President, ANAP[e]
Sixto Batista	(alternate)		Member	General of Division Chief, FAR[f] Political Directorate
Jaime Crombet		Member	Member Party Sec'y --Pinar del Río	
Aldo Santamaría			Member	Vice Minister, FAR Navy Chief of Staff
Senén Casas	(alternate)		Member	Member (CS) General of Division
Abelardo Colomé			Member	General of Division
Ulises Rosales			Member	General of Division Chief of General Staff

Table 8.2 (cont.)

| | Position | | | | |
| | Party | | | State/Government |
Name	Political Bureau	Secretariat	Central Committee	
Luis Domínguez			Member	Member (CS)
Isidoro Malmierca			Member	Minister of Foreign Relations
Humberto Pérez	(alternate)		Member	Vice-President (CM) President, JUCEPLAN[g]

[a]Council of Ministers
[b]Council of State
[c]Committees for Defense of the Revolution
[d]Confederation of Cuban Workers
[e]National Association of Small Farmers
[f]Revolutionary Armed Forces
[g]Central Planning Unit

Osvaldo Dorticós, a former president (1959-1976), member of the Political Bureau, and minister of justice, committed suicide in 1983. The new minister of justice is Brig. Gen. Juan Escalona. Arnaldo Milián, member of the Political Bureau, party secretary in Villa Clara, and minister of agriculture, died in 1983.

foundation of the self-perpetuating totalitarian state. As long as Castro lives, it is inconceivable that anyone else would hold any of the top positions or that he would be forced to share power or come to accept the idea of collegiality. Totalitarianism is not averse either to the cult of personality or to the all-powerful leader, as Mao's China, Stalin's Russia, and now Castro's Cuba prove. Cuba has not yet acquired that level of modernization which produces a "differentiated technocracy" presumably able to exert decisive bureaucratic influences on top policymakers. In a nutshell, Cuba has moved through the phase of institutionalization into the politics of stable totalitarianism, creating an imposing state without effectively circumscribing Castro's personal power.

The Judiciary

Cuba's People's Supreme Court is the foremost judicial unit; its decisions are final. Supreme Court justices are elected by the National Assembly, as are its president and vice-president, but the latter two have to be nominated by the head of state. Cuban courts do not constitute an independent branch of government that could check abuses of executive, legislative, or Communist party authority. That is a bourgeois conception of law and justice that is explicitly repudiated by Marxist teachings. Cuban courts are not charged with protecting individual rights and freedoms against the potential tyranny of government. Article 121 of the constitution lists among the courts' objectives "to maintain and strengthen socialist legality," "to safeguard the economic, social and political regime established in this constitution," and to increase citizens' awareness of their duty of loyalty to the homeland and the cause of socialism. Naturally, in the Cuban legal/juridical system, there is no recognition of separation of powers, and the courts are in fact subordinate to the National Assembly and the Council of State. Least of all are they immune from interference from the Communist party or the political leadership, and they do not exercise any authority or restraint on the latter.

Cuba has 169 municipal courts and 14 provincial courts exercising jurisdiction on criminal and civil matters, with the latter acting as appellate courts. Military courts also exist, as do labor councils with some quasi-judicial functions. Professional and lay judges for the municipal and provincial courts are elected by the respective assemblies following nominations from the Ministry of Justice. Popular courts functioned through the 1960s and early 1970s separate from the formal court structure. The popular courts had acquired broad but ill-defined jurisdiction over civil, political, and criminal matters, but their proceedings often degenerated into personal and political vendettas in the highly charged atmosphere of the period. Nevertheless, those tribunals imposed sentences ranging from public admonishments to incarceration, and in many of their cases the distinction—if any—between delinquency and political crimes was unclear.

PROVINCIAL AND LOCAL GOVERNMENT

In 1976, Cuba was divided into fourteen provinces from the six provinces that had existed since colonial times. The city of Havana remains as the capital, but it now constitutes a separate province with a population of 1.92 million, roughly 20 percent of Cuba's total population. Each province and municipality is governed by an Assembly of Delegates of People's Power, which are the local organs of state power. Delegates serve two-and-one-half-year terms.

Provincial and municipal assemblies act in close coordination with social and mass organizations and are charged with management of local services, as well as recreational, cultural, and educational activities. These bodies also "obey and help to enforce the general laws and regulations" from higher state organs and are led by Executive Committees elected from the membership. An interesting feature is the provision that the president of each municipal Executive Committee (169 individuals) is by right a delegate to his/her respective Provincial Assembly.

In October 1981, according to figures released by the Cuban government, 6,097,639 citizens elected 10,735 delegates (out of 22,726 nominations) to the Municipal Assemblies of People's Power. That represented 97 percent of all those registered to vote and constituted an increase of 283,872 votes since the 1979 elections. According to Cuba's National Electoral Commission,

843, or 8 percent, of the delegates elected were women; 2,429 or 23 percent were workers, both groups registering minor gains since 1979. It is clear from these figures that the number of women occupying positions of local political influence is quite small, even though they make up 49.7 percent of the total population. The figures also suggest that effective participation by women in local and mass organization affairs is limited in terms of decision-making power, since women as a group are heavily underrepresented in local positions of power.

As is the case with their participation in national institutions, as well as in the Communist party, women fail to share power proportional to their numbers at local levels. Traditional attitudes regarding male superiority in part account for this, as well as the fact that many women themselves may not feel comfortable in the political arena. Participation through mobilization is one thing; actually gaining the power to make binding decisions is something entirely different.

THE ELECTORAL SYSTEM

Elections in one-party states cannot be judged from a competitive democratic standpoint. Neither can one take seriously claims by the Cuban leadership that since 97 percent of those eligible to vote did so, Cuba's system is one of the most democratic in the world. Sociocultural pressures to vote combine with subtle and not so subtle forms of coercion to make nonvoting suspect behavior. A revolutionary, highly mobilized society frowns on apathy and political indifference, and voting is one more test of one's political commitment. This is not to suggest that large numbers of Cubans turn out to vote against their will. That may or may not be the case. The point is that the costs of noninvolvement are substantial, since voting is an indication about the "correctness" of one's political attitudes.

Second, elections in Cuba are not meant as a chance for citizens to select from competing candidates or policy alternatives. Rather, elections serve to legitimize established institutions, offering citizens the opportunity to ratify the leadership's choice of both candidates and policies. They are also meant for external consumption. Least of all are elections genuine political contests or effective means of showing one's displeasure with present policies. Finally, elections have absolutely no bearing on the selection of high government officials, because the selection of those officials is two stages removed from popular accountability and the leadership's choices are ultimately approved. All Cubans sixteen years of age and older can vote through secret ballot to elect delegates to the 169 municipal assemblies. That is the extent of their *direct* participation.

The size of the municipal assemblies varies according to population, and only "the Communist Party and the mass organizations have the right to distribute propaganda or organize electoral meetings. Therefore critics of the government cannot exchange opinions or information and do not have the right to association."[19] Communist party controls over elections are considerable, especially in the nomination process. Party monitoring and ultimate approval of nominees inhibits competition and reduces the number of non-Party contestants presented to the electorate. Regulations covering nomination and the two-tiered system of selecting national officials ensures that Party members will be elected in large numbers at all levels. For example, 92 percent of the deputies elected to the NA for the 1976–1981 period were either PCC members or candidates; according to Robert Wesson, all 499 NA deputies for the 1981–1986 period are Party members.[20] Party influence is also strong at municipal and provincial levels. Thus, "since Party directives are binding for Party members, those who sit in (local) assemblies are obligated not only to follow those directives but also to convince non-members of the correctness of the Party's position."[21] Finally, to the delight of the leadership, voter turnout was expectedly high, 95 percent in October 1976 and 97 percent in October 1981; in the latter, Matanzas, Villa Clara, and Pinar del Río provinces registered a 98 percent turnout and the City of Havana around 95 percent.

THE CUBAN COMMUNIST PARTY

The Cuban Communist Party (PCC) today occupies the central role in Cuba's government and institutions. Its position is recognized in the constitution, which describes the Party as "the organized Marxist-Leninist vanguard of the working class" and as "the highest leading force of the society and the state." The Party's goals are to guide common efforts toward the construction of socialism and progress toward a communist society. Democratic centralism is its operative decisional principle, namely ratification and approval by lower party structures of decisions made at the Party's highest level, the Political Bureau.

The PCC's first congress was announced for 1967 but never took place; it was rescheduled and then canceled in 1969 but finally held in December 1975. A second congress took place at the stipulated five-year interval in December 1980. At the 1980 Party congress, attended by seventeen hundred delegates elected throughout the nation, Castro reported on the country's economic performance of the previous five years, assessed current economic and social conditions, stressed the need for greater sacrifices, and praised the delegates for their proven militancy and commitment. In his report, Castro also outlined the economy's prospects for the next five-year period, warning that prior expectations could not be satisfied across the board, but still asserting that politically and economically, the system was sound. In his closing speech, speaking directly to incoming U.S. President Ronald Reagan, Castro also repeated his view that Cuba was willing to resist the U.S. "blockade for one hundred years," even if it meant hardship and more sacrifices.

Party membership has risen dramatically since the 1960s. In 1965, membership was 70,000, but by 1969 it had declined to 55,000, rising to

170,000 in 1973 and 202,807 in 1975. According to figures disclosed by Castro in 1981, current membership stands at about 434,000. In addition, the proportion of workers (47 percent) and women (17.5 percent) in the Party has risen, though not dramatically. Accepting Castro's figure of current membership at 434,000, that means that 4.3 percent of Cuba's total population belongs to the PCC.

As is the case with other communist parties and in keeping with the Leninist method, the principle of democratic centralism governs intra-Party affairs. Top organs and leaders decide crucial policy matters, make critical appointments, assess trends in foreign and domestic politics, and then solicit and obtain ratification and approval for their decisions from lower party organs. The PCC has in fact been enshrined as Cuba's ruling institution, and the process of institutionalization has led to an "internal strengthening of the Party" as well as the "assertion of its hegemony over Cuba's other political institutions, most especially the administrative bureaucracy."[22]

Continuity at the top characterizes the Party's ruling elite. Following the 1975 Party congress, thirteen individuals made up the Political Bureau, with the Castro brothers as first and second secretaries. After the 1980 congress, Political Bureau membership rose to sixteen, but control was retained by a small clique of Castroite loyalists, and most were duly "re-elected" (see Table 8.2).

In addition to being top Party officials, several members of the Political Bureau also occupy high positions either in the state bureaucracy, the Party Secretariat or the armed forces, illustrating the interlocking nature and overlapping membership characteristic of communist regimes. Still, in terms of power and influence, the Political Bureau is "the elite of the elite," with its members assuming role transferability due to their Party positions as well as to their integrity and personal loyalty to Fidel Castro.

The Central Committee of the PCC, besides "electing" the top Party leadership and on occasion serving as a deliberative body, has assumed some importance. It has begun to meet regularly, and its work involves intra-Party affairs, national economic matters, and budgets and reviews of foreign policy matters. Its central role "is to act as the principal forum through which the top leadership of the Party establishes and disseminates Party policy" to the lower cadres and to provincial and local Party bodies.[23] The Central Committee is organized in departments—for example, America Department, Department of Revolutionary Orientation, Department of Economy—through which the Party monitors and offers guidance in specific issue areas. Following the Second Party Congress in December 1980, total membership expanded from 112 to 148 individuals, with its members coming from the Party organization itself, the government, the military, police, and the mass organizations.[24]

The third top Party organ is the Secretariat, functioning as a second executive branch of the PCC. The Castro brothers are its first and second national secretaries, and its membership fluctuates between six and eleven members. The Secretariat has provincial and municipal branches; in addition,

Party cells exist in work centers, factories, state farms, government offices, and military units. Although information on the Secretariat's activities is extremely difficult to find and is seldom disclosed by the regime, it is reasonable to assume—based on what other communist parties' secretariats do—that it is responsible for Party organization at all levels and that it may well have enforcement capabilities, both in terms of disciplining members as well as in the area of policy guidance. Unlike the Political Bureau, the Secretariat is not a policymaking body, but it clearly serves as a mechanism through which compliance with Party decisions is monitored at administrative and functional levels.

MASS ORGANIZATIONS

Cuba is a highly mobilized and partially controlled society in which citizen participation is encouraged via speeches by the leadership, calls from state-controlled media, and new norms in the political culture. Participation in this context, however, should not be equated either with individual or group autonomy or with genuine mass spontaneity. Participation through membership in the Committees for Defense of the Revolution (CDR), the Federation of Cuban Women (FMC), labor unions, or the Communist Youth Union (UJC) means discussing local affairs, doing volunteer work, receiving "guidance" from party officials, marching in the streets against fellow citizens who choose to emigrate, attending mass rallies, and engaging in other revolutionary duties. In addition, mass political behavior is at times characterized by coerced or tacitly forced participation, since nonparticipation is costly. In the Cuban context, individual participation signals the depth of one's commitment to the new order. Social apathy and political indifference are scorned by the revolutionary ethos, which demands "full integration" and ostracizes political bystanders.

The limits of political participation are explicit. Antisocialist or dissident conduct is proscribed, and it is the regime that defines acceptable or intolerable behavior. Widespread mobilization demanded by the regime should hardly be perceived as spontaneous mass participation, nor can one take huge popular rallies and congregations as firm measures of citizens' commitment to the system. Least of all should one conclude that participation translates into effective influence. Often disguised as mobilization and encouraged by the regime in order to demonstrate national unity, participation is subject to manipulation, constituting neither an influence nor a restraint on the behavior of the political elite.

Cuba's brand of tropical communism once appeared vibrant, sure of itself, confident of the future. To some extent, institutionalization took the "feeling" out of the body politic, making political life more predictable. In addition, the tightening up of control in the area of mass culture and the arts has ended any hope that institutionalization might lead to greater personal or intellectual freedom. But in the 1980s, crisis-induced, episodic mobilization persists, and it is at such junctures that popular passions become evident.

Either a major domestic crisis such as the storming of the Peruvian embassy by ten thousand people in 1980 or a foreign policy defeat such as the one Cuba suffered in Grenada in 1983 stimulate mass behavior. At such times, militancy is revived, those who wish to leave are denounced as *escoria* (social scum), the Yankees are reviled, and the society turns inward for strength. Otherwise, revolutionary fervor appears to be tapering off, and there is a generalized awareness that the future is not very promising. One writer advances the view that "what was known as the Cuban Revolution in fact belong[s] to the past," attributing the decline in popular enthusiasm to the organizational model imposed in the 1970s and 1980s.[25] I tend to agree with that assessment.

Committees for the Defense of the Revolution

Founded in 1960, the Committees for the Defense of the Revolution are the backbone of the Revolution at the grass roots, serving different purposes and generating popular mobilization when the occasion requires it. Started as neighborhood committees designed to protect the Revolution from its internal enemies and emphasizing vigilance or outright persecution of suspected counterrevolutionaries, the CDRs gradually assumed other functions without ever giving up their original mission. In actual practice, the CDRs have organized neighborhood work campaigns, outfitted volunteer brigades, and promoted educational and cultural activities. CDR leaders have encouraged voluntarism, helped in public health campaigns, and called for unremitting revolutionary consciousness. CDR militants have also hounded "nonintegrated" individuals, denouncing and condemning all forms of parasitic and antisocial behavior, as well as collaborating with local authorities in policing neighborhoods. In 1980, according to eyewitness accounts from Mariel refugees, the CDR sponsored "repudiation meetings" designed to chastise, browbeat, and humiliate citizens who wanted to leave Cuba. Often, these meetings turned into violent and vituperative mob action.

Among the CDRs' most important functions are monthly meetings of "political-ideological education circles," during which various materials suggested by the Party leadership are studied and debated. Thus, the CDRs serve as an important agent of political socialization. Their activities are regularly monitored by the Party, and members are fully aware that their political attitudes are the subject of intense scrutiny.

Membership in the CDRs has risen dramatically since 1960 but has been stable since 1981. As seen in Table 8.3, roughly 56 percent of Cuba's total population of 9.7 million are members. Since one has to be at least fourteen years old in order to belong, CDR membership includes a much higher percentage of the adult population.

CDRs draw their members from across Cuba's transformed social structure, but their hard-core followers come disproportionately from the

Table 8.3.   Total CDR Membership, Selected Years

Year	Total Membership
1961	798,000
1966	2,237,652
1971	3,500,125
1976	4,800,000
1981	5,500,000
1983	5,500,000+

Sources: Jorge Domínguez, Cuba: Order and Revolution (Cambridge, Mass.: Belknap Press, 1978),
p. 262; Granma Weekly Review, 1 November 1981,
p. 6; 28 August 1983, p. 9.

popular sectors. According to the Party's newspaper, *Granma*, members must be in agreement with the Revolution, be ready to defend it, maintain an attitude consistent with its principles, and solicit membership in their neighborhoods or zones. The basic organizational cell is the neighborhood CDR, and the national hierarchy includes municipal, provincial, and national organs led by elected representatives.

Federation of Cuban Women

According to the 1981 census, women make up 49.7 percent of Cuba's population, numbering 4,796,783 out of a total population of 9,723,605. The role of women in Cuban society has changed during the last twenty-five years, especially for younger members of the first revolutionary generation, in keeping with the Revolution's thrust toward greater social and sexual equality. The 1976 constitution (Article 63), for example, states that "women have the same rights as men in the economic, political and social fields as well as in the family." It also asserts that in order to ensure the exercise of equal rights, taking into account the need that women work, "the state sees to it that they are given jobs in keeping with their physical makeup."

On occasion, Castro has referred to the role of women in a revolutionary society. He is not unmindful of the sexual prejudices persisting in contemporary Cuban life, rooted in deeply held values and beliefs asserting the superiority of the male. Despite fundamental changes in class and property relations, Cuba continues to be a male-dominated society. But Castro has recognized distinct feminine contributions to the building of socialism, stating that although socialist society has to eradicate sexual discrimination, special consideration needs to be paid to those who "are the natural factory where life is formed, the creators of the human being."[26] Incidentally, the highly acclaimed film *Lucía* depicts the changing role of women from colonial times to the present.

Red Sunday, observed in November, is dedicated to the memory of the October Revolution and the casualties in Grenada. Murals in Havana's docks on Red Sunday 1983 exhorted dockworkers to honor the slogan of defense production and commit themselves to load and unload all ships under any circumstances, in order to demonstrate to the imperialist "yankis" that Cuba cannot be intimidated.

Founded in 1960, the Federation of Cuban Women (FMC) is the major national organization promoting women's interests and causes. Membership is rewarded and is something of which Cuban women are proud; it demonstrates one's socialist and revolutionary commitment and brings prestige and social rewards. As is the case with other mass organizations, the FMC subordinates its members' interests to national goals, and these, objectively, are seldom seen in conflict. The FMC is thus not an independent political organization; its role is to support the regime's social policies insofar as these may have an impact on women's lives. "The FMC has been characterized as a mass organization directed from above, with women's goals pursued only when they coincide with those of the government and coming always after national goals and priorities have been set by the regime."[27]

Membership in the FMC has quintupled since 1960. As of mid-1980, roughly 80 percent of the adult female population—some 2 million women— belonged to the organization. Vilma Espín, Raúl Castro's wife, is FMC president and is also a member of the Central Committee of the PCC and the Council of State. There are no women members of the Political Bureau or the Secretariat, and relatively few in the Central Committee. Two of the best-known women of the Revolution, the legendary Celia Sánchez and Haydeé Santamaría, veterans of the guerrilla struggle, died in 1979 and 1980 respectively, the latter committing suicide.

Summing up, although the FMC is recognized in the constitution as one of the leading mass organizations, the emancipation of Cuban women has a long way to go. In the clash between revolutionary demands and individual psychological attachments, the latter often prevail. Though women make their mark in the professions, in technical fields, to some degree in athletics, in the militia, and in the society's educational and cultural life, their gains in politics are limited. Their political influence may expand, or it may stabilize at present levels.

Additionally, some women are still ambivalent regarding their political role in a revolutionary society, in terms of what is ultimately expected of them individually, as members of a family, or as a class.[28] Cultural barriers and traditional attitudes persist, even among women themselves, to the extent that the idea of full sexual equality may not be central in their value systems.

Confederation of Cuban Workers

In Marxist societies, the interests of the working class allegedly coincide with those of the state and nation. Marxist theory holds that the construction of socialism proceeds through the dictatorship of the proletariat toward the communist utopia. During the transition, the working class assumes the reins of state power, governing in its own name as well as that of peasants and the intelligentsia, looking to conclude its historical mission.

In practice, however, due to the contradictions between Marxist dialectics and Leninist political theory, it is the vanguard of the proletariat, namely the Communist party, that appropriates for itself the leadership role. As a consequence, workers' organizations such as the Confederation of Cuban Workers (CTC), to which numerous unions belong, become satellites of the ruling Party, lose much of their autonomy, cannot challenge Party policy, and do not represent the interests of workers except in the most formal terms. Given the fusion between the state, the Party, and theoretically, the proletariat, workers' organizations in Marxist societies cannot assume adversarial or independent economic and political roles. Strikes, for example, have been banned in Cuba since the early 1960s. Nothing like Poland's Solidarity has surfaced, and certainly no one like Lech Walesa.

CTC objectives are in line with the official view that workers should promote society's collective interests rather than pursue selfish, gain-oriented aims. Statutes unveiled at labor congresses and subsequently endorsed by the leadership in the early 1970s defined union objectives as (1) support of the government, (2) participation in vigilance and defense activities, (3) cooperation in order to improve managerial efficiency, (4) maintenance of labor discipline, and (5) raising workers' political consciousness.

Undoubtedly, the CTC is a captive organization. Nevertheless, workers are often consulted about proposed laws, regulations, production goals, and administrative matters affecting labor. At other times, they are asked to ratify government measures. Material incentives are now emphasized over moral ones, and workers are constantly urged by officials to increase their productivity, make greater sacrifices, improve workmanship, and heighten efficiency. Cuban labor has lost its political autonomy, but it has gained benefits in terms of health care, vacations, pension coverage, and other rewards. Wage differentials have been introduced in response to functional specialization while "advanced" workers are recognized as the most productive and others are urged to emulate them.

On the other hand, if Cuba does not suffer the chronic unemployment problems common to preindustrial developing societies, Cuban workers have little mobility. The state is the largest and practically the sole employer; there is no free labor market and one's advancement often hinges on political criteria. In addition, regimentation and strict supervision of workers by plant managers is normal; a workers' record and performance are also closely monitored through government-issued identification cards. Thus, the process of institutionalization did not change the unions' dependent character, nor did they gain positive associational rights. In fact their role is still to "cooperate with the state, the party and the enterprise manager in the improvement of production and discipline of labor . . . the new participatory powers of labor are small and essentially related to production; labor does not intervene in key decisions affecting the national economy, their own enterprise, or their own welfare."[29]

Cuban workers may be resigned to their lot, and many of them are ardent revolutionaries, but their expectations of what lies ahead are shaped by an environment in which scarcity and centralization prevail. Life is not a bowl of cherries for the average worker's family; there is always difficulty in obtaining basic items, and rationing affects the quality as well as quantity of consumer goods. Free health care, adult education programs, scholarships for their more intelligent offspring, and other social services make life bearable, but workers cannot expect quantum improvements in the quality of life. Obviously, a society that values social egalitarianism is not geared to the emergence of a moderately affluent working class. Lastly, one doubts that average workers see themselves as members of a class with a singular historical mission—the revolutionary proletariat—or that they in fact feel able to influence the regime's domestic or foreign policies.

THE MILITARY

During the 1970s, Cuba's armed forces became more professional and modern, in keeping with the institutionalization process. The duties of the military became separate from those of civil sectors, and its functions and responsibilities distinct from those of the state and the Communist party. Soldiers are no longer directly involved in production. The army has reassumed its traditional role of national defense, but its involvement in "internationalist missions" demonstrates its offensive capabilities. As is

Shoppers wait in line outside a food market in Havana's Vedado district. Cuba has rationed goods since the early days of the Revolution. Many items are unrationed but scarce, so Cubans still spend hours in lines.

common in other communist systems, however, several dozen military men sit in the Central Committee, and some occupy high government positions. For example, Senén Casas, Abelardo Colomé, and Sixto Batista occupy top political as well as military positions, underscoring the armed forces' emergence "as a major political actor within the Cuban regime."[30]

The size of Cuba's regular armed forces increased in the 1970s, as seen in Table 8.4; estimates including military reservists go as high as 600,000 men, or roughly 6 percent of the population. In 1981, in response to the perceived threat from the United States, the Militias and Territorial Troops (MTT) was created, numbering some 400,000 to 500,000 men and women.

Since the mid-1970s, Cuba has received large quantities of sophisticated military equipment from the USSR, including MiG-23 and MiG-27 fighters and Foxtrot-class submarines. The total value of arms transfers from the USSR to Cuba between 1976 and 1980 was $1.1 billion, the second highest in Latin America.[31] The Soviets have also sent technicians and advisory military personnel to Cuba, and have provided training in the USSR for Cuban military personnel and intelligence officials. A Soviet combat brigade of some 2,600 men is stationed in the island, along with some 2,000 Soviet military advisers, and 6,000–8,000 Soviet civilian advisers. Soviet naval

Table 8.4. Size of Cuban Armed Forces, Selected Years

Year	Total
1976	125,000
1977	200,000
1978	210,000
1979	375,000
1980	375,000

Source: United States Arms Control and Disarmament
Agency, World Military Expenditures and Arms Transfers
1971-1980 (Washington, D.C.: USACDA, 1983), p. 45.

task forces make periodic visits to Cuba, and long-range reconnaissance aircraft continue routine flights between the Soviet Union and Cuba. In 1981, according to U.S. State Department figures, the USSR supplied Cuba with over 66,000 tons (some 60,000 metric tons) of military equipment, their largest delivery since 1962.[32]

At the time of this writing, some 20,000 Cuban troops remain in Angola and an additional 12,000–15,000 in Ethiopia. In both cases they help maintain Marxist pro-Soviet regimes in power, and in the absence of a settlement, their presence, especially in Angola, is indispensable. In March 1984 the Cuban and Angolan governments restated their commitment to a pullout of Cuban troops if South Africa withdraws from Namibia and stops supporting UNITA rebels. But difficulties remain, which are likely to retard the achievement of a regional settlement. In total, some 50,000 Cuban troops and military advisers serve in several countries, from South Yemen to Nicaragua, supporting Marxist and revolutionary movements.

As this brief discussion points out, Cuba's military capabilities are considerable; the Cuban armed forces are superior to any in the Caribbean and Central America and are quite capable of resisting an invasion. As the African campaigns showed, Cuba's forces, with logistical assistance from its superpower patron, can help to achieve foreign policy goals in instances in which the leadership deems military power to be an essential element of its foreign policy strategy. That obviously was *not* the case in Grenada in 1983.

There is no evidence that the military, especially its top ranks, are not committed to the existing system or Castro's personal leadership. Party cells throughout the military hierarchy further ensure the leadership's political control, enabling the latter to detect any "rumbling in the ranks." Castro's skills as a professional conspirator also minimize the probability of any institutional takeover. Finally, serving in the armed forces offers pride, distinction, and rewards for many young Cubans. The leadership encourages militancy, honor, and outright bellicosity against aggressors, propagating an ethos of "study, work, and the rifle" in which military service is another manifestation of one's revolutionary, patriotic, and if necessary, "international proletarian" duties.

SUMMARY

Economic difficulties, Soviet pressures, and the need to define the proper role of the Party in government, politics, and administration forced the Cuban leadership to veer away from the experimentation and arbitrariness of the 1960s into the "stable totalitarianism" of the 1970s and 1980s. In doing so, the state has acquired the stability that formal ruling institutions offer; political order and legality are now valued above continued change. A full-fledged Marxist-Leninist regime with institutional life and explicit normative preferences governs through tacit consent, ideological uniformity, and still-effective leadership.

If the process of institutionalization has wrought a sense of political maturity, it has also dampened the society's revolutionary fervor while inducing a greater sense that a national political community is viable even under conditions of permanent austerity. But Kalman Silvert's premonition that "national community is double-edged, creating the legitimacy and consensual acceptance of authority that may produce the unaccountable totalitarian state"[33] has largely come true.

The existence of national institutions also creates opportunities for limited political mobility, especially for competent members of the first revolutionary generation whose entry into the system is not entirely dependent on direct ties, or proven loyalties, to the Castroite elite. That elite has in fact become something of a club, whose prerogatives, privileges, and episodic profligacy are encouraged by the multiple roles its members play and by their access to various consumer goods and "socialist luxuries" unavailable to most citizens. New forms of corruption are known to exist. Periodic shakeups attempt to root out those who abuse their authority, or grant political favors, but these efforts are not always successful.

Finally, the new ethos seeks to integrate communist loyalty with economic competence in order to extract maximum individual performance and firm up political attitudes. The set of rights that presumably prevent excesses against those who choose to live at the political margins, or those who opt for various forms of social or political resistance, are not effective against the monolithic state. Institutionalization, in sum, is not equivalent to constitutionalism, producing neither political liberalization nor a relaxed cultural atmosphere. Limits on personal liberties, such as governmental denials of permission for regular travel abroad, perpetuate the society's isolation. But it is extremely unlikely that the extant limits on political freedom or dissent may recede through a vigorous assertion of individual rights, since the latter have in fact, disappeared.

NOTES

1. See Edward Gonzalez, "Castro and Cuba's New Orthodoxy," *Problems of Communism* 25 (January-February 1976):1–11.

2. Opening Speech by Raúl Castro to the First Congress of the PCC, *First Congress of the Communist Party of Cuba* (Moscow: Progress Publishers, 1976), p. 5.

3. A very helpful unpublished draft on which I relied for parts of this chapter is Andrés Suárez, "La Construcción del Socialismo en Cuba: El Papel del Partido," draft for discussion at the Institute of Cuban Studies' Seminar on the Process of Institutionalization in Cuba, Caracas, Venezuela, March 1975.

4. This view and others appear in "Cuba: La Institucionalización de la Revolución," *Estudios Cubanos* 8, 1 (January 1978). For earlier discussion, see Nelson P. Valdés, "La Institucionalización," paper presented at the Institute of Cuban Studies' Seminar on the Process of Institutionalization in Cuba, Caracas, Venezuela, March 1975.

5. Crane Brinton, *The Anatomy of Revolution* (New York: Vintage Books, 1965), pp. 207–214.

6. Cole Blasier, "COMECON in Cuban Development," in *Cuba in the World*, ed. Cole Blasier and Carmelo Mesa-Lago (Pittsburgh: University of Pittsburgh Press, 1979), p. 248.

7. For an expanded discussion, see Sergio Roca, "Cuban Economic Policy in the 1970s: The Trodden Paths," in *Cuban Communism*, 4th ed., ed. Irving L. Horowitz (New Brunswick, N.J.: Transaction Books, 1981), pp. 83–117.

8. Carmelo Mesa-Lago, *Cuba in the 1970s*, rev. ed. (Albuquerque: University of New Mexico Press, 1978), p. 91.

9. Jorge I. Domínguez, *Cuba: Order and Revolution* (Cambridge, Mass.: Belknap Press, 1978), pp. 235–236.

10. Luis Salas, *Social Control and Deviance in Cuba* (New York: Praeger Publishers, 1979), p. 221.

11. The "Guantanamera" is a very popular Cuban tune from prerevolutionary times. Literally, its title refers to "the girl from Guantánamo," since 1976 the capital city of Cuba's easternmost province.

12. The incident and its consequences are discussed in Maurice Halperin, "Culture and the Revolution," in *The New Cuba: Paradoxes and Potentials*, ed. Ronald Radosh (New York: William Morrow, 1976), pp. 190–210; Carlos A. Montaner, *Secret Report on the Cuban Revolution*, trans. Eduardo Zayas-Bazán (New Brunswick, N.J.: Transaction Books, 1981), pp. 115–128; Lourdes Casal, *El caso Padilla: Literatura y revolución en Cuba* (New York: Ediciones Nueva Atlántida, 1972).

13. "Statement of the First National Congress for Education and Culture, Havana, 30 April 1971," in Montaner, *Secret Report on the Cuban Revolution*, pp. 119–125. First three quotes on p. 124; last quote on p. 122.

14. For a statement on the regime's cultural policies, see Armando Hart, "Opening Speech in the meeting of intellectuals for the sovereignty of the peoples of Our America." Havana, 4 September 1981.

15. Domínguez, *Cuba: Order and Revolution*, p. 287.

16. For a copy of the 1976 constitution, see "Constitution of the Republic of Cuba," Center for Cuban Studies, New York, 1976.

17. Domínguez, *Cuba: Order and Revolution*, p. 244.

18. *The Situation of Human Rights in Cuba, Seventh Report* (Washington, D.C.: OAS General Secretariat, 1983), p. 37.

19. Ibid., p. 34.

20. Robert Wesson, "Checklist of Communist Parties, 1982," *Problems of Communism* 32 (March-April 1983):94–102.

21. William LeoGrande, "The Communist Party of Cuba Since the First Congress," *Journal of Latin American Studies* 12, 2 (November 1980):417.

22. Ibid., p. 419.

23. Ibid., p. 409.

24. For an extended assessment of economic conditions, political changes in the hierarchy, and prospects, see Jorge I. Domínguez, "Cuba in the 1980s," *Problems of Communism* 30 (March-April 1981):48–57.

25. Maurice Halperin, *The Taming of Fidel Castro* (Berkeley: University of California Press, 1981), p. 333. For a once-hopeful view of what the 1970s and 1980s might have, but in fact failed to bring about, see C. Ian Lumsden, "The Ideology of the Revolution," in *Cuba in Revolution*, ed. Rolando E. Bonachea and Nelson P. Valdés (Garden City, N.Y.: Anchor Books, 1972), pp. 529–544.

26. Speech by Fidel Castro to the FMC, cited in Montaner, *Secret Report on the Cuban Revolution*, p. 96.

27. Max Azicri, "Women's Development Through Revolutionary Mobilization: A Study of the Federation of Cuban Women," in *Cuban Communism*, ed. Horowitz, p. 281.

28. See the interviews, interpretations, and analysis in Oscar Lewis, Ruth M. Lewis, and Susan M. Rigdon, *Four Women* (Urbana: University of Illinois Press, 1977).

29. Mesa-Lago, *Cuba in the 1970s*, p. 97.

30. Edward Gonzalez, "Institutionalization and Political Elites," in *Cuba in the World*, ed. Blasier and Mesa-Lago (Pittsburgh: University of Pittsburgh Press, 1979), p. 21.

31. Peru received $1.5 billion, $900 million of it from the Soviet Union.

32. U.S. Department of State, Bureau of Public Affairs, *Cuban Armed Forces and the Soviet Military Presence*, Special Report No. 103, August 1982.

33. Kalman H. Silvert, *Essays in Understanding Latin America* (Philadelphia: Institute for the Study of Human Issues, 1977), p. 91. The Silverts' essay is titled, "Fate, Chance, and Faith: Some Ideas Suggested by a Recent Trip to Cuba," written in 1974.

9

Dilemmas of a Revolution

Twenty-five years after the triumph of Fidel Castro's revolutionary movement, Cuba's monolithic government, its largely egalitarian social system, its centrally planned economy, and its collectivist and militant political culture are direct outcomes of systemic change. Profound changes in society, government, culture, and foreign relations have in turn reshaped individual and elite attitudes and behavior, but the process of political socialization is still to be completed. Specifically, a political order whose prerevolutionary democratic impulses were often thwarted by authoritarian forces has been replaced by a one-party totalitarian state dominated by an aging *caudillo*. Both are largely immune to pressures from below.

In contrast, though the pace and direction of political change have slowed dramatically in the postinstitutionalization period of the 1980s, the system's institutional performance, as well as the means through which it allocates its political and socioeconomic goods, is compatible with the populace's limited expectations. The compatibility of these two factors is the key to understanding the system's political and social stability. In a thoroughly politicized environment with few politically meaningful cleavages, clashes that might occur due to unresolved political disputes or still unsatisfied demands are unlikely to assume system-threatening proportions. In no small measure, egalitarian and distributive policies have blunted the edges of potential social conflicts, having in fact produced more than a minimum level of satisfaction for most human needs. Cultural affairs, laden with revolutionary themes, now reach across the social spectrum, and U.S. influences are much reduced.

The overwhelming coercive capabilities the state can bring to bear on those elements that might conceivably turn disaffection into open defiance maintain the political status quo and are an effective deterrent. For example, no credible political opposition to the regime, or to the communist system, has emerged in the past two decades, nor have Solidarity-type mass movements articulated the need for substantial internal reforms. Simply put, the system has moved through the institutionalization phase into the politics of stable totalitarianism without suffering either a major crisis at the top or destabilizing declines in its legitimacy.[1]

President Fidel Castro spoke to the Cuban people to commemorate the twenty-fifth anniversary of the Revolution and repeatedly criticized the United States. From the same balcony he addressed the nation on the night of the revolutionary victory in Santiago, as Batista fled the country from Havana.

In this final chapter, I will assess how the predictable politics of stable totalitarianism pose new dilemmas for the regime, look at what the major socioeconomic and cultural achievements have been, and evaluate the effects of sustained socialization and the system's near-term prospects. Particularly, the underlying costs of socialism are examined, namely bureaucratization, planned austerity, minimal political accountability, and economic dependence. Lastly, this chapter summarizes the major themes explored in the work in an attempt to settle these overriding questions: Has the Revolution crystallized Cuba's identity and fulfilled its sense of nationhood? Have the politics of controlled participation and mobilization increased the leverage of the few over the many, or vice versa? And have structural changes enhanced the system's viability?

CHANGE THROUGH ORDER:
THE POLITICS OF PREDICTABILITY

Cuba's domestic politics in the 1980s have acquired a markedly predictable character, due largely to the "routinization of charisma" and to the decade-long institutionalization process, which in effect set limits on domestic political change. The adoption of a constitution and the creation of new national institutions regularized the political process; defining the rights, duties, and obligations of citizens and *recognized* mass organizations set limits on individual and organizational behavior. The polity has changed from one in which authority was exercised capriciously (in the 1960s) to one in which the state is truly omnipotent but in which the legal buffers between the community and its rulers are more explicitly understood and respected. Thus, the means through which institutions govern are more likely to be seen as legitimate.

On the other hand, ruling effectively through institutional means has not led to any sort of democratization, especially at the national level, where the PCC is dominant and where the top leadership's wishes are now "legal fiats." It is also clear that abandoning the "revolution at all costs" approach of earlier periods meant a depersonalization of Castro's central role without discarding the utility of his charisma. Consequently, the regime evolved out of its personalist and autocratic character—through the period of institutionalization—into a stable totalitarianism in which the charismatic factor is present but is no longer dominant. In fact, the regime's basic character amalgamates charismatic features with the inclusiveness of monolithic rule and is likely to remain thus as long as Castro asserts his central roles. In the final analysis, basic definitional problems will not be resolved for some time, awaiting the system's passage through its first and sure-to-be formidable succession crisis. At that point, either the "Yugoslav model," in which a legendary leader, Tito, was succeeded by a plural executive with rotating leadership, the more unsettled pattern of the Brezhnev-Andropov-Chernenko transition in the Soviet Union, or perhaps even a third path may be followed. It is nonetheless a dilemma that will invariably confront the leadership.

So far, the issue of succession has hardly been broached, but there has always been speculation about what Cuba's political system will look like without Castro. This issue will be particularly crucial for Cuba, since the colorless personalities surrounding Castro in the Political Bureau (see Table 8.2) have been neither genuinely popular nor nationally acclaimed. This situation suggests that a collective arrangement will be instituted when the time comes, or even as it approaches.

In my judgment, the main political achievement of revolutionary rule is the apparent crystallization of a strong national consciousness buttressed by a history of struggle and defiance. That has in turn produced a clear sense of purpose and identity, fostering feelings of community and effective ties to the *patria* (fatherland). In other words, even if governing institutions imported from the Soviet Union shape the formal character of the state, binding loyalties to the nation constitute a core value transcending today's political arrangements. For instance, though the Soviets' support is recognized, Cubans are frequently reminded that theirs is a history rich in struggle, whose roots go back to the Ten Years' War and the Cuban War of Independence. That reinforces the idea that the nation, if need be, can take care of itself. Thus, it is plausible to argue that Cuba's unfulfilled search for political autonomy continues despite its adoption of alien political forms, in this case the one-party, centrally controlled Soviet model. It is not inconceivable that the peculiar conditions of a dependent, tropical, and Latin "sugar island" may prove to be incompatible with Soviet-style management and bureaucratization.

One of the major shortcomings found in Cuba's political development stems from its failure to create channels through which the masses can effectively restrain the political elite. A revolution carried out in order to create a system whose viability partly depended on generating feelings of attachment to a new order has ended up restricting the people's ability to make leaders sit up and take notice. The PCC is an elite institution, for instance, and mass behavior is reactive rather than spontaneous. In fact, revolutionary dynamism has given way to political lethargy, and there is reason to doubt the zeal of second-generation cohorts.

There is little question that the new political institutions process some political demands, but these do not involve important issues of domestic or foreign policy. Typically, debate in the National Assembly revolves around the performance of a minister, the quality of services provided by the state, some budgetary transactions, and routine matters of domestic legislation. For instance, during the assembly's fourth session in July 1983, it approved a special report presented by the Ministry of Public Health as well as several decree-laws issued by the Council of State between sessions of the assembly. These decrees dealt with the hereditary rights of small farmers, social security for farmers in cooperatives, rights and patents of inventors, and other matters. In the foreign policy field, the deputies approved documents appealing for peace in the region, supporting agreements of the World Parliament for Life and Peace (issued in Prague), and an agreement of solidarity with the Chilean people.[2] These are not real issues of war and peace. Questions of greater magnitude, involving Cuba's overseas expeditions, regional security, ties to the Soviets, and others, are not subject to public debate. Deliberation in these areas remains secluded within the top political and military leadership and is not open to discussion by the average deputy or the wider public. Such facts severely undermine the position of those who see Cuba as the prototypical socialist democracy, in which the public attentively debates crucial domestic and foreign policy matters. Nothing could be further from the truth. The Cuban public, largely uncritically, assents to what the leadership wants; the feeling that "father knows best" is part of the new political culture.

An additional distinction that is often obscured when the performance of revolutionary-turned-totalitarian regimes is assessed centers on the claim that unitarianism is more compatible with a mature sense of national identity than pluralism. In fact, that is the argument that generations of Latin American dictators and their intellectual supporters, for example, the Venezuelan Laureano Vallenilla, have made: that only through order can

President Fidel Castro on the twenty-fifth anniversary of the Revolution.

national viability be achieved. Revolutionaries speak a similar language, in the sense that they equate legitimate political differences among contenders with efforts to foster political disunity. That is why, for instance, the process of political socialization and the materials and symbols used to educate the populace to a new political consciousness emphasize notions of order, militancy, sacrifice, and struggle rather than individual or group interests. In Cuba's case, the institutions charged with socialization have fostered a unitary political culture, achieving remarkable congruence between the traditional symbols of nationhood and the revolutionary process itself. For instance, as frequently seen on television screens in the United States, whenever Castro launches into his marathon tirades "in front of one million people" in the Plaza of the Revolution, huge posters of Marx and Engels look out upon the crowd alongside those of Martí, Maceo, and Ché. The message in those political murals is clear: Communism, *cubanidad*, and internationalism are all parts of the same whole. This is the new trinity, revered symbolically and emulated in practice.

On the other hand, it is not clear to what extent individual attitudes have changed as a result of the broader process of transformation and how deeply those values associated with a socialist ethos have penetrated individual consciousness. Recent efforts to create parallel markets and to reinstitute material incentives in order to encourage labor's productivity suggest that the regime is less than confident that "socialist altruism" is a strong motivating force. Others have pointed out that "dissimulation," that is, "pretending to be satisfied and happy with the system" in order to stay on the good side of the authorities is one way in which individuals mask their real beliefs and attitudes.[3] Finally, the Mariel exodus of 1980, part of a much longer process of migration from the island, indicates that substantial numbers of people reject the socialist system, its supporting values, and its promises for the future. In fact, research on the political outlook of Mariel refugees suggests overt hostility to the "culture of austerity" as well as political disagreements with the communist regime itself. Political and economic dissatisfaction, in other words, continues to exist, materialist attitudes are found across the social structure, and the expectation of finding a better life outside of Cuba continues to influence migration.[4]

In contrast, the very fact that the Revolution has survived in the face of enormous domestic difficulties and external threats has had a strong unifying impact on the body politic. The struggles of these twenty-five years have fostered a sense of confidence and maturity going beyond a circumstantial survivalist ethos. One senses that there are authentic reasons that the people feel in control of the nation's destiny that have little to do with the "lifeboat syndrome," that is, that impending doom forces individuals to band together. Rather, because Castro "has been a genuine national leader, and a great many Cubans have backed him and the revolutionary government as part of a national epic in which they themselves have participated," the regime can still count on a reservoir of unspent energies.[5]

To recapitulate, the domestic political achievements of the revolutionary regime are the following: (1) the creation of a national state whose legitimacy stems from Marxist-Leninist principles and popular consent; (2) the establishment of ruling institutions that offer indirect representation as well as forum(s) for the expression of nonsystemic grievances; (3) a collectivist political culture that gives meaning to individuals' behavior in terms of greater social good; and (4) a generalized popular consciousness of nationhood cognizant that Cuba's evolution is part of an unfinished struggle for autonomy. Supporting these achievements, an ethos of militant defiance and a national disposition toward unity are frequently expressed chauvinistically, but they are also congruent with more traditional Latin-Iberian authoritarian inclinations. If strengthened, these macrocultural traits could constitute barriers against real and alleged fears of "capitalist contamination" and/or political decay.

SOCIALISM AND ITS CONTINUING COSTS

Consciously or by design, if socialism has brought about cultural integration, national unity, social egalitarianism, and stable totalitarianism, it logically follows that other forms of social and political organization have been rejected. In fact, Cuba represents a good case in which the choice of modernization through socialism imposes what Peter Berger has called a high "calculus of pain," involving sacrifices today in order that future generations may benefit. That, incidentially, has been a constant theme for the present generation, but its sacrifices are not about to end. In addition, one must note that "sooner or later, avowedly or covertly, all policy considerations involve choices between values, and all policy decisions are value-charged."[6] This is particularly true when change has been directed from above, when the objective—(reaching communism)—has been explicitly defined, and when the populace has constantly been told by its leaders that enduring sacrifices is essential for the sake of a better future.

It is the judgment here that the disappearance of political freedoms and associated civil rights represent the highest cost borne by the revolutionary generation, a cost that will continue to be imposed as long as the political model of stable totalitarianism is maintained. To put it differently, the regime explicitly sacrificed freedom in order to improve equality, seeking order over political pluralism, statization over a mixed economy, and ideological secularization rather than openness and diversity. After a generation, there is substantial evidence that the original choices have produced political inertia and permanent austerity, so that the argument that the present *has* to be sacrificed in order *perhaps* to save the future has lost its credibility. Even if its more noteworthy social, cultural, and economic achievements are impressive by, say, conventional Third World standards, the failure to promote authentic democratic practices that challenge the prerogatives of the ruling elite and afford protections against the monolithic state stands out as a major flaw. In any assessment, therefore, one must consider that "it is in the choosing that enduring societies preserve or destroy those values that suffering and necessity expose. In this way societies are defined, for it is by the values that are foregone no less than by those that are preserved at tremendous cost that we know a society's character."[7]

One should not frivolously downgrade the efforts of a generation. Clearly the choices were—and continue to be—painful, but one should not defer critical judgment because some progress has been made. Intellectual honesty is likewise demanded, since judging the Cuban case is for many an emotional experience with lasting cathartic effects. One tends to agree with Horowitz in that "the greatest dilemma in Cuban studies has been the near total conviction that truth is a function of ideology," but that what is needed is "found neither in mindless criticism nor pious celebration."[8]

As is by now well established, Cuba's indexes of life expectancy (seventy-three years), literacy (96+ percent), and infant mortality (17 per 1,000 live births) are among the highest in Latin America, comparing favorably with those of more advanced countries.[9] Aspects of its educational system are also impressive, and Cuba is moving aggressively to train more and more young men and women for careers in science, technology, health services, and medicine. Unquestionably, opportunities have expanded, and individuals from the popular classes—among them blacks and women—benefit from ongoing educational programs. Cultural life has also been popularized. Cuba now can boast a creditable theater and cinema as well as internationally renowned athletic and sports programs. Winning performances in international competition are considered political assets for the regime. Medals in the Olympics or in the Pan American Games enhance Cuba's reputation. If the victory is at the expense of the United States, it is a cause for national jubilation. Soviet and Eastern European techniques and methods are used in training athletes, and as is the case elsewhere in the communist world, athletes are a privileged group. For example, Teófilo Stevenson (boxer) and Alberto Juantorena (runner) are both Olympic gold medalists and genuine national sports heroes. But Cuba's athletic programs are not trouble free. Two of its weight lifters were expelled from the Ninth Pan American Games in Caracas in 1983 due to their use of anabolic steroids. Of course, athletes from the United States, Canada, and other countries were also guilty of similar violations. Altogether, these advances leave little doubt that judged exclusively on the material quality of life, the system meets the basic physical needs of its citizens. If by the standards of the affluent middle sectors of the area "most Cubans are not well off, in comparison with the majority of Latin America, they are doing quite well indeed."[10]

On the other hand, though in some aggregates the performance is impressive, new difficulties have appeared and some older problems remain unsolved. For instance, Sergio Roca argues that "Cuba seems unable to generate substantial and permanent improvement in the quality of consumer goods, and in the delivery of public services," something which has already produced a critical backlash.[11] Roca also points to poor conditions in the administrative and qualitative aspects of national education, losses in productivity due to inadequate inputs in industry and elsewhere, inadequate living conditions in parts of the rural areas, a severe housing shortage, and low motivation by some workers. It is also a fact that scarcity rather than abundance prevails in the planned economy, that rationing is still in effect and is severe, that moderate materialist expectations exist without being satisfied, and that life is subject to daily hardships. Life for the average Cuban, though improved, is far from comfortable. Lastly, recent evidence suggests that demographic trends in general and fertility levels in particular have "been influenced [downward] to a great extent by the poor performance of the Cuban economy," which continues to have a sobering effect on individuals' and families' expectations.[12] It is thus probable that maintaining the levels of social and economic satisfaction achieved during the last decade or so will be difficult, and it is not inconceivable that living standards may decline. In some areas the quality of goods and services is not going to improve dramatically, and availability itself may be restricted or reduced. In short, whether gains can be sustained remains an open question.

Table 9.1.   Cuba's Production and Exports of Sugar,
Selected Years (thousands of tons)

Year	Production	Exports
1978	7.66	7.28
1979	7.88	7.26
1980	6.80	6.19
1981	8.03	7.03
1982	8.20	

Sources: "Cuba: Evolución reciente de su economía,"
Comercio Exterior 32, 1 (January 1982):25-35;
Lawrence Theriot, "Cuba Faces the Economic Reali-
ties of the 1980s," in Joint Economic Committee
Print, East-West Trade: The Prospects to 1985
(Washington, D.C.: U.S. Government Printing Office,
1982).

Continuing difficulties in the domestic economy stem partly from
Cuba's dependent status. Originally, socialist planners expected that dependency would be substantially reduced, if not altogether ended, by
shifting Cuba's economic ties from the capitalist world to the socialist bloc.
Many also felt that the stranglehold to which the United States subjected
Cuba's economy needed to be broken in order to establish genuine economic
sovereignty. To those, capitalism meant dependence.

It is now recognized and accepted that developmental socialism has
brought a new structure of dependency to Cuba, which is still anchored
on production and export of sugar for a major overseas market. Sugar
exports bring in 85 percent of the country's foreign exchange; agreements
signed between Cuba and countries belonging to the Council of Mutual
Economic Assistance (CMEA) in 1981 make the island the socialist bloc's
main sugar supplier. This is part of a longer process of Cuba's economic
integration into the CMEA dating back to 1972.

The critical importance of sugar is evident in Table 9.1. Some two-
thirds of all sugar exports from Cuba go to the Soviet bloc, indicating
that Cuba has failed to diversify its export structure and has not been
able to sell large amounts of sugar to nonsocialist markets. To some extent,
the fixed prices for Cuban sugar paid by the USSR compensate for low
prices in the world market, where Cuba often sells. For example, between
1975 and 1979, the Soviets paid Cuba between $0.305 and $0.44 per
pound, well above world market prices, which by 1979 had plummeted
to $0.09 per pound. This in effect is a subsidy to Cuba from its largest
trading partner, but it is insufficient to alleviate Cuba's chronic balance of
payments problems.

As a matter of fact, Cuba's balance of payments picture continues to
show large deficits; the value of Cuba's imports—foodstuffs, oil, machinery,

agricultural equipment, and various raw materials—exceeds the value of Cuba's exports of sugar, nickel, frozen fish, and citrus fruit. Cuba ran a negative trade deficit between 1970 and 1973 and between 1975 and 1980; its only surplus (11 million pesos) came in 1974 and was due largely to favorable trade with capitalist countries. In 1980 alone, Cuba's trade deficit totaled 542 million pesos, the second largest for the entire decade.[13]

Cuba's bilateral trade with the Soviet Union deteriorated markedly in 1979 and 1980, following a series of favorable surpluses. In those two years, Cuba ran a deficit of nearly 730 million pesos, but in 1980 it was able to obtain a surplus of 182 million pesos from its trade with capitalist countries. In 1981, Cuba's major capitalist trading partners—Canada, Mexico, France, Japan, and Spain—accounted for only 20 percent of the country's imports, showing not only how small is the degree of flexibility in Cuba's external trade relations, but also the limitations imposed by the lack of hard currency.[14]

It is also true that the maintenance of the U.S. embargo continues to have an economic impact, though the Cuban economy has had time to readjust. More than a matter of commerce, the embargo is a bilateral political issue. It is unlikely to be lifted by Washington until a process of normalization is evident or Havana makes some major foreign policy concessions. Castro frequently boasts that Cuba is prepared to endure economic sacrifices for the foreseeable future if the lifting of the embargo means that Cuba will be asked to compromise "vital principles." The impasse illustrates how the tools of foreign economic policy are often utilized by strong actors in order to force changes in the behavior of smaller states. In this case, however, the embargo has not precluded Cuba from aggressively pursuing its revolutionary objectives, nor does it cause, at this juncture, major economic dislocations for Cuba. The embargo, however, "continues to narrowly restrict Havana's economic development options, necessitating an ever growing dependence on CMEA, especially the U.S.S.R."[15]

Cuba's staggering trade deficits, its failure to diversify its structure of foreign commerce, its continued reliance on Soviet aid and subsidies, and the global recession of 1980–1982 aggravated a mounting debt crisis. But several Latin American nations, including capitalist petro-powers Mexico and Venezuela and mostly agricultural Costa Rica, have also had major financial difficulties. Interestingly enough, because Cuba is largely insulated from international capitalist market forces, and because its centrally planned economy can maintain artificially low prices, Cuba's rate of inflation is quite low compared to that of its Latin American neighbors.

Through the 1970s, Cuba borrowed substantial sums from Western financial institutions, taking advantage of moderate interest rates and liberal lending policies. Many of the loans were syndicated through European and Japanese institutions, with some participation from Canadian and Arab bands.[16] By that time, the United States had ceased to pressure some of its allies against granting loans or credits to Cuba, partly because of

improvements in East-West relations and also because European governments and bankers refused to link lending policies to Havana's foreign
adventures. But by mid-1982, Cuba found itself unable to make payments
on notes that would shortly come due, forcing the government to request
the rescheduling of part of its hard-currency debt of $3.5 billion.

The government's view of the crisis focused on falling sugar prices,
high interest rates, rising prices for imports, and restrictions placed on the
availability of credits to Cuba allegedly through pressures from the United
States.[17] During the second half of the Carter administration and under
President Reagan, the idea of linking Havana's "adventurism" to its need
for funds was revived. In effect, Washington hopes to moderate Havana's
behavior through economic pressures, and in 1983 the Reagan administration
reinstituted the ban on travel to Cuba that Carter had lifted.

Additional factors contributing to Cuba's debt crisis included shortfalls
in expected income from tourism, Soviet reluctance to assume some of the
burden or extend new loans and credits to Cuba, and even Cuba's overseas
military ventures. The latter did not inspire confidence in some Western
governments that might otherwise have supported Cuba's claims that due
to U.S. economic aggression, the request should be viewed as a "special
case." But an explicit linkage between Cuba's financial needs and its foreign
policy has never been established by the Europeans. Lastly, the poor growth
record of the Cuban economy in the early 1980s, and the less than
satisfactory prospects for a sustained recovery, tend to make prospective
lenders wary.

In the spring of 1983, the government reached an agreement with
its creditors. The $1.2 billion Cuba sought to reschedule involved mostly
short-term notes maturing through 1985; Cuba committed itself to making
interest payments, but it wanted these negotiations to focus on short-term
obligations, not on its total outstanding debt. Officials of the Cuban National
Bank (BNC) met with creditors from Austria, Spain, West Germany, and
other governments until a settlement was concluded in March 1983 allowing
Cuba to reschedule some $413 million owed through that year. Under the
terms of the agreement, Cuba will repay 95 percent of the principal in
ten installments between 1986 and 1991, with the other 5 percent to be
paid in 1984 and 1985. Negotiations are also expected to continue on an
additional $800 million in debt not covered in this first round.[18] In no
way are these agreements connected to an additional $7.5 billion owed
by Cuba to the USSR. Repayment of part of that debt is to begin in 1986.

It is clear that poor growth at home and external constraints abroad
place Cuba in a double vise, locking its economy into a cycle of high
indebtedness and economic dependency.[19] In addition, "energy constraints
[Cuba imports 98 percent of its oil from the USSR] and dependence on
traditional [agricultural] exports will continue to condemn Cuba to a stop-
go cycle of economic development, inevitably linked to volatile swings in
world sugar markets."[20] Finally, an examination of revolutionary Cuba's
aggregate economic performance in terms of trade dependency, composition

of exports and imports, trade partner concentration, and foreign indebtedness concludes that "the analysis of the mechanisms of external economic dependency shows little change between the prerevolutionary and the revolutionary situation, with a tendency to worsen in the 1970s perpetuating the island's vulnerability."[21] It is thus clear that developmental socialism has neither enhanced the society's economic autonomy nor improved its capabilities in managing a new, though admittedly different, structure of dependence.

THE NONPOLITICS OF DISSIDENCE: A FINAL COMMENT

One of the arguments in favor of Marxist socialism is that it is possible to move away from capitalist poverty and exploitation into socialism while preserving traditional freedoms, that is, that it is possible to "build socialism with a human face." The fact that the state becomes the principal agent for change is not considered a threat to political and civil freedoms because it is assumed that those holding power will not monopolize it indefinitely. It is also assumed that once private property is abolished, the principal source of oppression will be removed and all will share more equally in the benefits of development. Many saw Allende's Chile as holding the promise of building socialism without the horrors of repression, and many once hoped that revolutionary Cuba would move in that direction. A few stubbornly cling to that illusion.[22]

A second view is that even if some freedoms are sacrificed in order to lift a society from underdevelopment to relative prosperity, doing so is entirely justifiable because freedom of expression, for example, or the right to make a meaningful choice of rulers is not as important as ensuring that everyone eat, be educated, and be employed. In short, material rights are more fundamental than political or civil rights and objective conditions often force societies to make unpalatable choices. A revolution is not a dinner party, and if a few (or many) malcontents must go to prison or be shot so that others can get on with the job of building a new society, then so be it.

That is why no assessment of Cuba's political system is complete until the issue of dissidence is joined, as well as the question of why the regime still holds some 1,000 political prisoners, many of whom qualify as prisoners of conscience. The view that secular freedoms and other human rights have to be suppressed until the development process permits such luxuries is unacceptable for two reasons. First, freedom of thought, conscience, and expression are consubstantial (*consustanciales*) with humanness itself. To deny these rights constitutes an assault on the human spirit whose elevation and sustenance must be nurtured in spite of the political expedient of the day. No state should willfully violate such basic human rights. Second, since there is no evidence that communist dictatorships disappear once a certain level of material wealth and comfort have been accumulated and distributed, incarcerating someone simply because he chooses to march to the beat of a different drummer is not going to produce any demonstrable economic or social gain. There is no overt reason, in short, why those who point out that development (or Revolution or "liberation") must not lead to totalitarianism have to be silenced or deprived of their liberties.

In fact, in communist dictatorships the state and the hegemonic party define not only what is right but what is true, reaching into the social fabric as no authoritarian regime can. On the other hand, the history of Latin America is full of examples of authoritarian regimes giving way to pressures for democracy, as the cases of Brazil, Argentina, and Peru in the 1980s convincingly show.

Totalitarian as well as authoritarian regimes lie on a continuum, with some more repressive than others. Cuba in the 1980s is closer to Eastern European polities than to Stalin's Russia or Mao's China, and one does not find in Cuba the widespread persecution and political violence associated with some Latin American authoritarian regimes.

Organized dissidence as such does not exist in Cuba, but individual dissidents—including writers, poets, intellectuals, and disaffected revolutionaries—are found. As conventionally understood, these elements do not constitute a political threat to the regime or to the socialist system. Their resistance is moral, personal, symbolic, and unpublicized. Resisters include persons concerned with the absence of workers' rights, such as those individuals sent to jail in May 1983 for their alleged promotion of a Solidarity-type union organization.[23] Or it may simply be the type of painful resistance of the poet Angel Cuadra (who has been tortured and is in jail), the sociologist Ricardo Bofill, and many others. For instance, Andrés Vargas Gómez, a grandson of one of Cuba's national heroes, Máximo Gómez, spent over twenty years in jail after having been sentenced for "counterrevolutionary activities" and had been told that he will never be permitted to leave the country.[24] But in a calculated gesture intended to embarrass the Reagan administration, the Cuban government allowed Vargas Gomez and twenty-five other former prisoners to leave Cuba, presumably at the behest of Rev. Jesse Jackson during his unofficial trip to Cuba in June 1984.

Since the moral-cultural ethos of Cuba's revolutionary culture conspires against the expression of values, ideas, and symbols opposed to scientific socialism, it is doubtful that a dissident counterculture can flourish, or that its numbers will grow substantially, as has happened in other sovietized countries. There is the additional fact that the regime's control of the media and other instruments of socialization allows it to closely monitor cultural affairs, especially through the writer's union (UNEAC). For example, according to Carlos Ripoll:

> Literary criticism has since 1970 been the handmaiden of official policy on culture. The function of criticism has been reduced to spotting books that will serve as tools for mass indoctrination and to presenting them in a favorable light with the appropriate sprinkling of remarks on style or aesthetic

achievement, real or imagined, even though such considerations are lip service to values that no longer matter in Cuba.[25]

On the other hand, writers whose views are more tolerant of the revolutionary process and whose work stays within the bounds of what is deemed acceptable by the cultural authorities manage to get some works into print. According to Peter Winn, the result in these cases "is a revolutionary literature that is as serious as art and politics," produced by "promising young novelists who have begun to transform their generation's experiences into literature and make the Cuban revolution into myth."[26] Some literature of the 1970s and 1980s reflects a "liberalization that appears to be due to a feeling of security in the revolution," and literary commentary and criticism appear to be moving away from sectarianism.[27] Some of Cuba's finest novelists and poets—Reinaldo Arenas, Heberto Padilla, Guillermo Cabrera Infante, and since 1982, Armando Valladares—as well as lesser-known figures, have gone into exile for a variety of reasons. Alejo Carpentier, author of Los Pasos Perdidos and El Recurso del Método and probably Cuba's best-known novelist, was a supporter of the Revolution, but he spent a considerable amount of time outside Cuba. Nicolás Guillén, active in cultural affairs since the 1930s and today a member of the PCC's Central Committee, is well known and has been honored as Cuba's national poet for his erotic and Afro-Cuban pieces. Roberto Fernández Retamar, a poet whose work is less than compelling, is vice-president of the publishing house Casa de las Américas. He and Guillén are unconditional supporters of the regime.

The absence of widespread political dissidence is due to a number of factors. First, the regime has proven its repressive capabilities by imposing harsh penalties on those who challenge its authority or question the moral value of the socialist system. Second, it is doubtful that deeply held antiregime views exist in the larger public. The dynamics of revolutionary development have led to the satisfaction of many basic needs, reducing the probabilities that political opposition would spring from a widespread feeling of deprivation. Third, the regime's mobilizational capabilities, its ability to detect antiregime attitudes and behavior, and the strong sense of unity that nationalist fervor sustains, all contribute to the population's political quiescence. Liberal notions of dissidence are neither part of Cuba's political tradition, nor are they compatible with revolutionary values of unity and sacrifice. No mass movement seeking to overthrow the regime and change the system's character has emerged in the last two decades. Individual resistance occurs, but only in limited contexts. Under certain conditions, it may expand and acquire a broader social and political meaning, as was the case during the Mariel crisis of 1980, but so far it has been neither politically earthshaking nor prospectively threatening.[28]

It is also clear that the government rules through more than sheer terror. As a stable totalitarian government, its repressive outbursts are episodic and selective and no longer indicative of its essential nature. It is a harsh government, but it does not depend principally on systematic coercion for its survival nor is it unmindful of the domestic and external costs of ruling through fear. Since there is no domestic threat to its survival, psychological pressures, subtle or overt intimidation, sanctions of various kinds, and direct confrontation are more appropriate means through which politically suspect behavior can be effected.

But as the record of the past twenty-five years plainly and incontrovertibly shows, the regime has dealt severely with many of its opponents. Summary justice with little regard for the accused's legal rights was often employed during the eminently political trials of the early revolutionary period. Numerous executions also took place (according to some accounts they continue, though sporadically), and the death penalty is still in effect. Until the early 1970s, the line between civil offenses and political crimes was terribly blurred, allowing the regime to arbitrarily charge individuals with political offenses that might properly be considered civil or common. This situation clearly enhanced the executive's discretionary authority, probably led to harsher sentences than normal, and created a climate of personal insecurity. Most important, the regime itself, not any formal legal code as such, "defined what was and was not a political offense."[29] Offenses against the system of socialist property, or involvement in the black market, were often judged to be political crimes. Lastly, justice administered by popular tribunals (phased out in the early 1970s) was arbitrary and individuals were often unable to defend themselves. On the whole, the courts could not be used as a means through which legal protections might be obtained.

As mentioned in Chapter 8, judicial reform has been part of the process of institutionalization. In 1979, a new criminal code was adopted, reclassifying crimes such as burglary, theft, and impersonation of public officials as common crimes. Under this code, crimes are grouped "in relationship to the similarity of the activity contained in the group," differentiating crimes against the security of the state from those against public order, or labor crimes.[30]

In the final analysis, neither the universities, the mass media, the churches, nor any other institution challenges the state's monopoly on defining reality. An adversary intellectual culture does not exist. Clichés, sloganeering, and unremitting ideological uniformity substitute for critical thinking and inquiry. Cuban communism does not permit challenges either to the PCC's hegemony, to the official ideology, to the economic system, or to the structure of political power. That is why the regime is totalitarian, despite the legal reforms of recent years and the absence of mass terror.

The Catholic church, the several Protestant denominations, and the state coexist peacefully. Cuba maintains diplomatic relations with the Vatican, and a Papal Nuncio maintains an office in Havana. But church life is nearly moribund and attendance is extremely low, mostly the elderly and those who still practice their faith in a society where atheism is officially sanctioned. Beliefs have been thoroughly secularized through intense socialization. The Catholic church has no schools and religious education is proscribed. Holy Week and holidays like Christmas and the Epiphany were abolished long ago. A few Catholic seminaries remain open, but few Cuban youths choose to study for the priesthood. Seminaries and convents are relics of a distant past. Catholic weddings are rare and fraught with difficulties because one priest must serve several congregations. Lastly, religious symbols have no part in the new political culture. Many congregants feel alienated from the broader culture and are subject to subtle forms of discrimination. A believer, for instance, cannot belong to the PCC.[31] A small Jewish colony survives in Havana.

Finally, one comes to the issue of political imprisonment. The regime's view is that people are incarcerated in Cuba not for their beliefs, thoughts, or political views, but for their actions. Yet there are numerous cases over the past decades of individuals having been sent to jail when, acting on their beliefs, they expressed opposition to the revolutionary regime.[32] The connection between thought and action is illustrated by the fact that even after the new constitution was adopted in 1976, writings that are in any way interpreted as being against the socialist state constitute a crime against the internal security of the state.

The number of political prisoners held by the regime has varied. During crises, for example, during the Bay of Pigs invasion in 1961 or during the difficult economic conditions of the late 1960s, arrests and imprisonment for political reasons were more common than today. Castro himself told the U.S. journalist Lee Lockwood in 1965 that the government held 20,000 political prisoners, though exile estimates consistently challenged this figure as too low. In the early 1970s, the French photographer Pierre Golendorf, himself a political prisoner for thirty-eight months, wrote upon his release that he estimated the number of political prisoners at around 20,000 but that older prisoners placed the figure somewhere between 80,000 and 200,000.[33]

A few years later, due to completion of sentences by individuals, a diminution in both internal and foreign threats, work-release programs, and a policy of "rehabilitation," the number had dropped to between four and five thousand. In November 1978, amid a dialogue between the Cuban government and members of the exile community in the United States, Castro indicated a "willingness to release three thousand persons imprisoned for crimes against state security," as well as an additional six hundred who had been incarcerated for "illegal departures."[34] According to Castro, these represented 80 percent of the total number still held. Lastly, in its *Sixth Report on the Situation of Political Prisoners in Cuba* (1979), the Inter-American Commission on Human Rights (IACHR) estimated that some one thousand political prisoners were still held in Cuba, including some condemned for crimes committed during the Batista period and some one hundred "intransigent" individuals opposed to rehabilitation. The commission noted that (1) there are individuals in Cuba who are in prison for the mere fact of having expressed their opposition to the system; (2) the precriminal and postcriminal security measures in some cases serve to intimidate and oppress individuals for having expressed their political views; and (3) the handling of "intransigent" prisoners is characterized by mistreatment, absence of medical attention, lack of proper food, and lack of due process. At the time, the commission commended the government for the release of the thirty-six hundred prisoners in the "hopes that this step is just the first in a process aimed at putting an end to political imprisonment in Cuba."[35] In sum, it is irrefutably clear that the revolutionary regime has imprisoned thousands over the past twenty-five years. No less deniable is the fact that many of these prisoners (including a number of women) have lived under appalling conditions, often for extended periods of time. Many died as a result. Those costs must be mentioned in any assessment of Cuba's socialism.

SUMMARY AND CONCLUSIONS

Cuba in the mid-1980s is an example of a society struggling to realize full nationhood. Modernization through socialism has modified the pre-revolutionary feelings that Cubans were incapable of controlling their own destiny and the view that foreign influences (in government, art, culture, and lifestyle) were somehow superior to what Cuba itself could produce. In addition, adversity and "the politics of crisis" have tempered the national character, bringing some sense of confidence and achievement to a people whose cultural isolation left them to their own devices. But out of the struggles of the past generation a more complete society is still to emerge, one that reconciles material improvements with secular liberties.

Within the space of a generation, Cuba has also managed to reduce the extremes between wealth and poverty typically found in many Latin American countries and throughout the developing world. It is also a country whose heritage of struggle and heroism is central to any understanding of its contemporary life and popular attitudes. It is a culture that thrives on adversity; defiance is perhaps the most visible manifestation of, paradoxically, fear and security. Also, a generalized, partly messianic belief nourishes feelings that Cuba has a larger mission, infusing its domestic politics with intense pride, and its foreign policy with what Horowitz calls "small power chauvinism."[36]

But the structural realities that assign Cuba a less than autonomous role and impinge on its economic sovereignty have not disappeared. Sugar is still king. Monoculture is alive. The country is deeply in hock, and the calculated generosity of the socialist superpower is both humiliating and onerous. Cuba, in short, is not well, hardly more than a low-ranked producer in the socialist world's "international division of labor."

In contrast, Cuba's politics are largely its own, and the country has been able to resist the degree of open meddling by the Soviets evident in the latter's Eastern European empire. Foreign ambassadors do not make or unmake governments, as was once the case; Cuba's national interests are at times independently pursued. With little doubt, Cubans live under a totalitarian state, but neither systemic terror nor the fear of death or merciless persecution rules most people's lives. Cuba's totalitarianism is imposing and harsh, but the system has not yet lost all of its *fidelista* flavor. By the same token, the country's political evolution has been stunted by the failure to liberalize the polity and by the conscious suppression of individual freedoms. For that, as well as for the choices which they continue to make, the leaders of the revolutionary generation must assume full responsibility.

Finally, Cuba asserts its identity in the face of persistent, often hostile influences. Its assertiveness stems from its existential conflict with the United States, unabated, often furious, riddled with paradoxes, but still dangerous. In fact, the proximity of the United States induces a kind of "positive paranoia" in the island, strengthening the collective will while perpetuating a psychologically debilitating siege mentality. The historical dilemma of "what are we to do about the United States" permeates the revolutionary experience. At the same time, one gets the impression that eventually Cubans want recognition and admiration for their modest achievements. In sum, the process of attaining nationhood and creating a society "with all and for the good of all" (*con todos y para el bien de todos*) remains incomplete. Martí's ideal that the republic "honor the dignity of every one of its sons" is still a vision and a goal, not yet a reality.

NOTES

1. The Mariel crisis of 1980 could be an exception, since it is clear that the widespread disaffection evident in Cuba since 1979 had social overtones. The exodus itself produced a major political crisis for the regime, compounded by the reports of physical and psychological abuse to which substantial numbers of those willing to leave Cuba were subjected. For some commentary, see Irving L. Horowitz, "El éxodo: causa y efectos," *Opiniones* 3, 7 (October 1980):38–41; Juan M. del Aguila, "El exilio: fórmulas y política," *Opiniones* 3, 7 (October 1980):42–46.

2. "Efectuado en La Habana el Cuarto Período Ordinario de Sesiones de la Asamblea Nacional del Poder Popular," *Granma Resumen Semanal*, 24 July 1983, pp. 2–3.

3. Carlos Alberto Montaner, *Secret Report on the Cuban Revolution*, trans. Eduardo Zayas-Bazán (New Brunswick, N.J.: Transaction Books, 1981), p. 165.

4. See Robert L. Bach, Jennifer B. Bach, and Timothy Triplett, "The Flotilla Entrants: Latest and Most Controversial," *Cuban Studies* 11, 2; 12, 1 (July 1981-January 1982):29–48. Also Gastón Fernández, "Comment—The Flotilla Entrants: Are They Different?" in the same issue of *Cuban Studies*, pp. 49–54.

5. Jorge I. Domínguez, "Cuba in the 1980s," *Problems of Communism* 30 (March-April 1981):57.

6. Peter L. Berger, *Pyramids of Sacrifice: Political Ethics and Social Change* (Garden City, N.Y.: Anchor Books, 1976), p. 150.

7. Guido Calabresi and Philip Bobitt, *Tragic Choices* (New York: Norton, 1978), p. 17.

8. Irving L. Horowitz, "Introduction to the Fourth Edition," in *Cuban Communism*, 4th ed., ed. Irving L. Horowitz (New Brunswick, N.J.: Transaction Books, 1981), pp. 4–5.

9. According to official figures, infant mortality rates continue on the downward trend begun in 1978. In 1978, the rate was 22.3 deaths per 1,000 live births; in 1980, 19.6 per 1,000; in 1982, 17.3 per 1,000. In addition, a life expectancy of 73.5 years places Cuba on a level with the most developed countries. The regime attributes such good results to its sustained expenditures for health services and its continued commitment to training doctors, nurses, and health service personnel. "La salud pública y la revolución," *Granma Resumen Semanal*, 17 July 1983, pp. 9–10.

10. Gary W. Wynia, *The Politics of Latin American Development* (Cambridge: Cambridge University Press, 1978), p. 296.

11. Sergio Roca, "Cuba Confronts the 1980s," *Current History* (February 1983):75.

12. Sergio Díaz-Briquets and Lisandro Pérez, "Fertility Decline in Cuba: A Socioeconomic Interpretation," *Population and Development Review* 8, 3 (September 1982):533.

13. "Cuba: evolución reciente de su economía," *Comercio Exterior* 32, 1 (January 1982):25–35.

14. See Castro's speech on "The 29th Anniversary of the Attack on Moncada," *Granma Resumen Semanal*, 8 August 1982, p. 4.

15. Lawrence H. Theriot, "Cuba Faces the Economic Realities of the 1980s," in U.S. Congress, Joint Economic Committee, *East-West Trade: The Prospects to 1985*, Joint Committee Print (Washington, D.C.: Government Printing Office, 1982), p. 107.

16. Ernesto Betancourt and Wilson Dizard III, *Castro and the Bankers: The Mortgaging of a Revolution* (Washington, D.C.: Cuban-American National Foundation, 1982).

17. "Por qué y cómo Cuba renegocia parcialmente su deuda externa," interview with Ismael Morera, Vice-President of Cuba's National Bank (BNC), *Granma Resumen Semanal*, 13 September 1982, p. 7.

18. "Suscriben acuerdo para refinanciamiento de la deuda externa de Cuba," *Granma Resumen Semanal*, 7 March 1983, p. 3.

19. For an assessment, see Susan Eckstein, "Capitalist Constraints on Cuban Socialist Development," *Comparative Politics* 12, 3 (April 1980):253–274.

20. Theriot, "Cuba Faces the Economic Realities of the 1980s," p. 135.

21. Carmelo Mesa-Lago, *The Economy of Socialist Cuba* (Albuquerque: University of New Mexico Press, 1981), p. 186.

22. The reasons why such attitudes prevail, especially among intellectuals, are brilliantly analyzed in Paul Hollander, *Political Pilgrims, Travels of Western Intellectuals to the Soviet Union, China and Cuba* (New York: Harper and Row, 1981).

23. See *Latin American Political Report*, 83-19 (May 1983):12; "A General for the Justice Ministry as Dissent Grows." *Latin American Political Report* 83-41 (October 1983) p. 2. It is reported that ten judges and lawyers, all state employees, were detained for expressing dissatisfaction with the procedures employed in trials of counterrevolutionaries. It also mentions that two French journalists were arrested, but subsequently released, after meeting Ricardo Bofill, a well-known dissident. Brigadier General Juan Escalona was appointed as minister of justice.

24. "Inside Castro's Prisons," *Time*, 15 August 1983, pp. 20–22. A personal account by Armando Valladares.

25. Carlos Ripoll, *The Cuban Scene: Censors and Dissenters* (Washington, D.C.: Cuban-American National Foundation, 1982), pp. 11–12.

26. Peter Winn, "The Cuban State and the Arts," in *Cuban Communism*, ed. Horowitz, p. 360.

27. See Roberto González-Echevarría, "Criticism and Literature in Revolutionary Cuba," *Cuban Studies* 11, 1 (January 1981):14.

28. One of the principal reasons is that migration has constituted a natural escape valve. Some 10 percent of Cuba's population has gone into exile, relieving the regime of politically troublesome elements. Also, not having as many mouths to feed, houses to provide, or people to care for frees up already limited resources. For commentary, see Silvia Pedraza Bailey, "Cubans and Mexicans in the United States: The Functions of Political and Economic Migration," *Cuban Studies* 11, 2; 12, 1 (July 1981-January 1982):79–97.

29. Jorge I. Domínguez, *Cuba: Order and Revolution* (Cambridge, Mass.: Belknap Press, 1978), p. 251.

30. Luis Salas, *Social Control and Deviance in Cuba* (New York: Praeger Publishers, 1979), pp. 44–45.

31. For assessments of religious life in Cuba, see Manuel Fernández, "La crisis actual del catolicismo en Cuba," *Reunión* 93-94 (January-February 1977):2–3, 8. See also interview with Mons. Carlos Manuel de Céspedes, the secretary of the Cuban Bishops Conference, by Jordi López Camps, "Cuba: Una Iglesia Bloqueada," *Reunión* 129-130 (January-February 1980):4–5.

32. For an account of three famous cases, see Lorrin Philipson, "Huber Matos, the Undefeated," *National Review*, 20 February 1981, pp. 153–158, 184; "Dangerous Manuscripts, A Conversation with Reinaldo Arenas," *Encounter* 58, 1 (January 1982):60–67; "Cuba's Tropical 'Gulags'," *Miami Herald*, 26 December 1982 (a conversation with Armando Valladares).

33. Pierre Goldendorf, *7 Años en Cuba, 38 meses en las prisiones de Fidel Castro* (Barcelona: Plaza & Janes, S.A., 1977), p. 255.

34. The "dialogue" was an effort by Cuban exiles in the United States to seek resolution of differences with the Cuban government in three areas: family reunification, release of political prisoners, and visits to Cuba by exiles. Referring to the exiles as "members of the Cuban community in the United States" (rather than the vituperative "worms" so frequently heard before and since), Castro allowed that "I believe that the conditions have been created—conditions which did not exist before—for us to meditate a little on each of these problems." Some attribute the subsequent release of most prisoners to the "dialogue"; others condemned the visits as humiliating cave-ins to Castro's seductions. "Illegal departures" is the legal charge levied against persons caught attempting to leave Cuba clandestinely. Thousands have left in this manner over the years, but the regime has also caught many.

35. See *Sixth Report on the Situation of Political Prisoners in Cuba* (Washington, D.C.: OAS General Secretariat, 1979). For more recent information, see *Amnistía Internacional, Informe 1982* (London: Publicaciones Amnistía Internacional, 1982), pp. 113–114. For an excellent testimonial, see *El presidio político en Cuba comunista* (Miami: Instituto Internacional de Cooperación y Solidaridad Cubana, 1983).

36. Horowitz, "Introduction to the Fourth Edition," p. 5.

Abbreviations

ABC	Secret cellular society of the 1930s. A represents top cell, B the next lower level, C the next, and so on.
ALN	National Liberating Alliance
ANAP	National Association of Small Farmers
ARO	Acción Revolucionaria Oriental
BAGA	Bloque Alemán–Grau-Alsina
BNC	Cuban National Bank
CDRs	Committees for the Defense of the Revolution
CIA	Central Intelligence Agency (U.S.)
CM	Council of Ministers
CMEA	Council of Mutual Economic Assistance
CNC	National Council of Culture
CS	Council of State
CTC	Confederation of Cuban Workers
DR	Revolutionary Directorate
ECLA	Economic Commission for Latin America
ELN	National Liberation Army
FALN	Armed Front of National Liberation
FAR	Revolutionary Armed Forces
FEU	University Students Federation
FLN	National Liberation Front
FMC	Federation of Cuban Women
FMLN	Farabundo Martí National Liberation Front
FNLA	National Front for the Liberation of Angola
GNP	gross national product
GMP	gross material product
ICAIC	Cuban Institute of Arts and Cinematography (Instituto Cubano del Arte e Industria Cinematográficas)
ICAP	Cuban Institute of Friendship with the Peoples
INAV	National Institute of Savings and Housing
INIT	National Institute of Tourism
INRA	National Institute for Agrarian Reform

JUCEPLAN	Central Planning Board
M-26-7	26th of July Movement
MPLA	Popular Movement for the Liberation of Angola
MR-13	13th of November Revolutionary Movement
MRP	People's Revolutionary Movement
MRR	Rescue Revolutionary Movement
MTT	Militias and Territorial Troops
NA	National Assembly
NAM	Non-Aligned Nations Movement
OLAS	Organization of Latin American Solidarity
ORI	Integrated Revolutionary Organizations
PCC	Cuban Communist Party
PLO	Palestine Liberation Organization
PRC-A	Cuban Revolutionary Party–Authentic
PSP	Popular Socialist Party
PURS	United Party of the Socialist Revolution
SAR	Society of Friends of the Republic (Sociedad de Amigos de la República)
SELA	Latin American Economic System
SPD	Social Democratic Party
SWAPO	Southwest Africa People's Organization
UJC	Communist Youth Union
UNEAC	National Union of Cuban Writers and Artists
UNECA	Union of Caribbean Construction Enterprises
UNITA	National Union for the Total Liberation of Angola